Jesus the Distressed Migrant Today

Jesus the Distressed Migrant Today

Biblical, Theological, Socio-Economic and Political Factors, Impacts and Responses

Prakash Louis
Peter Ignatius

Christian World Imprints

First Published in 2025 by

Christian World Imprints
Christian Publishing & Books from India
A-71 Group, Wazirpur Industrial Area
Delhi-110052
cwidelhi2017@gmail.com
www.ChristianWorldImprints.com
Phone: +91 11 41526079

ISBN: 978-93-6065-648-5 (HB)
ISBN: 978-93-6065-543-3 (PB)

Printed in India.

A Snapshot of the Lives and Struggles of the Migrants

Migrants are needed but not wanted people

It is ironic that the government sees everyone attempting illegal entry at the border with Mexico as a potential terrorist, while the perpetrators of the 9/11 tragedy all came in on legal visas

The average hourly wage for a manufacturing job in Mexico is $2.17 (Rs. 169.26), while in the United States it's $18.24 (Rs. 1,422,72)

Migrants are needed for development but socially discriminated

Migrants are exploited at source, transit and destination

A migrant's social location gives her/him a better vantage point than a non-migrant's own from which to understand social and theological realities.

Migrants are the crucified people of today

industrialisation was necessary for development, but migration was not desirable

migration is a 'problem' emerges in the state's narrative time and again,

We are forced to work like an ox.

Contents

Preface

Migration talks about the movement of people. People migrate for various reasons. It could be within and or outside a locality or intrastate and interstate. Migration is also both within the national territory or transnational. Migration could be to mitigate the distressed situation or to enhance employment and economic prospectus. These types of migrations have played a key role in shaping the local, regional, national and global communities, economies and cultures.

Human mobility is as old as human history and herstory. The need to avail of better opportunities for survival has been the main motive for such movement of people. In recent centuries, the pattern of growth and development and or underdevelopment has increasingly conditioned available opportunities for workers. This reality which is often termed as 'push and pull factors' speak of what probably happens in the lives of the migrants. Migration continues to go on unabated irrespective of all the noise made about the policies and programs by the ruling elite. Migration also goes on without end due to dire need of survival of those who are at the periphery of society. It is their hard labour and toil which keeps the economy of many families and countries ticking.

This book begins with the Catholic Social Teachings which is moved to the Catholic Social Praxis, typically of Pope Francis through this document, "Responding to Refugees and Migrants: Twenty Action Points by Holy Father Francis to the United Nations in 2017." This document by Pope Francis is an invitation to accompany and assist migrants. This document captures various aspects of the program of action that need to be attended to by all the stakeholders who are concerned about the plight of the migrants and want to respond individually and collectively.

This book offers the opportunity to raise fundamental questions regarding the lives and struggles of distressed migrants. This book is not the first book on migration nor on distressed migration. This is not the last book on distressed migration. It basically tries to capture the various aspects of migration in general at the global level and migration in particular at the Indian level; it is an attempt to highlight the issues faced by the migrants in general and distressed migrants in particular; it is an effort to resist from viewing migrants as faceless numbers but as fellow human beings who are marginalised and pulverised. It is the lives and struggles of these marginalised migrant people and communities who form the core of the discourse of this book.

This book came about from the challenges posed while accompanying distressed migrants. Having worked among the marginalised in the last two decades and now among the migrants, there was a strong sense to articulate the lives and struggles of the migrants as living human beings. This book also came about by the agony one went through in accompanying and assisting the migrants both in source and destination ecosystems. It also was an outcome of the very understanding of the fact that Jesus himself was a migrant and refugee. In a sense, he epitomises the lives and the struggles of the migrants today, right from birth to death. Hence, the title, 'Jesus the Distressed Migrant Today.'

This book will be useful for all those who are concerned about the issues of the migrants, all those who are trying to respond to this issue and the policy makers who can focus on best practices to address the vulnerability of the labourers and migrants of India and elsewhere. The Church of India can make use of this to delve deep into the various aspects of the distressed migrants whose number and vulnerability is on the increase. Lots of individuals and institutions are addressing the issues of migrants. But there is lot more to be seen, understood, experienced and based on which individuals and institutions can accompany and assist the distressed migrants.

This book is not the first book on migration nor on distressed migration. This is not the last book on distressed migration. This book basically tries to capture the various aspects of migration in general at the global level and migration in particular at the Indian level; it is an attempt to highlight the issues faced by the migrants in general and distressed migrants in particular; it is an effort to resist from viewing migrants as faceless numbers but as fellow human beings who are marginalised and pulverised. It is the lives and struggles of these marginalised migrant people and communities who form the core of the discourse of this book. As stated in the sub-title, here an attempt is made to unpack the biblical, theological, socio-economic and political factors that influence migration, the outcome of migration on the marginalised and the responses made by various agencies to address the issue of distressed labour migration.

It is with pride and pleasure, but above all with humility and humanity, we offer this book, "Jesus the Distressed Migrant Today: The Biblical, Theological, Socio-Economic and Political Factors, Impacts and Responses" to wider audience, who like us are concerned about the growing marginalisation and oppression of the distressed labour migrants.

This is not an academically grounded book. Nor is it fully action oriented. It has taken a mid-path, so as to engage in an action research and also delineating pathways to accompany and assist the distressed migrant labourers of India and the world. We have also tried to base this book on sound biblical and theological principles so as to draw strength from our own resources.

We are grateful to all those who have contributed in various ways in the preparation, publication and distribution of the book. Our gratitude is first and foremost for the migrants who by their lives and struggles have taught us what is to live in the most discriminated and vulnerable conditions both at home and in the destination. The determination, perseverance, hope, grit and gratitude they have continue to inspire us. We are grateful to all the sources from which we have drawn both inspiration and information for the wholeness of the book. We have tried to acknowledge their work. If we have failed, we ask sorry about it. We thank Mr. Sudhanshu Kanda of Christian World Imprints of New Delhi, who within a short span of time got this book printed and agreed to be the publisher too.

We also apologise to all if we erred in any way. May everyone find a home, peace, prosperity, dignity, joy, justice and hope.

Responding to Refugees and Migrants Twenty Action Points Holy Father Francis to the UN. 2017

Pope Francis issued a 20-point action plan to governments on refugees and migrants to try to galvanise their response to an issue seen by the Vatican as one of the biggest global challenges of the 21st century. His intention was to lay the ground for the drafting of two global compacts on refugees and migrants, which are expected to be adopted at the UN General Assembly in September 2018.

The roadmap was published on Monday, 21/08/2017 by the Vatican's migrants and refugees section, which was set up by Francis last year and operates under his direction. The action points were personally approved by the pontiff.

In a message issued before publication, Francis said he had "repeatedly expressed my particular concern for the lamentable situation of many migrants and refugees fleeing from war, persecution, natural disasters and poverty." The situation was "undoubtedly a 'sign of the times,'" he said.

The document, Responding to Refugees and Migrants: Twenty Action Points, says the world is facing "the largest movement of displaced people in recent memory." The document's 20 points are grouped in four calls to action: to welcome, to protect, to promote and to integrate. Their "ultimate goal is the building of an inclusive and sustainable common home for all."

Before detailing the action plan, the authors suggest that distinguishing between migrants and refugees, as the UN does in its separate compacts, is problematic. "Empirical evidence shows that migration is more and more mixed. This makes it difficult to maintain a clear-cut distinction between migrants and refugees. Often their needs are very similar if not identical," the document says.

Among its action points are the creation of legal pathways for safe and voluntary migration and resettlement, and a ban on arbitrary and collective expulsions. It suggests states make wider use of humanitarian, student and family reunification visas. The document says greater support should be available for countries that have borne the brunt of migration: more than half the world's displaced people are in Africa and the Middle East, with 17% in Europe, according to the UN.

In his message, Francis said personal safety and dignity should be prioritised over national security and, "for the sake of the fundamental dignity of every human person, we must strive to find alternative solutions to detention for those who enter a country without authorisation."

Francis indicated that migration should be a major Vatican focus in the run-up to the 2018 UN General Assembly. He has made the issue central to his papacy since visiting the Mediterranean island of Lampedusa, where thousands of migrants have landed, within weeks of his election. He has also housed several Syrian refugee families in the Vatican.

Matteo Salvini, the leader of Italy's anti-immigrant Northern League party, wrote on Facebook: "If you want to do it in the Vatican, go ahead. But as a Catholic, I don't think Italy can welcome and support the whole world." But undeterred by these criticisms, Pope Francis continued to voice the lives and struggles of the migrants and refugees.

Responding to Refugees and Migrants: Twenty Action Points

For centuries, people on the move have received the assistance and special pastoral attention of the Catholic Church. Today, facing the largest movement of displaced peoples in recent memory, the Church feels compelled to continue this work in solidarity with them and in cooperation with the international community.

While massive numbers of people have been forced to leave their homes due to persecution, violence, natural disasters and the scourge of poverty, migration should nevertheless be recognized, not as a new phenomenon, but rather as a natural human response to crisis and a testament to the innate desire of every human being for happiness and a better life. This reality, with its important cultural and spiritual dimensions, is having a significant impact on attitudes and reactions all over the world.

Even amidst the current crisis, experience teaches that effective, shared responses are available. The Church looks forward to working together with the international community to promote and adopt such measures to protect the dignity, rights and freedoms of all persons currently on the move, including forced migrants, victims of human trafficking, asylum seekers, refugees and internally displaced persons.

The United Nations processes to produce Global Compacts, one on safe, orderly and regular migration, and the other on refugees, are a unique opportunity to respond together through international cooperation and shared responsibility.

The Church has already taken a stand on many of the issues which will be included in the Global Compacts and, drawing on its diverse and longstanding pastoral experience, would like to contribute actively to the two processes. To support this contribution, the Vatican's Section on Migrants & Refugees (Dicastery for promoting Integral Human Development), consulting with various Bishops' Conferences and Catholic NGOs working in the field, has prepared the following Twenty Action Points. They have been approved by the Holy Father. They are grounded on the Church's best practices responding to the needs of migrants and refugees at the grassroots level. They do not exhaust the Church's teaching on migrants and refugees, but provide practical considerations which Catholic and other advocates can use, add to and develop in their dialogue with governments towards the Global Compacts.

The 20 Points advocate effective and proven measures which together constitute an integral response to the current challenges. In accordance with Pope Francis's teaching, the points are grouped under four headings: to welcome, to protect, to promote, and to integrate. Each is an active verb and a call to action. Starting from what is currently possible, their ultimate goal is the building of an inclusive and sustainable common home for all. Our sincere hope is that these Action Points will provide welcome guidance to policy-makers and everyone concerned with improving the situation of migrants, refugees, asylum seekers and internally displaced persons, especially those who are most vulnerable.

Empirical evidence shows that migration is more and more mixed. This makes it difficult to maintain a clear-cut distinction between migrants and refugees. Often their needs are very similar if not identical. Accordingly, let the drafting and negotiating strive for the greatest possible harmony between the two Global Compacts. Moreover, both Compacts should have a real impact on people's lives and should, therefore, include targets and goals to be met as well as reporting mechanisms.

The Migrants & Refugees Section offers the Twenty Action Points as a contribution to the drafting, negotiation and adoption of the Global Compacts on Migrants and on Refugees by the end of 2018. Guided by Pope Francis, the Section stands behind the principles embodied in these Points and looks forward to working with the international community toward their inclusion in the Global Compacts.

1. To Welcome: Enhancing Safe and Legal Channels for Migrants and Refugees

Migration should be safe, legal and orderly, and the decision to migrate voluntary. With this in mind, the following action points are suggested:

1. **Encourage States to Ban Arbitrary and Collective Expulsions.** The "non refoulement" principle should always be respected. This principle is based on the individual situation of the person and not on how "safe" a country is generally claimed to be. States should avoid using safe country lists, as such lists often fail to meet the refugee's needs for protection.
2. **Encourage States and all actors involved to expand the number and range of alternative legal pathways for safe and voluntary migration and resettlement, in full respect for the principle of non-refoulement.**

Examples of such avenues would include:

a. Adopt the practice of extending humanitarian visas, or if already present, expand their use as a national policy priority.

b. Encourage the wider use of student visas, including for apprenticeship and internship programmes as well as all levels of formal education.
c. Adopt humanitarian corridor programs that grant legal entry with a humanitarian visa to people in particularly vulnerable situations, including those forced to flee conflict and natural disasters.
d. Adopt legislation which enables local integration through community and private sponsorship by citizens, communities and organizations.
e. Adopt resettlement policies for refugees or, if already present in the legal framework, increase the number of refugees resettled on a scale that would enable the annual resettlement needs identified by the Office of the United Nations High Commissioner for Refugees to be met. f. Provide family reunification visas or, if already available, expand the number of such visas issued, particularly for the reunification of all family members (including grandparents, siblings and grandchildren).
f. Adopt national policies which permit those forced to flee armed conflict, persecution or widespread violence in their countries of origin to be received immediately, even if temporarily, by neighboring States through, for example, the granting of temporary protection status.
g. A responsible and dignified welcome of migrants and refugees "begins by offering them decent and appropriate shelter. The enormous gathering together of persons seeking asylum and of refugees has not produced positive results. Instead these gatherings have created new situations of vulnerability and hardship. More widespread programmes of welcome, already initiated in different places, seem to favour a personal encounter and allow for greater quality of service and increased guarantees of success."[1]

3. **Encourage States to adopt a national security perspective that fully takes into account the security and human rights of all migrants, asylum seekers and refugees entering its territory.**

[1] Pope Francis, Address to Participants in the International Forum on Migration and Peace, 21 February 2017.

For example:

a. Provide training in international human rights law and international refugee law to public officials and law enforcement officers who work in border areas.
b. Adopt national policies which respond first to the needs and vulnerabilities of those seeking admission, including access to basic services, before addressing an applicant's legal status.
c. Adopt national security policies that prioritize the safety and protection of refugees and asylum seekers fleeing armed conflict, persecution or widespread violence to find safety quickly by ensuring an expeditious screening and admission process.
d. Adopt national policies which prefer alternatives to the detention of those seeking access to the territory.

2. To Protect: Ensuring Migrants' and Refugees' Rights and Dignity

The Church insists on the importance of taking a holistic and integrated approach, with a focus on the centrality of the human person. A holistic approach remains, indeed, the best way to detect and overcome harmful stereotypes, and to avoid stigmatizing anyone in respect to a few specific aspects, to take account of all dimensions and fundamental aspects of the person as a whole. "The proper implementation of human rights becomes truly beneficial for migrants, as well as for the sending and receiving countries. The measures suggested are not a mere concession to migrants. They are in the interest of migrants, host societies, and the international community at large. Promoting and respecting the human rights of migrants and their dignity ensures that everyone's rights and dignity in society are fully respected."[2]

Migrants, asylum seekers and refugees should be received as human beings, in dignity and full respect for their human rights, regardless of their migratory status. While it is the right of every State to manage and control its borders, migrants and refugees must be received in conformity with applicable obligations under international

---

[2] Statement of the Permanent Observer of the Holy See to the United Nations and Other International Organizations in Geneva at the 29th Session of the Human Rights Council Interactive Dialogue with the Special Rapporteur on Migrants Geneva, 15 June 2015.

law, including international human rights law and international refugee law. The more alternative and legal pathways are available to the migrant and refugee, the less likely they are to be taken advantage of by criminal networks and to find themselves victims of human trafficking, or victims of exploitation and abuse in the context of the smuggling of migrants. The right to life is the most basic guarantee of civil and political freedom. Article 6 of the International Covenant on Civil and Political Rights states that "every human being has the inherent right to life. This right shall be protected by law. No one shall be arbitrarily deprived of his life."[3]

Every response to migrants, refugees and asylum seekers, particularly in search and rescue operations, should be directed primarily to ensure and protect the right to life of all, regardless of their status. With this in mind, the following action points are proposed:

4. Encourage States with significant labour migrant outflows to adopt policies and practices which provide protections for citizens choosing to emigrate.

For example:

a. Create national pre-departure information systems and training which alert and educate citizens and employers, as well public officials and law enforcement officers who work in border areas, to identify signs of forced labour or trafficking.
b. Require national regulation and certification of employment recruiters.
c. Establish, at the Ministerial level, a department dedicated to diaspora affairs.
d. Adopt national policies that protect the interests of and assist diaspora and migrant communities abroad, including through consular protection and legal services.

---

[3] GA res. 2200 A (XXI), 21 UN GAOR Supp. (No. 16) at 52, UN Doc. A/6316 (1966); 999 UNTS 171; 6 ILM 368 (1967).

5. Encourage States with significant labour migrant inflows to adopt national policies which protect against exploitation, forced labour, or trafficking.

Some examples would be:

a. Enact legislation which forbids employers from withholding the passports and other forms of identification from their employees.
b. Enact national policies which provide foreign residents with access to justice, regardless of their migratory status, allowing them to report human rights abuses and violence without fear of reprisal, including detention and deportation.
c. Enact national policies which allow migrants to open private, personal bank accounts that also permit direct deposits by employers.
d. Adopt national minimum wage laws which require the regular and predictable payment of wages, at least on a monthly basis.

6. Encourage States to adopt national policies which enable migrants, asylum seekers, and refugees to make the best use of their skills and capacities, in order to better contribute to their own and their communities' well-being.

For example:

a. Grant refugees and asylum seekers freedom of movement and provide work permits as well as travel documents which allow for their return to the host State, particularly for those that find employment in other States.
b. Adopt programs engaging local communities in hosting small groups of asylum seekers in addition to larger reception and identification centers.
c. Enact legislation which allows asylum seekers, refugees and migrants the ability to open bank accounts, establish enterprises, and conduct financial transactions.
d. Enact national policies which allow migrants, asylum seekers and refugees to access and use telecommunications, such as internet or sim cards for mobile telephones, without burdensome procedures or fees.

e. Enact national policies which allow repatriated and returning migrants and refugees to have swift access to employment opportunities in their countries of origin, thus encouraging their reintegration into society.

7. **Encourage States to comply with their obligations under the Convention of the Rights of the Child (CRC) when enacting domestic legislation to address the vulnerable situation of unaccompanied children or minors separated from their family.**

For example:

a. Adopt alternatives to mandatory detention, which is never in the best interest of the child, no matter their migratory status.

b. Provide foster care or guardianship for unaccompanied children or minors while they are separated from their family.

c. Establish separate processing centers for families, minors and adults.

8. **Encourage States to comply with their obligations under the Convention of the Rights of the Child (CRC) when dealing with all migrant minors and recommend the following actions, among others:**

a. Adopt procedures that guarantee legal protections to minors approaching the age of majority. In particular, enact legislation that preserves their legal status and prevents them from becoming undocumented and thus subject to detention and deportation.

b. Adopt procedures that permit minors that are close to the age of majority to continue their education without interruption.

c. Adopt policies that require the registration of all births, providing each newborn with a birth certificate.

9. **Encourage States to adopt national policies that provide equal access to education for migrant, asylum seeker and refugee learners of all levels.**

For example:

a. Enact national or regional policies which provide migrants and refugees with access to primary and secondary education level no matter their migratory status.

b. Enact policies which provide that the primary and secondary education to which migrants and refugees have access meets the same standards of education received by citizens.

10. Encourage States to adopt legislation which provides migrants and refugees with access to adequate social protections.

For example:

a. Enact legislation which ensures the right to health of migrants and refugees, including access to primary health-care services, regardless of their migratory status and immediately upon arrival.

b. Enact legislation that grants access to national pension schemes and that guarantees the portability of social security coverage and benefits between and among countries to prevent migrants and refugees from losing entitlements due to their migration status.

11. Encourage States to enact legislation to prevent migrants and refugees from becoming "stateless."

In particular:

a. Enact legislation granting adequate protection and standards of treatment in respect of rights and freedoms as established by international conventions addressing statelessness and human rights treaties and provisions relevant to the right to a nationality.

b. Enact legal and policy reforms that are necessary to address statelessness effectively, working in the four areas of statelessness – identification, prevention, reduction and protection – and aiming at granting citizenship to children at birth.

3. To Promote: Advancing Migrants' and Refugees' Integral Human Development

At the present time the average duration of exile for those who have fled armed conflict is 17 years. For labour migrants as well, the time away from home can amount to many years. Hosting states, rather than providing merely emergency responses and basic services, should assure structures which allow those staying long-term to develop as human beings and to contribute to the development of the host country. Moreover, since a basic principle of the 2030 Sustainable Development Goals is to "leave no one behind", the international community should take care to include refugees, asylum seekers and labour migrants in their development plans. The following action points are suggested:

12. Encourage States to enact legislation that enables the recognition, transfer and further development of the formal skills of all migrants, asylum seekers, and refugees residing in the host country.

For example:

a. Enact policies which provide access to tertiary education as well as support for qualified migrants, asylum seekers and refugees.
b. Enact policies which provide equal access to apprenticeship and internship programmes for qualified migrants, asylum seekers and refugees on the same basis as citizens.
c. Enact policies which facilitate the assessment, validation and recognition of academic and vocational education, including higher education, of migrants and refugees through, for example, inter-university arrangements as well as bilateral and multilateral agreements.

13. Encourage States to adopt laws, policies and practices which facilitate the local integration of migrants, asylum seekers and refugee populations.

For example:

a. Where they do not already exist, enact laws that recognize the right of asylum seekers and refugees to freedom of movement and freedom to choose their place of residence.
b. Where they do not already exist, enact laws that recognize the right of asylum seekers and refugees to work, at the time of registration with appropriate national authorities.
c. Adopt policies which provide access to classes and training in the local language and customs as well as the printing of public notices and information in those languages most common among migrant and refugee populations within the host country.

14. Encourage States to adopt policies and practices which promote and preserve the integrity and well-being of the family regardless of migratory status.

For example:

a. Enact laws which allow for the reunification of refugees and migrants with their families and that recognize the right of these family members to work. A minimum level of income, or proof of the ability to provide financial support, should not be a requirement for the reunification of minors with their parents.

b. Enact laws which expand the scope of family reunification policies to include all family members (including grandparents, siblings and grandchildren) in order to allow the entire family to remain united in the resettlement process.

c. Enact policies which facilitate family tracing and reunification.

d. Enact laws which prohibit and actively prevent the abuse of minor workers, ensuring that the work is safe and does not harm their health, well-being or jeopardize their educational opportunities

15. Encourage States to adopt policies and practices that provide migrants, asylum seekers and refugees with special needs or vulnerabilities with the same opportunities as other disabled citizens.

For example:

a. Enact policies which provide all disabled with access to assistance devices to the disabled (for example, wheelchairs, guide dogs, hearing aids) regardless of migratory status.

b. Enact policies which promote rapid access to special education or vocational training as well as health care for unaccompanied or separated minors who are disabled.

16. Encourage the international community to increase its share of development and emergency assistance to States which host and support large influxes of refugees and migrants fleeing armed conflict so all may benefit, regardless of migratory status.

For example:

a. Encourage donor States to tailor aid and assistance to include the development of medical, educational, and social services infrastructure in hosting areas upon arrival. For example, paying for the construction of additional classrooms and funding teacher training where local capacity has been overwhelmed or exhausted.

b. Encourage donor States to adopt policies that set aside a percentage of the direct assistance, as well as access to programmes and services, provided to refugees and migrants, for the benefit of local families experiencing similar economic and social disadvantages.

17. Encourage States to adopt policies and practices that guarantee the freedom of religion, in both belief and practice, to all migrants and refugees regardless of their migratory status.

4. To Integrate: Enriching Communities through wider Participation of Migrants and Refugees

The acceptance of migrants and refugees is an opportunity for new understanding and broader horizons, both on the part of those accepted, who have the responsibility to respect the values, traditions and laws of the community which takes them in, and on the part of the latter, who are called to acknowledge the beneficial contribution which each immigrant can make to the whole community. Both sides are mutually enriched by their interaction, and the community as a whole is enhanced by a greater participation of all its members, both resident and migrants. This is also true for the migrant or refugee who chooses to return home. The following actions points are suggested:

18. On the basis that integration is neither assimilation nor incorporation, but a "two-way process," which is essentially rooted in the joint recognition of the other's cultural richness, encourage States to enact legislation which facilitates local integration.

For example:

a. Adopt laws and constitutional provisions aimed at granting citizenship at birth.
b. Adopt laws which provide timely access to citizenship for all refugees.
c. Adopt a rights and needs based approach to the granting of citizenship. Citizenship should not be contingent on economic status or the ownership of property.
d. Adopt laws that grant citizenship without "new language requirements" for older applicants (over fifty years of age).
e. Adopt laws which facilitate the legal migration of family members of foreign residents.
f. Adopt laws which allow for the regularization of status for long term residents of the host country.

19. Encourage States to adopt policies and programmes which actively promote a positive narrative on migrants and refugees and the solidarity towards them.

For example:

a. Provide subsidies to municipalities and faith-based communities to host events which showcase positive aspects of the culture of the members of the foreign community.
b. Engage in public campaigns that identity and promote positive examples of individuals and groups hosting refugees and migrants and integrating them into their local communities.
c. Require public announcements to be issued in the language spoken by larger groups of migrants and refugees.
d. Enact policies that promote hospitality within the local communities, and which actively seek to welcome and integrate migrants into the local community.

20. When foreign nationals are forced to flee from violence or environmental crisis in the host country, they are often eligible for voluntary repatriation programmes or evacuation programmes. In these cases, the host State, donor states or the State of origin should be encouraged

to adopt policies and procedures which facilitate the reintegration of returnees.

For example:

a. Increase donor funding for enhancing the infrastructure in areas of return or transitions assistance for returning workers caught up in foreign crisis.

b. Enact laws that recognize and allow for the transfer of educational or other credentials earned abroad by returning citizens and permit rapid access to labour markets for those with professional or vocational credentials (e.g. trained teachers, electricians, medical personnel and heavy equipment operators).

Source: https://holyseemission.org/index.php

1

Introduction

Migration, labour migration, seasonal migration, circular migration, internal migration, distressed migration, forced migration, involuntary migration, disaster induced migration, poverty caused migration, conflict driven migration, development generated migration are the terms[1] one hears constantly these days when one talks about social issues. As the reality of migration unfolds itself on the global scenario and in a powerful bang by the lives and struggles of the distressed migrants, migration as personal, social and inter-national phenomenon challenges us.

Migration talks about the movement of people. People migrate for various reasons. It could be within and or outside a locality or intrastate and interstate. Migration is also both within the national territory or transnational. Migration could be to mitigate the distressed situation or to enhance employment and economic prospectus. These types of migrations have played a key role in shaping the local, regional, national and global communities, economies and cultures.

Human mobility is as old as human history and herstory. The need to avail of better opportunities for survival has been the main motive for such movement of people. In recent centuries, the pattern of growth and development and or underdevelopment has

[1] Various terms are used to understand and address this historical, massive, expanding human reality called migration. Each of this term highlight various aspects of this reality. This book repeatedly uses the term distressed labour migration or distressed labour migrant.

increasingly conditioned available opportunities for workers. This reality which is often termed as 'push and pull factors' speak of what probably happens in the lives of the migrants. Migration continues to go on unabated irrespective of all the noise made about the policies and programs by the ruling elite. Migration also goes on without end due to dire need of survival of those who are at the periphery of society. It is their hard labour and toil which keeps the economy of many countries ticking.

In turn, these workers - many of them migrants - have been the main contributors to growth and prosperity. Despite the increased ability of society and governments to ameliorate the costs of migration, the most vulnerable among the migrants pay heavy price. At times, even with their lives. At the same time, the benefits of growth and development that has accrued to them have been disproportionately small. This means, their labour and the sacrifices they and their families make benefit others but not them.

Migration is a heterogeneous phenomenon, with significant variety among migrants in terms of initial levels of education, skills, and economic background. Internal migrants are from varying backgrounds. Evidence suggests that in India the better-off segment of the population is migrating more in the post-globalization period. But this is only part of the story. The movement of the poor and vulnerable segment is also increasing. Most of this group remains undocumented. Labour migrants and seasonal migrants generally occupy the lower end of the labour market. They are self-employed and regular wage workers, as well as casual workers. Social networks play an important role in facilitating internal migration. But labour intermediaries or what is called agents also play a very significant role in mobilizing migrant workers for a number of industries.[2]

Migration is a process of movement. It is a movement that moves people, cultures, resources and ideas from one place to another. It has changed and challenged the existing cultures, ideas, resources, etc., and also has enhanced them for betterment. Migration has emerged in the last few years as a crucial socio-political, economic and policy matter. In a special way, it highlights issues like employment,

---

[2] Ravi Srivastav and Amit Kumar Pandey. *Internal and International Migration in South Asia: Drivers, Interlinkage and Policy Issues*. UNESCO: New Delhi. 2017.

displacement, disenfranchisement, integration, safe migration, disintegration, etc.

Migration directly impacts employment and labour markets in the source areas, as well as the income, assets and expenditure of households. Internal migration also has significant links with development, both in source areas – through remittance inflows, increase in investment, knowledge flows and skill enhancement – and in destination areas, principally through labour market impacts. Migration is also a coping strategy for the poorest migrants. Out-migration reduces unemployment and underemployment. However, large-scale out-migration can affect emotionally, intellectually, culturally, religiously, spiritually, socially, economically, politically the women and elderly people who are left behind.

In South Asian countries like India, Bangladesh, Sri Lanka and Nepal, domestic remittance inflows are an important source of income to migrant households. These inflows lead to a reduction in poverty.[3] But there is an ongoing debate about whether they also contribute to growing inequality. The impact of migrants on destination labour markets is very important. The migration of labourers eases the labour supply at destination and makes accumulation and growth possible. Employers prefer migrant labour because it is flexible, easy to control, cheaper and loose labour rules and no labour unions.

Migrants generally work in the informal sector,[4] often in those sectors where local labourers are reluctant to work, and they have flexible hours. Sometimes, migration is the exit mechanism from the existing social hierarchy. However, migrant workers are denied basic rights and decent working conditions. Their wages are often below that of local labourers and lower than the legal minimum wage. In many places, migrant workers work in sub-human conditions, and in violation of labour laws. Poor migrant workers lack access to entitlements at destination. This has an effect on their living and health conditions. They lack proper housing and are concentrated in

---

[3] Imran Khan. *An Impact Analysis of Remittance Inflows on Reducing Income-based Poverty in South Asia.* Sage Journals. October 26, 2023.

[4] In India, informal labour constitutes a significant portion of the workforce, with over 85% of jobs falling under this category. This sector is characterized by a lack of formal contracts, job security, and social benefits, often affecting the welfare and livelihoods of those employed.

slum areas of urban centres. In the absence of proper urban planning and development, rural–urban migration creates pressure on facilities in destination areas. As a consequence, policy-makers view internal migration negatively. There is a tendency to restrict internal migration flows, especially to cities.

In terms of number of migrants, there are differences of opinions, estimates, informations and data. For example, as of 2024, India became the most populated nation in the world, with 1 in 7 humans on the planet identifying themselves as an Indian. Thus, India has taken over from China as the first most populous country. Among these individuals, an estimated 600 million or 60 crore Indians are internal migrants. Due to lack of well planned and executed survey on internal migrants, there are more estimates than actual number. This also goes to state the fact that compared to international migration, internal migration is not a priority to the government of India.

According to the 2011 Census, the number of internal migrants in India was 450 million, that is, 45 crores. As per the data of 2011, Uttar Pradesh and Bihar were the largest source of inter-state migrants while Maharashtra and Delhi were the largest receiver states. Around 83 lakh residents of Uttar Pradesh and 63 lakh residents of Bihar had moved either temporarily or permanently to other states. Around 60 lakh people from across India had migrated to Maharashtra by 2011.[5] These numbers could be even more due to the distress the labourers are facing, due to the loss of jobs post-covid, lack of livelihood from agriculture, lack of employment and due to policies and programs of the government.

It is good to pay attention to the links between internal and international migration. The segmentation that is observed between internal and international migration appears to be a matter of degree. The main distinguishing features between internal and international migrants are the regulatory barriers they face, their skills, financial endowments, social networks and access to other recruitment channels. Migrants who have low skills and social networks suffer from lack of information about the labour markets, are engaged through intermediaries, employed at the lower end of the labour

[5] It is pertinent to note that the census 2011-2020 was undertaken but the government of India has not released the census report yet. Also, we are in 2025, but census work has not begun. Due to this one can only estimate the volume of migration.

market, and are likely to suffer from a strikingly similar range of deprivations, both as internal and international migrants. The decision to embark upon boils down first to whether potential migrants have access to networks and recruitment channels, and second, whether they can meet the higher costs of migration.

While, international migration is a preferred movement of the people by the people and the government, the hardships, discriminations and sufferings these labour migrants go through is painful and avoidable. For instance, 400 migrants from Gopalganj district of Bihar were stuck in Saudi Arabia as reported in most of the dailies on 19th May, 2025.[6] As reported for the last 8 months they do not have job, they do not have payment and some of their passport has been taken away by the company which recruited them from India. These labourers are in touch with their family members to get them back to their homes. This is the matter to be handled by the labour department. But since the migrants are in a foreign country, it is placed under the external affairs ministry of Government of India. The external affairs ministry is busy selling out 'Operation Sindoor,'[7] hence it does not bother about the plight of these migrants.

Interestingly, the government of India has pre-departure training manual for international migrants but nothing for internal migration. Titled, "Important Information for Migrant Workers: Handbook on Pre-Departure Orientation was jointly prepared by the government and India Centre for Migration, New Delhi. This is a good attempt to prepare the international migrants. But there is nothing like this for internal migrants.[8] One of the ways this awareness can be created is by placing big cut outs or play related clips it on the screens in railway stations and bus stands.

Workers can use migration ladders – internal or intra-regional migration to acquire resources or networks, and then migrate abroad.

---

[6] Bihar, Bengal and Uttar Pradesh migrant labourers stuck in Saudi Arabi. Dainik Jagaran. 19/05/2025.

[7] Operation Sindoor is the name given to the war with Pakistan by the present Indian government. Now it is busy selling the idea that it did not go for war but was forced to do so, due to terrorist activities from Pakistan.

[8] Realising this need, the Bihar Migrant Hub has prepared "Migrant Labour's Pre-Departure Training Program' in English and Hindi and during campaign and festival times when the migrants return home or leave home, we inform migrants many aspects they need to keep in mind.

Skills demand and supply can also be a major issue in both international and internal migration. Migrants in both streams are predominantly low-skilled, but the national market and the international market both have a demand for skills, and individuals with skills can compete for the more attractive segment of the job markets in these professions. If training is provided at the lower skill levels also, it is very likely that it will have a favourable impact on job conditions. Thus, despite the differences, there are obvious links between internal and international migration which can be configured into national policies.

From the foregoing pages, we can see that we have stated the fact that the focus of this study is internal migration. This is due to the fact that often times, the internal migrants get very limited attention from various stakeholders, especially the government. Secondly, the number of internal migrants outweigh the external migrants. Thirdly, the condition of the internal migrants is more deplorable than the external migrants.

Our focus is not those who migrated due to marriage.[9] Numerically, migration due to marriage appears to be one of the factors. There are also others who go to exploit the so-called economic boom. For instance, the people of Bihar migrate to Jharkhand since Jharkhand is a mineral rich state and the scope for employment is great. During an economic boom, some individuals or groups may take advantage of the situation by engaging in activities that benefit them financially, even if these activities are not in the best interest of the broader economy or society. Business corporates like Adani and Ambani's moved out and continue to move out to maintain their business empire. But this book focuses on those who migrated to eke out a living.

This discussion on labour migration is placed against the ongoing debates on the changes in patterns of employment and job creation in India, during the period of economic liberalisation, under the 'Inclusive Growth' policies since 2004, and under the impact of the global financial crisis, in the context of around 93% of India's workforce currently being in 'informal employment', and growing inequalities. Migration patterns, to some extent, mirror the changes in labour markets and the dominance of informal employment more

[9] It is unfortunate that the national census continues to focus on marriage as a major factor in migration but pays limited attention on the labour migration.

generally, but not completely, and too little attention tends to be placed on the study of migration, particularly its changes over time. Too often, also, existing analysis is caught in simple two-sector models, neglects the diversity of labour mobility within India as elsewhere.[10]

The subject of migration remains contested, for a variety of reasons. Politically, while there is generally a preference for or at least an acceptance of people moving when there is a demand for labour, there are at least equally strong voices strengthened in times of crises calling for reducing the number of migrants. Academically, questions remain regarding the causes and impacts of migration, and how mobility relates to inequality and poverty. Disciplinary differences regarding approaches to understanding migration continue to exist. It is a fact that while there are general lessons regarding migration, the links between migration and poverty are deeply context-specific.[11] This can be spelt out in this manner.

First, the movement of people is much more common than is usually assumed, and has existed for much longer than is often acknowledged. Both recorded and unrecorded data indicate the movements of people, especially of the labour class from ages. Unfortunately much of that, therefore, remains unrecorded. Labour migration also assumes many forms, of which the classic rural–urban transition is only one: the movement of entire households is only one of them, and the (usually) more common form is the movement of one member of the household, who retains links with her or his origins, migrating for varying and often a-priori unknown periods of time.

Second, the question of who migrates does not have a simple answer. In different contexts, different individuals and socio-economic groups migrate, prompted by different capabilities, opportunities, and differentiated access. Different regions and countries have varying propensities for migration, to different types of destinations and opportunities: simple push-pull models tend to be inadequate to explain the complexity of segmented migration streams. but often the poorest people (or those lacking sufficient labour within households) may not be able to migrate, and the poorest areas do not necessarily have the largest number of migrants. The phenomenon of

---

[10] Arjan de Haan. *Inclusive Growth? Labour Migration and Poverty in India. The Indian Journal of Labour Economics,* Vol. 54, No. 3, 2011, p. 387.

[11] Ibid. p. 388.

chain-migration leads to a great deal of path dependency—though not determinism—in terms of migration patterns.[12]

Globally, with technological change, migration has tended to become more selective, thereby offering fewer opportunities for unskilled workers. This is a reality in a much more literate and educated communities and countries. But less literate and less educated communities and countries like India, technology surely plays a positive role regarding migration. But to conclude that technology propels migration may be bit farfetched for India.

Third, caste, class, gender, age and location constitute the key elements to understanding migration processes. There are no generalities about whether men or women migrate, though a great deal of path dependency and gender stereotyping exist. While in most places, young men might be over-represented amongst migrants, thus constituting particular gendered and household impacts, women have always been mobile as well with outside movement for marriage being a dominant reason for migration in India, and moving for engaging in 'traditional' female occupations and newer ones,[13] including unskilled and semi-skilled manufacturing and service sector jobs.[14] Female migrants tend to be particularly vulnerable, and suffer from labour market discrimination and violence, but migration also has an impact on gender identity and relations.

Fourth, the reasons for migrating are diverse, with 'push-and-pull' being differently configured for different types of migrants. Statistical data tend to record only one reason for migration, thus under-estimating the complexity of migration. Migration often arises from desperation, lack of work, or indebtedness. Seasonal migration, including rural–rural and rural–urban, for many households, is part of regular household strategies. but a lot of migration is also driven by

---

[12] Chain migration is the social process by which immigrants from a particular area follow others from that area to a particular destination.

[13] ILO. (2024). Gendering internal labour migration corridors Migrant women workers in southern India's garment industry. Young women from Odisha and Jharkhand are moving into the garment industries in south India. Interestingly, those girls who worked as workers in garment factories later become agents to supply girls for same work. There is also competition between women and men agents.

[14] Arianne M. Gaetano and Brenda S. A. Yeoh. (2010) *Introduction to the Special Issue on Women and Migration in Globalizing Asia: Gendered Experiences, Agency, and Activism, International Migration,* 2010 Vol. 48, No. 6, pp. 1-12.

the hope or idea of better opportunities and broadening horizons, or is part of rites of passage of young men and women.

Fifth, as the reasons and patterns of migration are diverse, so also are its impacts. At the household level, migration usually improves incomes and well-being, but often tends to maintain levels of living. For example, illustrated by a common expression that remittances allow farmer households to plough their land as opposed to losing land. The areas of origin usually show clear signs of migrant remittances,[15] but there appear to be relatively few cases of transformation of areas, thereby also suggesting that migration tends to be part of the regions' economies rather than initiating economic development, or causing severe brain drain.[16] The question of impacts on the areas of destination has received relatively a lot of attention, but assessments tend to vary, such as migrants being positively seen as enhancing growth and well-being, to being negatively perceived as a drain on local economies as well as upsetting local cultures.

Studies that have been undertaken in the recent past about migration, show that rural people have become even more mobile in the last few years, with deteriorating employment prospects locally and emerging opportunities elsewhere. With the exception of the poorest of the poor, the largest landowners and successful businessmen, nearly all others including medium farmers and forward castes are migrating. While the most educated and wealthy, usually upper caste but not always migrate for secure and well paid jobs on a more permanent basis, the vast majority of migrants go for periods ranging from 3 to 9 months. Scheduled Castes and Economically Backward Castes are engaged in both short distance and long distance migration but usually in the lowest paid jobs.

Farm labouring work, casual labouring work in construction, work in brick kilns and rickshaw pulling are the four most important categories of work for the poorest, unskilled, landless and lowest caste migrants. This includes, but is not limited to the Musahar, Manjhi, Dom, and other SCs. They are prevented from breaking away

---

[15] International remittances have received a great deal of interest over the last decade, for example because they now far outstrip official ODA flows and many governments have become increasingly welcoming of remittances as a source of foreign earnings.

[16] Economic and human development increases people's capabilities and aspirations and therefore tends to coincide with an increase rather than a decrease in emigration.

from such jobs because of their limited skills, education and social networks.

Discrimination at the destination is also a factor in keeping certain castes in certain jobs and perpetuating the strong segmentation that exists in migrant labour markets. There are also strong indications that many migrants belonging to the broad and diverse category of Other Backward Castes (OBCs) have become upwardly mobile, graduating from farm work to work in a variety of industries where earnings are higher. Simultaneously they have become more spatially diversified, using their social networks to switch between destinations that are often quite far from each other, in order to move up the job ladder in occupations that require similar skills. The result is that migrants from Bihar have now spread their networks to destinations all over India in a way that was not evident a decade ago. The choice of destination is strongly determined by social networks – people from a particular caste and village tend to go to the same destination and into similar occupations. Distance and transport facilities are not as important in determining the choice of destination.

Brick Kiln and Migrant Economy

India is estimated to produce about 250 billion bricks annually, i.e., about a tenth of global production. The industry is characterised by low capital-intensity and seasonal employment, and is located in rural areas and urban peripheries, i.e., it will not be captured as usual rural urban migration, but as rural to rural migration. Employment estimates vary widely, from 10 million by ILO to 1.5 mn. by NSSO. Employment is for about seven months, beginning in early winter till the onset of monsoon. Men and women prepare arrange and transport bricks. Accompanying children can also help out on site. Injuries are commonly reported. Medical expenses are reportedly met initially by the contractor, but later deducted from wages. Accommodation on work sites is provided by the contractor, but it usually comprises structures of bricks and plastic sheets, lacking basic facilities like water and sanitation.[17] While the owner of the brick kiln and the contractors make money, the migrant labourers pay by their labour and at times by life.

[17] GoI. Report of the Working Group on Migration. Ministry of Housing and Urban Poverty Alleviation. January. 2017.

A large number of people belonging to the Musahar caste migrate from Bihar to brick kilns in Uttar Pradesh and West Bengal where they stay for 7-8 months in a year. The Musahar (literal translation is rat-eaters), are classified as a scheduled caste and they have remained largely on the periphery of society. They are usually found in the least paid and most degrading jobs with the worst terms of employment. Apart from brick kiln work, large numbers of Musahar work in crop harvesting, which is also one of the least well paid occupations. Recruiting for brick kiln work is done through an agent who gives their families a wage advance. Thus brick kiln workers continue to work without any form of social protection or social security and the overall benefit for the migrant is being able to eat regularly. However in the absence of education and health systems that cater to migrants, the costs have remained very high.[18]

Factors that Lead to Migration

Most studies have highlighted the fact that the movement of people from one place to another, is driven by a complex interplay of "push" and "pull" factors. Push factors, such as poverty, lack of opportunities, natural disasters, and conflict, force individuals to leave their homes. Pull factors, like better job prospects, higher wages, and improved access to education, attract people to new locations.

1. **Better Employment Opportunities:** This in addition promises improvement in the standard of living. In this scenario, people seek migration as a way to cope with unemployment and poverty.
2. **Education:** Better education opportunities motivates people to move.
3. **To Overcome Poverty And Improve The Quality of Life:** Escaping from poverty is one of the major reasons for migration.
4. **For Security and Safety:** It is difficult to survive in a place where someone's basic rights are violated. Hence, the person either individually or with family moves out to safer locations.

[18] Priya Deshingkar and Shaheen Akter. Migration and Human Development in India. Human Development Research Paper 2009/13.

5. **Marriage And Family Reunification:** Marital stability is one of the most common reasons for migration to secure the stability of the family.
6. **Better Healthcare:** Better healthcare services motivate people to migrate.
7. **Religious, Cultural, And Lifestyle Reasons:** Migration has also been seen due to the suitable personal cultural beliefs and religious practices occurring in some places.
8. **Political Instability And Turmoil:** Political turmoil, uncertainty, crisis and violence are also common reasons for migration.
9. **Natural Disasters And Climate Change also leads to migration.**
10. **Discrimination And Disharmony:** Discrimination based on caste, class, ethnicity, gender, language, religion and region can also force people to move out.

While these factors propel motivation in general, the distressed labour migrants we are concerned in this book is a special focus group for our understanding, accompaniment, providing assistance and advocating their cause.

There is a high level of diversity in labour migration in India. Progressive analysis of both macro data and micro studies reveals that labour migration across different age groups and genders is not limited to rural or urban areas or any specific states or regions. To offer a singular explanation of what drives labour migration is thus quite difficult. The nature and magnitude of internal labour migration need to be located in the broader political economy and development context of India. The key drivers of migration are summarized in the subsequent sections (ILO 2020, p. 13).

Among the workers who make temporary moves within India, there is an over-representation of Adivasis, Dalits, religious minorities, the poor, the less educated, the landless, those from rural areas and those who were engaged in agriculture in their source region. The National Commission for Enterprises in the Unorganised Sector (NCEUS), using secondary and macro-data, established a nexus of poverty, vulnerability, type of employment and social status of workers. Because of these reasons, these workers tend to undertake the riskiest, lowest paying and most hazardous jobs, with clear patterns of segmentation by caste and gender. This signifies how social inequalities are replicated in the segmentation of the labour markets.

Disadvantaged caste groups, for example, embrace migration as an opportunity to escape unfair practices in their villages, such as caste based discrimination in accessing employment, opting for other livelihood options. It plays a crucial role as a poverty interrupter in the case of households in remote rural areas or for those in chronic poverty. Natural disasters, climatic conditions and conflicts also contribute to migration in search of livelihoods.

The economic model is focused on cities and certain sectors of economic growth. This has led to the creation of both spatial (between rural and urban) and sectoral (between primary and tertiary) inequalities. The agrarian crisis in India, with reduction in person-days of available farm work and reduced public investment in the primary sector, intensified migration for work. The resultant decline in real earnings, lower consumption by the rural poor and growing landlessness left people with limited choice but to migrate out for livelihoods. Connectivity has also been another important driver of labour migration in the country. Enhanced access to road and rail networks, communication channels and information about availability of work has also given a boost to migration in India.

Migration also occurs in pursuit of better livelihoods and socio-economic mobility. Migrant workers aim to enhance their consumption and standard of living by migrating to major cities that offer better resources, better educational facilities for children and a wider range of livelihood options. Migration also helps workers to finance expenses for marriage or to enhance their asset base, by means such as improving housing or even buying land.

Invisibility, Fragmentation and Informality

Migrant workers remain un-enumerated and unrecognized at the local, regional and national levels. The interface between migrant workers and public systems and services can be established only if there are reliable databases at all levels of governance. It is challenging for local self-governments (LSGs) and labour departments to engage with high labour mobility as it is characterized by informality and lack of documentation. The labour market is highly fragmented, wherein production processes are often outsourced to smaller units in the supply chains that engage migrant workers. These supply chains are heavily subcontracted in a way that makes it difficult to establish the relationship between business owners and workers, with no clear lines of accountability resulting in unfair labour practices. Informally employed in casual work arrangements and frequently paid on a piece rate basis, these workers remain outside the purview of employee welfare. The existing gap in the unionization of migrant workers is also an important reason for the precarious nature of their employment. In the absence of adequate bargaining power and representation, migrant workers may not be able to demand their rightful wages and decent working conditions. Language barriers also add to the challenges faced by migrant workers.[19]

Informal settlements[20] in open spaces, such as public or private land, on road pavements, under flyovers and near railways tracks are a prominent typology of how migrants choose to live in cities. While such arrangements allow them to live among their community members, they also expose them to the risk of frequent evictions and alienate them from access to basic amenities such as water and sanitation. Construction sites and factories doubling up as night shelters are common forms of housing for migrant workers. This not only aggravates their alienation from the city, but also exposes them greatly to the toxicity at the workplace, compromising physical safety and well-being.

An absence of dignified housing is further aggravated by a lack of adequate water, sanitation and hygiene (WASH) facilities. Despite the installation of public toilets through a slew of schemes in urban areas, their availability may not be adequate in migrant-dense clusters. Moreover, the affordability of such services may create barriers to access for low-waged migrant workers. Women and girls bear the burden of the implications of inadequate provisions for dignified

[19] IL O. Road map for developing a policy framework for the inclusion of internal migrant workers in India. International Labour Organisation. 2020.

[20] Informal settlements, also known as slums, shantytowns, or squatter settlements, are residential areas that lack formal government recognition and often lack basic services and infrastructure. They are characterized by informal housing, often built near roads, railway tracks, river bands, etc. These people are displaced from these at any time under beautification, security reasons, VIP visits, etc.

housing and sanitation while also increasing their vulnerability to harassment and sexual abuse.

Financial Insecurity

In India, one in three workers does not receive minimum wages, with casual workers forming the large proportion of that group. Migrant workers, who are in most cases casual workers, are paid on a piece-rate basis and form the bulk of workers falling outside the ambit of minimum wage laws. The report of the NCEUS, that is, National Commission for Enterprises in the Unorganised Sector[21] also highlights the significant overlap between the most impoverished sections of the populations and migrant workers. Wage protection laws remain unimplemented in the case of migrant workers due to their inability to prove formal employment relations, with wage fraud (wage theft) being a common occurrence.

Poor financial inclusion and low levels of literacy of migrant workers compromise their access to social security schemes. While a major chunk of migrant workers in the country is in the construction sector, they are not aware of the Building and Other Construction Workers Welfare Board (BOCW). A paradigm shift occurred during the 41st Labour Ministers Conference in May 1995.[22] Recognizing the urgent need to address challenges faced by construction workers, a consensus emerged which led to the enactment of the Building and Other Construction Workers (Regulation of Employment and Conditions of Service) Ordinance, 1995. This marked a crucial step towards regulating employment conditions, enhancing safety standards, and improving the welfare of construction workers nationwide.

Several government programmes exist to offer social security benefits to migrant workers and are implemented through the banking systems. However, overburdened bank branches have little room to counsel migrants about the details of each scheme or to enroll workers

---

[21] In August 2005, the National Commission published an ambitious plan (The Unorganized Sector Workers Social Security Draft Bill) aiming to provide a minimum level of social protection benefits to some 300 million informal economy workers. But this remained at the most a document to be quoted and referred to.

[22] These kinds of ministerial level meetings are not organised anymore and hence issues of labourers are not taken up for deliberations and action.

in them. The financial institutions in India need to, therefore, cater to the requirements of this segment of the population.

Special efforts should be made to address the banking requirements of migrant workers taking into account their work timings. Since remittances are the lifeline of many migrant households, the Jan Dhan Bank accounts promoted by the GoI should take into consideration the requirements of the migrant workers and ensure their financial inclusion and participation through this scheme. Linguistic barriers further add to the problem, resulting in migrants often falling prey to financial frauds in their attempt to access social security.

Forced Labour Conditions

Migrant workers may end up working in conditions of, or akin to, forced labour. In situations where workers live within the worksites, such as manufacturing units, brick kilns, construc-tion sites, or, for domestic workers, their employer's residence, by packaging the accommodation as a "perk", this arrangement could place migrant workers in highly exploitative circumstances where they are available to the employer for work round the clock. Other situations may include deceptive or coercive recruitment, such as when migrant workers are recruited without providing full and correct information about the nature of work, wages or working conditions; excessive deductions purportedly for food and accommodation; or being forced to migrate on account of an often intergenerational debt bondage. Such situations may also amount to human trafficking.

Further, the migrant workforce is a heterogeneous category, with several highly vulnerable subpopulations. These include women, children, older persons, persons with disabilities and historically marginalized communities who have specific vulnerabilities at their work destinations because of social stigmatization. These vulnerabilities make migrant workers highly dependent on contractors/employers for addressing their needs, and end up creating forced labour conditions. Unwritten and unilateral contracts with and debt-based attachments to the employer are some other examples of such conditions. There are also instances where women and children have been trafficked for labour.

Labour Burden on Women

Migrant women face severe gender-based challenges in the regions to which they migrate. These challenges include, among others, discrimination in labour markets, vulnerabilities in living spaces, and a lack of access to public spaces. They are more invisible in comparison to their male counterparts. This lack of visibility is "marriage migrants." However, women who move with their husbands after marriage tend to work in the destination regions.

Migrant women are largely concentrated in sectors where they are not identified as workers. They are employed as helpers to carry and lift materials in the construction sector along with their spouses or male relatives. This role, which is at the lowest end of the labour chain, is almost exclusively reserved for them. They are often not paid at par with their male co-workers. Perverse payment practices such as the *jodi*-based system, where husbands or male relatives are paid the price of 1.5 labour units[23] when they are employed as a couple, have been observed in some construction labour markets.

For a significant section of women migrants, worksites are within households. More than half of the migrant women in Mumbai and Delhi were reported to be domestic workers. Among these, live-in workers face additional challenges of work conditions akin to forced/bonded labour, including a lack of privacy, defined working hours, and access to trade unions or other organizations working with domestic workers. With multiple employers and the non-applicability of labour laws, domestic workers struggle to access minimum wages, social protection or workplace safety and health, all of which are integral to the decent working conditions of a domestic worker as stated in the ILO Domestic Worker Convention, 2011 (No. 189).

Many migrant women employed in the small manufacturing sector, especially textiles and garments, tend to be home-based workers, who receive orders from agents and subcontractors. They do not have formal employment relationships and are paid on a piece-

[23] This is the height of the exploitative nature of the caste, feudal and patriarchal world view and behaviour. For instance, women are treated as second class citizens. Labourers are also treated as second class citizens. If the person is a labourer and a women, then that person is doubly oppressed and exploited. Thirdly, this will not be done to an upper caste, high class, educated, sophisticated, English speaking women. Hence, when one hears that Indian women have achieved empowerment, this refers to only the women of top echelon. They are in army, navy, air force, IT sector, corporates etc.

rate basis, with very low remuneration based on their output. They fall completely outside the ambit of labour legislations as they are considered self-employed, even though their work is survivalist in nature and highly vulnerable.

Migrant women also constitute a substantial proportion of intra-state or rural-to-rural migration, to work in hazardous sectors, under unsafe conditions, often forming family-based or single-female labour in sectors such as brick kilns, mines or agriculture and other allied sectors. They face complete exclusion from state systems and public consciousness due to the invisibility of these migration streams. Harassment, accidents, trafficking and bondage are common in these highly vulnerable migration streams.

Impacts of Migration: From various studies it is clear that migration can have positive as well as negative effects on the life of the migrants. Here we are looking at migrants as a general category. When we look at the distressed migrants, the discourse would be different.

Positive Impact

- Unemployment is reduced and people get better job opportunities.
- Migration helps in improving the quality of life of people.
- It helps to improve social life of people as they learn about new culture, customs, and languages which helps to improve brotherhood among people.
- Migration of skilled workers leads to a greater economic growth of the family and region.[24]
- Children get better opportunities for higher education.
- The population density is reduced and the birth rate decreases.

Negative Impact

- The loss of a person from rural areas, impact on the level of output and development of rural areas.
- The influx of workers in urban areas increases competition for the job, houses, school facilities etc.

[24] Priya Deshingkar, Sushil Kumar, Harendra Kumar Choubey and Dhananjay Kumar. *The Role of Migration and Remittances in Promoting Livelihoods in Bihar.* Overseas Development Institute: London. December, 2006.

- Having large population puts too much pressure on natural resources, amenities and services.
- It is difficult for a villager to survive in urban areas because in urban areas there is no natural environment and pure air. They have to pay for each and everything.
- Migration changes the population of a place, therefore, the distribution of the population is uneven in India.
- Many migrants are completely illiterate and uneducated, therefore, they are not only unfit for most jobs, but also lack basic knowledge and life skills.
- Poverty makes them unable to live a normal and healthy life.
- Children growing up in poverty have no access to proper nutrition, education or health.
- Migration increased the slum areas in cities which increase many problems such as unhygienic conditions, crime, pollution etc.
- Sometimes migrants are exploited.
- Migration is one of the main causes of increasing nuclear family where children grow up without a wider family circle.

Daniel Groody of the US stated, "It is ironic that the government sees everyone attempting illegal entry at the border with Mexico as a potential terrorist, while the perpetrators of the 9/11 tragedy all came in on legal visas."

Juan Rivera, a Notre Dame accounting professor, said the North American Free Trade Agreement has not worked because "**you are dealing with unequal partners**." The average hourly wage for a manufacturing job in Mexico is $2.17, while in the United States it's $18.24. Mexicans are lured to this country not only by this income differential but by the tempting 2,000-mile span of the border and by the illusion of unlimited opportunity as viewed on American television. This has been going on for ages.

Thus, how we treat the migrants depends upon how we view migrants. This introductory section tried to highlight some of these factors so as to make an entry into the lives and the struggles of the distressed labour migrants.

2

State of the Distressed Migrants

Karu Manjhi was from Shivala village of Danapur Block of Patna District of Bihar. He along with 2 of his villagers was going in 2014 to Bengaluru being paid by an agent with the promise of construction work. Travelling in general compartment in the summer heat, Karu Manjhi got down from the train at Vijayawada to fill some water. As he was filling water, he possibly saw a train moving and not knowing if that was his train or not, he rushed to get into the running train, slipped and fell between the platform and track and was run over by train. His companions informed his family but could not do anything in terms of getting his body or getting the compensation given by the railways in such cases. What was even more deplorable was when the other 2 returned to the village, Karu Manjhi's wife filled case against them alleging that they are responsible for her husband's death. The police were very happy since it could get money from both the parties. These hapless villagers had to borrow money from money lender to fight the case against each other.[25]

Karu Manjhi's case is not an isolated one. Distress migrants moving out of Bihar for eking out a living to save their families from starvation and death is an age old phenomenon. It is an undeniable fact that pandemic wreaked havoc on the already distressed migrants. One of the segments of the Indian population which was totally and

[25] Prakash Louis. Working in a rural development organisation in Manthan in Danapur, we witnessed such a case in 2014. But now these types of distressed migrant cases are on the increase.

fundamentally deceived and devastated by both the omission and commission of the government of India is the migrant labourers. From 25th March, 2020, the horrible plight of the migrant labourers has hit both the national and international media. It is this section of the population who come from the lower caste and class but is the backbone of Indian economy. But it is they who did not figure at all in the announcements and pronouncements, programs and plans, packages and reliefs of the government.[26]

Any discourse on distressed migrants raises the following questions: What development has taken place with 70 years of planned economy? Why is it that people like Karu Manjhi have to leave their village in search of work? Why is it that the rural economy is not able to provide them sufficient livelihood? What are the consequences of distressed migration? Are the consequences always as tragic as that of Karu Manjhi or are there some positive aspects of their migration as well? Who benefits from the hard labour of distressed migrants? What sacrifice distressed migrants have to make to eke out a living? What impact this has on the family that is left behind or moves with the migrants?

The Reality of Migration

The movement of workers across the Indian sub-continent is an age-old phenomenon. This depends on changing patterns of economic development, and is partly related to the levels of poverty, but with little evidence that migration contributes to a reduction in regional disparities, and to diverse migration patterns that challenge migration theories.[27] Poorest states like Bihar and Uttar Pradesh provide the largest numbers of migrants, who tend to move to richer areas like Delhi, and cities and rural production sites in Maharashtra and Gujarat. The patterns of movement are also prompted through chain migration, with the states of Kerala and Punjab being prime examples with respect to international migration (which is of relatively little importance for India's overall economy and labour force), but similar segmentation of migration streams exists within India. Patterns of labour migration

[26] Prakash Louis. Deceived & Decimated Citizens Divided, Defeated by the Political Elite of India. Indian Currents. 01 June 2020. p 12.

[27] A. Mitra. *Urban Poverty: A Rural Spill-Over. Indian Economic Review, Special Number.* 1992. Vol. 27, pp. 403–19.

in India can be observed in terms of the live characteristics mentioned above.

The patterns of migration change over time. Most recently, for example, international migration has become much more common from Uttar Pradesh, now surpassing Kerala in total numbers. A re-survey by Deshingkar and others[28] in Madhya Pradesh showed that circular migration had become more accumulative for the poor, with reduced uncertainty of finding work, increased wages and decreased dependence on contractors, but bringing greater returns to those with skills or strong social networks. Migration reduced borrowing for consumption, improved debt repayment capacity, and enhanced the migrants' confidence. Patterns of landownership amongst migrants, which are well documented in a range of studies, also illustrate diversity. Connell, et.al. (1976) showed that the landless were least likely to migrate. Yadava, et.al. (1996-97) found a positive relationship between landholding and migration in India, and that migrant households are socio-economically and educationally relatively better-off than the non-migrant ones.[29]

In a comparative study in the 1980s, Oberai, et.al. (1989) showed that in Bihar, the poor and landless were (slightly) more likely to migrate; in Kerala, the middle peasantry migrated more often, and in Uttar Pradesh, all landed groups, except the largest cultivators, migrated frequently. While there is some degree of path dependency, these patterns change over time, as Arvind Das (1985) narrated for a village in Bihar where sons of landowners were amongst the first to migrate, followed by the less well-off. A similar pattern has been detected with respect to the international migration from Punjab, where the better-off earlier migrants sponsored the less well-off ones (Pettigrew, 1977). Now the data shows that there are more and more distressed migrants who migrate to other parts of India.

This book in essence deals with the issue of migration, especially that of the distressed labour migrants as a global phenomenon. This is done to understand this ever growing migration in general and distressed migration in particular. At the same time, here the issues

---

[28] Deshingkar, Priya. et.al. *Circular Migration in Madhya Pradesh: Changing Patterns and Social Protection Needs*. European Journal of Development Research. February 2008.

[29] Arjan de Haan. Inclusive Growth? Labour Migration and Poverty in India. The Indian Journal of Labour Economics, Vol. 54, No. 3, 2011, p. 387.

of distressed migration is given as a case study so as to focus upon this issue in a localised manner. Within this framework of trying to understand the migrants, the focus in terms of the state of the migrants is Bihar, a dominant migration producing state.[30]

Interstate and intrastate migration from Bihar as well as in other parts of India is common phenomenon. This has been going on over several decades, with states like Bihar, Madhya Pradesh and Uttar Pradesh being some of the topmost migrant sending states. Unemployment, underemployment, extremely low wages, non-payment of wages, landlessness, assetlessness, minimum land holding, poor returns from agriculture, caste oppression, feudal exploitation, lack of educational facilities, devoid of industries, lack of financial support, etc. are some of the factors which force the poorest of the poor and the most marginalised to migrate. Most from these categories migrate so that the family members left behind can survive. Some of the studies of recent past also point to pull factor from urban centres. This is all the more the case with regard to youth who take up to migration for cash in hand, different clothing and mobile in addition to the reasons stated above.

But it is a known fact that the working and living conditions to which the migrant workers are subjected is another depressing story. They eke out a living in one of the most degrading atmospheres. They also live in some of the inhuman conditions. Though the problems of the distress migrants were not hidden from the government and public view, but it caught the attention of international community after a totally unplanned and unannounced nationwide lockdown announced on 24th March 2020. Those who followed this inhuman response of the government realised that the government not only demonstrated total neglect of the marginalised migrants, but it also rendered them stateless, further exposing them to misinformation, infections, insecurity, starvation, return home by foot for thousands of kilometres and humiliations.

[30] Bihar continues to be backward state and proverbial problematic state. In the past, it used to be clubbed together with Uttar Pradesh, Madhya Pradesh, etc., and used to be called 'BIMARU' state. We are not looking at migration from Bihar from this fact. We are examining distressed migrants from Bihar since it offers enough scope for serious exploration. We will be making reference to others states which are also migrant producing states.

Movement of Distressed Migrants

According to 2001 Census Report, 307 million or 30 crore people[31] migrated within the country for work either to cities or places which promised higher income. As expected migration within the state is on the higher side, migration to other states within India is on the increase.

Table 1: Number of Migrants by Place of Birth – India 2001

	Category	Migrations by Place of birth	Percentage
A.	Total Population	1,028,610,328	
B.	Total Migrations	307,149,736	29.9
B.1	Migrants within the state of enumeration	258,641,103	84.2
B.11	Migrants from within the districts	181,799,637	70.3
B.12	Migrants from other districts of the state	76,841,466	29.7
B.2	Migrants from other states in India	42,341,703	13.8
B.3	Migrants from other countries	6,166,930	2.0

Source: Table D1 India, Census of India 2001.

But this scenario changes as per 2011 census data. Over 455.8 million Indians were found to be "migrants" for various reasons during the enumeration exercises of Census 2011. The previous Census (2001) had recorded the number of migrants at 314.5 million, more than 30% lower than the 2011 figure. According to the 2011 Census, Uttar Pradesh and Bihar are responsible for the greatest number of migrants as 20.9 million people migrated outside the state from these two states alone.[32]

In some parts of India, three out of four households include a migrant. However, despite the large scale of migration in absolute numbers of people involved and India's long history of population and labour mobility, labour migration has rarely been reliably studied. Labour migration is complex. Streams differ in duration, origin, destination and migrant characteristics.

Economic and social impacts on migrants and their families vary. Migration often involves longer working hours, poor living and working conditions, social isolation and poor access to basic

---

[31] This was a very conservative estimate. Two decades after this estimate, there is another estimate which states that there are 30 crore migrants, among whom the most majority are distressed migrants.

[32] Census Data 2011. Government of India.

amenities. At destination, migrant labour affects markets, lowering the cost of labour. Migration also affects the labour market at the place of origin. Migrant earnings affect income, expenditure patterns and investment and changes relations at household and community levels.

While there seems to be some positive impact on incomes and investment, the major function of migration is to act as a 'safety valve' in poor areas. The impact on asset and income inequality is more mixed. Internal mobility is critical to the livelihoods of many people, especially tribal people, socially deprived groups and people from resource poor areas. However, because of lack of data, migration is largely invisible and ignored by policy makers. There is a large gap between the insights from macro data and those from field studies.[33]

Labour migration flows include permanent, semi-permanent, and seasonal or circular migrants. Much of the available data polls migrants in the permanent and semi-permanent categories, and considerably less large-scale statistical data are available on the numbers and characteristics of circular migrants.

Semi-permanent migrants are those who are likely to have precarious jobs in their destination areas, or lack the resources to make a permanent move. While they may reside in their destination cities for years or decades, they likely have homes and families in their sending district.

Seasonal or circular migrants, by contrast, are likely to move from place to place in search of employment, or to continue returning to the same place year after year. Such circular flows encompass migrants who may stay at their destination for six months or more at a time and hence need social services at their destination. Scholars have long characterized this migration as a type in which the permanent residence of a person remains the same, but the location of his or her economic activity changes.

Many of the women who migrate for marriage are also participants in the labour market, even if their primary reason for

---

[33] Ravi Srivastava and SK Sasikumar. An overview of migration in India, its impacts and key issues. This paper is one of twelve prepared for and presented at the Regional Conference on Migration, Development and ProPoor Policy Choices in Asia. The Conference was jointly organised by the Refugee and Migratory Movements Research Unit, Bangladesh, and the Department for International Development, UK, and took place on 22–24 June 2003 in Dhaka, Bangladesh.

migration is marriage. This is all the more the case of women from the lower social and economic category. The domestic maid industry in urban areas, for example, is a rapidly growing sector that employs women, most of whom are rural to urban migrants.[34] The domestic maid industry refers to the sector of employment where individuals are hired to perform domestic tasks in private homes for remuneration. Also known as domestic help, domestic worker, etc. There is an estimate that India has over 5 crore or 50 million domestic workers as of today. These are mostly assisted by informal sectors or voluntary agencies.

The crisis created universally by the pandemic Corona virus, the unplanned lockdowns after that, the aftermath of these two unexpected and unfamiliar events have altered the life of individuals, families, communities, countries and the globe once for all. It appears that life is not going to be the same any more. As the days proceed, the expectation of the people that life will return back to normal soon is getting converted into depression, faith giving way to frustration, marriages being cancelled, plans beings postponed for ever, dreams being destroyed, no work and no wages, no money to purchase food, starvation and death. The uncertainty all over eats into the very being of human persons.

Migration in and from Bihar – A Case

Table 2: Migration Trend of Bihar

Census Year	Total Population	Total Migrants	Internal Migrants	Interstate Migrants	International Migrants
1991	6,45,30,554	21529825 (33.36%)	2030129 (31.46)	1031566 (1.59)	190130 (0.29)
2001	8,29,98,509	2048076 (24.67%)	18649877 (22.47)	1619031 (1.95)	212015 (0.25)
2011	10,40,99,452	27244869 (26.17%)	25728400 (24.71)	1111954 (1.07)	398592 (0.38)

Source: Compiled from Census Data of India.

The North Indian states of Bihar and Uttar Pradesh have the highest percentages of rural population. These states are also the largest migrant sending states. Substantial flows of labor migrants

[34] Rameez Abbas and Divya Varma. *Internal Labor Migration in India Raises Integration Challenges for Migrants*. March 3, 2014.

relocate from Bihar and Uttar Pradesh to Maharashtra, Delhi, West Bengal, Punjab, Haryana, Gujarat, and other states across northern and central India. Other major migrant sending states are Rajasthan, Madhya Pradesh, Andhra Pradesh, Chhattisgarh, Jharkhand, and Orissa. Predictably, all of the major sending states are characterized by very low social and economic development indices and the major urban destinations are the growing economic magnets in an increasingly liberalized Indian economy.[35]

The cities of Mumbai, Delhi, and Kolkata were the largest destinations for internal migrants from northern and north eastern states of India. Many of the migrants to these cities are intrastate migrants, relocating from rural areas of Maharashtra and West Bengal. All three cities also absorb large numbers of people from other states across India. But this scenario has changed in the last two decades.

There are many factors which lead to migration. Some of them are: dismal performance of agriculture, aversion to agricultural work by the youth, and the lack of options in nonagricultural work, lack of skills for nonfarm employment, wage differentials, population pressure and the urge to have exposure to the modern life and better living conditions act as incentives for massive outmigration from the state. Labor migration in Bihar implies a massive outmigration of males, especially young men from the rural areas; while the women, children, and elderly are left behind in the village.

For the poor and the marginalized, migration is a way to cope with poverty and hunger. The data reveals that the most dominant migration stream is that of more than 8 months in a year, followed by migration which is of 3–8 months in a year. Bihari workers send remittances equivalent to about five percent of the state's GDP. The Remittance earned by migrants is a major source of income not only to the migrant households for their daily requirements but also to the local communities and the state. Thus, they contribute to the development of the state and the nation as a whole. Though the migrants contribute immensely to the growth and development of host locations, they are treated just like any other commodities.

[35] Ibid. Rameez Abbas and Divya Varma.

Studies undertaken by Mohamad Ansari[36] and Nandan Kumar cum R. B. Bhagat,[37] and others speak about the following phases of migration in and from Bihar:

1) **First Phase – During the Colonial Period towards East:** From 1830 to 1920 there were migrations from Bihar as indentured labourers[38] supervised by the British colonisers to Fiji, Mauritus, Trinidad, Namibia and British Guyana. Indian labourers were recruited mainly from eastern and southern Indian villages, who entered into five-year labour contracts with planters and sailed from the three major port cities of Calcutta, Bombay and Madras. It was a centralised system of labour migration from British India to colonial sugar plantations. It not only heralded the beginning of what came to be known as the Indian indentured (contractual) trade, but also a revival of slavery. This represented what was and what would become bonded labour system. Jan Breman in his study of Gujarat pointed out to the fact that on the one hand the labourers were exploited and on the other capital developed.[39]

---

[36] Mohammad Ansari. *Migration from Rural Region: A Study from Bihar in India.* Journal of Assam University. Vol. 6, No. 1, 2001.

[37] Nandan Kumar and R. B. Bhagat. *Out Migration from Bihar: Causes and Consequences.* Journal of Social and Economic Studies, Vol. XXII, No. 2, July December 2012, p. 135-136.

[38] Indentured labour is associated with the era of European colonization, beginning about 1500 and extending into the 20th century, though forms of indentured labour still exist. Its conditions were often severe enough to resemble slavery, even if local laws may have differentiated between slavery and indentured labour. Historical records state that in almost all places, local forms of slavery existed. Lower castes or scheduled castes or the Dalits are a segment of the Indian population who were subjected to inhuman slavery

[39] Jan Breman. *Of peasants, Migrants and Paupers: Rural Labour Circulation and Capitalist Production in West India.* Oxford University Press: Delhi. 1985.

Beyond this Day – 29th January 1838: Indian Indentured Trade and 'The First Crossing'. Royal Historical Society.

2) **Second Phase towards East:** In the latter half of the 19th century, an eastward trends of migration became well established, particularly migration from western part of Bihar to Bengal and Assam. The migration stream was dominated by lower caste and landless laborers, who were staying at bare subsistence level and ready to respond to the fair high wage gap between their native place and east. They found employment in the mills, factories, docks and coal mines, or on the roads and railways, or in harvesting the crops of other districts of West Bengal. This migration was mostly seasonal, and improved communication through railways made it possible for them to migrate easily and come back for agricultural and other activities at their native place.

3) **Third Phase towards North West:** The westward wave of labour migration from Bihar started in the decade of sixties, when the green revolution started in the northwestern part of India. Starting in the early 1970s with a small trickle to the rural areas of Punjab it soon took the form of a flood during the next one decade. Soon the influx of migrants spilled over to the

neighboring state of Haryana. In the 80s and 90s those who lived in Bihar and UP were witness to the migrant labourers to Punjab and Haryana travelling on the top of the train in one of the most precarious conditions.

4) **Fourth Phase towards West:** The fourth phase was the move of labour migration from Bihar towards big cities such as Delhi, Bombay, Surat,[40] Kolkata, and Hyderabad etc. Some studies have reported that the volume of migration also increased drastically since then. Outmigration started from all the sections of the state, cutting across the hierarchy of caste and class.

5) **Fifth Phase towards West and South:** Laborers are involved in a variety of occupations like those of security guards, rickshaw pullers and collies, etc. (Sharma, 2005). Migration is now viewed as finite stage of lifecycle of people of Bihar, as male member of household approach to a certain age, they send away to earn. The remittance is playing a critical role to support livelihood in the state.[41] According to this study over 30.49 lac people have migrated from Bihar for employment. But as per government record the number is rather low.[42]

6) **Sixth Phase towards South:** There are studies and reports trickling down that the most preferred destination now is to southern parts of India. These include, Kerala, Karnataka, Tamil Nadu, Andhra Pradesh and Telangana. Textile units like Tirupur have been having lacs of migrant workers from north India and especially from Bihar. While some of them still live in make shift sheds, others are slowly settling down here with families.

---

[40] Times of India reported in October 2018 that 'Migrants make up for 70% of the workforce in Surat. This is in agricultural sector to small and large factories, construction works, etc.

[41] Nandan Kumar and R.B. Bhagat. *Out Migration from Bihar: Causes and Consequences.* Journal of Social and Economic Studies, Vol. XXII, No. 2, July December 2012, p. 135-136.

[42] It is not argued here that migration fell under these neat categories but this was predominantly movement at this particular period from Bihar to destination states. For instance, during the colonial period itself there was substantial movement from Bihar to Bengal.

Factors behind Migration from Bihar

Various studies and theories tried to unearth the fact of forced migration, involuntary migration and distressed migration. The factors behind these are as follows:[43]

1. **Landlessness:** Vast majority of rural population, especially from the Dalit, most backward castes and Tribals are landless agricultural labourers. Since, they are not paid even the minimum wages and do not get work in farms throughout the year, many families face hardship and they are forced to migrate to elsewhere where they can find work and income.
2. **Poor Returns from Land:** Roy says that dismal growth of agriculture in Bihar, that is, 3.5 per cent during 2012-13 forced migration.[44] This growth does not provide for the survival of poor farmers and landless agricultural labourers. Though in the 90s, there was a slowing down of migrants from Bihar due to employment in infrastructural projects, once again there is increase in migration. Girish Kumar and Pranab Banerji claimed that 4.42 million people from Bihar migrate every year to various states of India.[45]
3. **Caste Oppression:** Irrespective of the fact that the country has attained freedom over 70 years ago and caste discrimination has been abolished, caste abuses are rampant in India. The dominated castes like the Dalits, most backward caste, etc., are subjected to exploitation and oppression even today. Earlier studies have pointed out that if the Dalit boys dress up well and are smart, girls from upper caste befriend them and are even ready to elope with them. But the dominant caste beat up the Dalit boys.[46]
4. **Feudal Exploitation:** The country has made progress in many areas. But even now the feudal mind set exists and subjects the most vulnerable to be subjects of abuse. If they resist they are

---

[43] Prakash Louis. *Distressed Migrants of Bihar: Factors, Causes and Responses.* XISR Working Paper. June 2022.

[44] Alok Gupta. Migration trends in Bihar are changing, causing labour shortage in several states. A few studies investigate the reasons and patterns. Down To Earth. 15/10/2014.

[45] Girish Kumar and Pranab Banerji. A Study of Bihari Migrant Labourers: Incidence, Causes and Remedies. Indian Institute of Public Administration. New Delhi. 2011.

[46] Prakash Louis. *People Power: The Naxalite Movement in Central Bihar.* Wordsmiths: Delhi p. 9095.

booked under false cases and thus they and their families face hardships.

5. **Lack of Employment Opportunities:** Since the agriculture itself is going through crisis, there is no employment in agricultural sector. India being an agriculture based economy, there is very limited alternative employment. This lack of employment and income severely forces the rural masses to migrate for seemingly better wage and employment opportunities. In 2017-18, the share of casual labour in Bihar (32.1%) was significantly higher than in India (24.3%). Further, nearly 40% of Bihar's youth had no jobs and the unemployment rate had jumped to 7.2% in 2017-2018 from 2.5% in 2011-12.[47]
6. **Lack of Quality Education:** For the rural masses and especially those who come from the weaker sections, educational opportunities are limited. If they get educated well, they can at least look for some public sector employments or in private sector. Due to lack of educational opportunities they are forced to remain wage earners. Since, wages in one's own place is less, they migrate.
7. **Lack of Skill Development:** Since the mindset of the ruling elite is to provide opportunities for skill development wherever there are industries and since Bihar is predominantly an agricultural state, no effort is made to provide opportunities for skill development. In this situation, the distress migrants loose out since they are skilled.
8. **Lack of Loan and Credit:** In Bihar, India's second poorest state, per capita income was just a quarter of the national average in 2004. Almost 90% of the population lives in rural areas, with limited opportunities for self-employment and little access to basic services. Although agriculture is the mainstay of the economy and employs over 80% of the population, the vast majority of farmers survive at subsistence and near subsistence levels. Without an adequate banking network, most poor people have to borrow from extortionist moneylenders or relatives and

---

[47] Santosh Mehrotra and Baikunth Roy. Will Bihar's Economy Rise to the Reverse Migration Challenge? The Wire. 23/06/2020.

friends to meet family expenses, often pawning tiny plots of land to repay old debts.[48]

Thus, the migrants of Bihar are caught in a web of exploitation and oppression. The pressure to survive in a most cruel social system can lead to this fact of young boys migrating to earn a living for the family. Gerry Rodgers, Janine Rodgers based on the study of Purnia district in 2008-2009 highlight this sad state of affairs. A form of migration that has developed recently concerns young boys aged 10 to 14, migrating to Moradabad, Delhi or Firozabad to work in factories making bangles, toys, carpets or steel pots and dishes. A contractor from outside the village advances their travel expenses and gets back a percentage of the children's wages (10% was mentioned). The boys concerned basically lived at the worksite, where they were given food, clothing and lodging, and a wage of Rs 600 to Rs 1,000 per month for the first year, and Rs 1,000 to Rs 2,000 thereafter. They would come back to the village from time to time especially for major festivals, but would be spending 8 to 10 months in the year away.[49]

In another study, it was reported that child migration from Purnia to towns in Uttar Pradesh and Bihar for work in 'dhabas' or hotels has been on the increase over the last 10 years. These children earn Rs. 300/ to 350/ per month with breakfast and meal. There are reportedly over 3000 to 4000 such child migrants[50] from Purnia. It is also reported that these are mainly children from SC families and they migrate for 8 to 9 months in a year for Rs. 500/ to 1500/ per month with food. Some of these children migrate up to Punjab, Madhya Pradesh and Chhattisgarh.[51]

---

[48] India: Liberating Bihar's Poor from the Debt Trap. World Bank Group. April 12, 2013.

[49] Gerry Rodgers, Janine Rodgers. *Inclusive Development? Migration, Governance and Social Change in Rural Bihar. Economic & Political Weekly*. June 4, 2011 vol. xlvi no. 23.

[50] Starting from 1990 to 2010, there were big increase in labour force. This period also marked the increase in child labour. Children from Bihar were taken to work in carpet factories in Banaras and Balia. Some of the NGOs got these child labours released following legal procedures. While, the NGOs were basking on their victory, the owners of these mills shifted the mills and the child labourers to Punjab at the borders of India and Pakistan.

[51] Priya Deshingkar, Sushil Kumar, Harendra Kumar Choubey & Dhananjay Kumar, *The Role of Migration and Remittances in Promoting Livelihoods in Bihar*, Overseas Development Institute, London , 2006. p. 2425.

Additional Factors Contributing to Migration

Migration patterns are key indicators of regional development. Recent research by Sarkar (2014) and 2011 Census D Series data reveal that Bihar and other EAG states, that is, Empowered Action Group"[52] sates experience higher rates of outmigration for employment reasons compared to other Indian states. This section analyzes migration reasons for Biharis, distinguishing between male and female migrants.

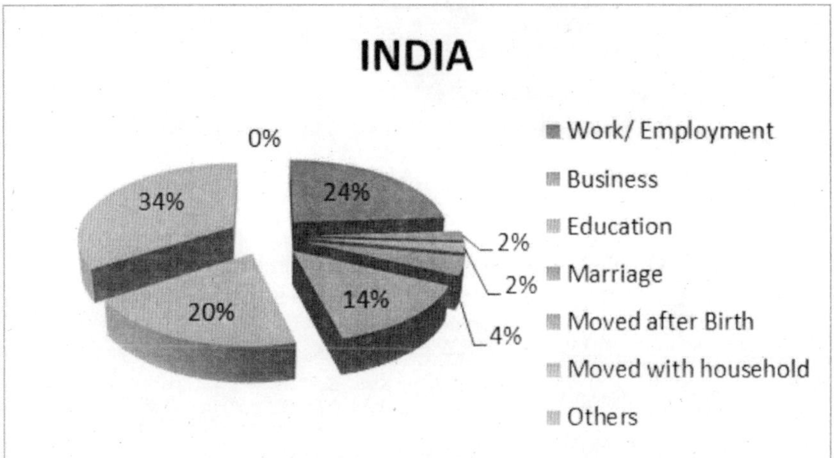

Graph1: Reasons for Male Migration In India
Source: Calculated using Census 2011, D Series data on migration.

Graph 1 indicates that, an average, 24 percent of male migrants across India relocate for work or employment reasons. In contrast, approximately 55 percent of male migrants from Bihar move for similar employment related reasons, which is more than double the national average. Additionally, while the national average for migration due to business reasons is about 2 percent, it is nearly 4 percent in Bihar.

[52] Bihar, Jharkhand, Madhya Pradesh, Chhattisgarh, Odisha, Rajasthan, Uttarakhand, and Uttar Pradesh. These ten are the EAG states.

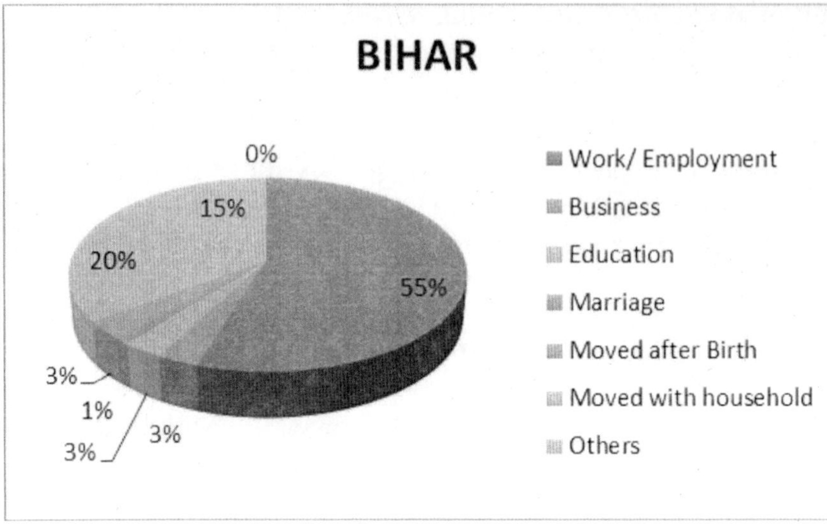

Graph 2: Reasons for Male Migration In Bihar
Source: Calculated using Census 2011, D Series data on migration.

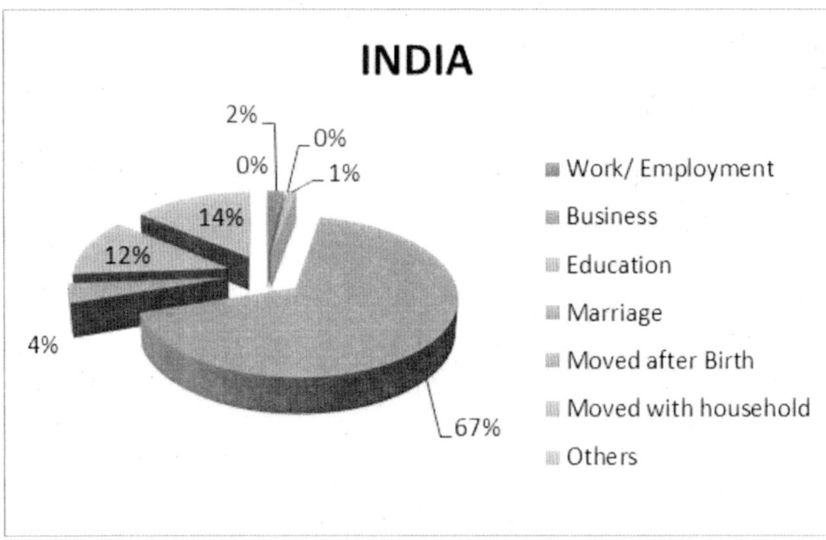

Graph 3: Reasons for Female Migration In India
Source: Calculated using Census 2011, D Series data on migration.

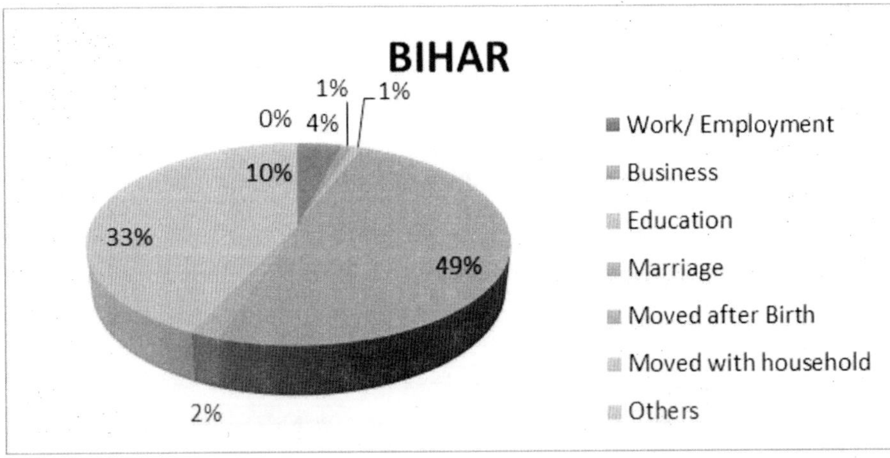

Graph 4: Reasons for Female Migration In Bihar
Source: Calculated using Census 2011, D Series data on migration.

Overall, migrants from Bihar are more than twice as likely to move for work or business reasons compared to the national average. Interestingly, while marriage is the primary reason for female migration nationwide, its impact is less pronounced in Bihar compared to the rest of India.

Migration from Bihar to Major Destination States: Interstate outmigration from Bihar has historically been high, primarily driven by economic factors. From a distressed migration to a survival migration to earning, becomes the line the migrants take from Bihar.

Table 3: highlights that Delhi is the top destination for migrants from Bihar, attracting 19.34% of them. Jharkhand and West Bengal are also major destinations, receiving 14.12% and 13.65% of migrants respectively. Maharashtra and Uttar Pradesh are significant but less prominent, with 10.55% and 10.24% of migrants. Haryana and Punjab receive smaller shares at 7.06% and 6.89%, while Gujarat attracts 4.79%. The "Rest of India" category encompasses 13.35% of the migration.

Table 3: Distribution of Male and Female Bihari People to Different States

Major Destination States for All Migrants from Bihar (distribution measured in percent)					
Migrants from Bihar		Migrants from Rural Bihar		Migrants from Urban Bihar	
Delhi	19.34	Delhi	20.05	Jharkhand	18.64
Jharkhand	14.12	West Bengal	13.81	Delhi	16.24
West Bengal	13.65	Jharkhand	13.1	West Bengal	12.97
Maharashtra	10.55	Uttar Pradesh	10.61	Maharashtra	12.38
Uttar Pradesh	10.24	Maharashtra	10.14	Uttar Pradesh	8.62
Haryana	7.06	Haryana	7.86	Gujarat	4.21
Punjab	6.89	Punjab	7.54	Punjab	4.02
Gujarat	4.79	Gujarat	4.92		
Rest of India	13.35	Rest of India	11.98	Rest of India	22.93
Total	100	Total	100	Total	100

Source: Calculated using Census 2011.

But this trend has changed considerably in the last one decade. The number of migrants going to Punjab and Haryana has reduced now. As per a study, in the year 2001, there were 3 lac migrants from Bihar to Punjab and 3.6 lac migrants from Bihar to Haryana.[53] But these were also those that were reported. It used to be stated that much of economic operations of Punjab and Haryana was due to the migrant labourers from UP and Bihar. But that scenario has changed now. These migrant labourers are not only diversifying location but also trying to diversify the type of employment.

COVID-19 and the Devastation of Migrants from Bihar

"Even if we are saved from Corona virus, we will die of Hunger." This was the cry of a distress migrant labourer who had returned to his home in Araria district of Bihar. While Adanis and Ambanis moved in the ladder of being billionaires during the pandemic, it was escalating poverty and the extermination for the poor. In the second week of April 2020, UN's International Labour Organization (ILO) claimed that about 400 million workers from India's informal sector are likely to

[53] Saurabh Senthil, Ranjit Singh Ghuman and Wilfred Isioma Ukpere. *Socio-economic Analysis of the Migrant Labourers in Punjab: An Empirical Analysis.* International Scholars Journal. September, 2013.

be pushed deeper into poverty due to COVID-19. There is no dispute that poverty in the country will worsen, but the question is, by how much? The Government of India has categorically stated that it does not have the necessary data about poverty or about the migrants. What this statement implies is that in the absence of 'reliable data' nothing can be done or nothing has been done.[54]

Thus, along with all the problems distress migrants undergo, the lockdown imposed without any plan and consideration for the marginalised added massive hardships. With an exodus of workers never witnessed before in Indian history, COVID-19 has posed deep and grave challenges to our understanding of labour, migration, differentiated citizenship, dignity, security, vulnerability, and deliberative democracy. There are several questions related to basic dignity that arise in this context: Why were workers ousted from cities, throwing them into hunger, starvation, and homelessness at four hours' notice? Nearly half of those in the exodus were women and children. Even while we try to grapple with the human rights implications of those graphic visuals, we were witness to for weeks on end; our questions are stacked along two tracks. The first and most obvious one is, of course, health – the range of concerns around the right to health generally, and policies for the containment and treatment of COVID-19 affected persons. The second set of questions pertain to our understanding of the intersections of caste, community, tribe, and class, each intersecting with gender in the reality unfolding before us.[55]

According to the State of Working India Report an analysis of labour market trends by the Centre for Sustainable Employment at Azim Premji University, Bengaluru, most Indian households work in the unorganised sector and face a low earnings problem. The report goes on to state that in 2015, of a workforce of 467 million, 47% were self-employed and 36.5% were casual wage workers, while only 17% were regular wage workers. Among these workers, in 2015, 92% women and 82% men earned less than Rs 10,000 a month. This is

---

[54] Prakash Louis. *Pandemic and the Plight of the Indian Poor.* Counter Currents. 21/10/2020.

[55] Asha Hans, Kalpana Kannabiran, Manoranjan Mohanty, and Pushpendra (et.al. ed). *Migration, Workers, and Fundamental Freedoms Pandemic Vulnerabilities and States of Exception in India.* Routledge: London. 2021, p. 1.

nearly half the monthly salary recommended by the Seventh Central Pay Commission of Rs 18,000 as a living wage, according to the report.

But Mukesh Ambani gets his place reserved in the world's richest businessmen. According to a report of the International Labour Organisation about 41% of casual labourers earned less than even the central government's indicative national minimum wages of Rs. 176/ per day. It is from this deplorable situation, the labourers migrate from Uttar Pradesh, Bihar, Jharkhand, West Bengal, Assam and Odisha to mega cities and rural areas in other parts of India where they get paid nothing less than Rs. 500/ Thus these migrant labourers not only earn a decent wage but are also contributing in the growth of the economy of the country.

But when the pandemic struck all, the migrant labourers were forced to walk back to their place of origin under the pretext of lockdown. Even millions of them die; the ruling elite of this country will not even shed crocodile tears since it does not matter to them. Irrespective of the fact that the migrant labourers were on the road walking hundreds and thousands of kilo meters from the month of March itself, there was no plan to reach them home or provide relief or make travel arrangements. Irrespective of many dying on the way, being killed, run over by train, etc. not even scant attention was paid to address their issues. It is becoming clearer that it is not due to lack of political will that the ruling elite failed to take care of them in the lockdown but it appears that they wanted them to be wiped out from the face of the earth.[56]

When we undertook a study of the state of affairs of the returnee migrants in 2020, the following were some of the critical issues that were highlighted:[57]

1) They lost livelihood, wages, security, etc., and some of them even lost their lives. Most of the labour migrants from Bihar were and are labourers from the historically oppressed

---

[56] Prakash Louis. Ibid. *Deceived & Decimated Citizens Divided, Defeated by the Political Elite of India*. Indian Currents. 01 07 June 2020. p. 12.

[57] Prakash Louis. *Study of the Migrant Labourers of Bihar, Jharkhand and Uttar Pradesh*. XISR: Patna. 2020.

communities stigmatized as untouchables and lower castes.[58] Having lost even the limited option of earning a living and saving their families from starvation gives a further blow to these marginalized.

2) Vast number of migrants are in unorganized sector. Unorganized sector is the backbone of Indian economy. Now this is in disarray due to lockdown and shutdown. Along with distress migrants, economy of the country also suffered a huge set back. In a rapid socioeconomic assessment study of the impact that COVID-19 had on children of migrant workers and their families in Bihar, it was revealed that along with the migrants, the economy of the country was also badly hit.[59]
3) In many of the formal sector one can work from home but this is not possible in unorganized sector where the physical presence of the labourer is needed. But with the lockdown and shut down none of these units of work are open and thus the migrant labourers are forced to return home.
4) Vast number of migrant labour force is from Bihar and Uttar Pradesh to other parts of the country. Come from Dalit, Tribal, MBC and Muslim communities. They are mostly landless, less educated, poor, rural based and hence are not able to handle the complications of the urban life. But due to survival needs migrate to eke out a living.
5) Migrant labourers are both unskilled and skilled labourers, agents and workers, single and group, youth and family, etc. Hence, when they were forced to return, those among these were unskilled and did not earn enough faced greater hardships.
6) Migrant labourers who are the backbone felt betrayed, illtreated, starved, dislocated, destroyed and ended up in depression.

---

[58] Indrajit Roy, "Labour Migration from (and in) Bihar: Continuities and Change," IGC working Paper, University of Oxford, January 2016. p. 4.

[59] Aditi Thakur, Naman Sreen, Shankar Purbey, Surya Bhushan, (study team), *A Qualitative Assessment of Impact of COVID-19 on Migrant Workers and their Families in Bihar*, Development Management Institute, supported by UNICEF.

7) Children are the worst affected in a time of crisis. This was the case during the lockdown. Irrespective of the best of the efforts of judiciary, state, media, civil society etc., it was witnessed that child labourers were greatly exposed to abuse and violence. Many reports suggest that economically distressed families, married off adolescent girls to alleviate their situation.[60]
8) At a time of deep crisis, instead of progressive labour laws, the rulers have opted for regressive 'reforms' violating domestic and international conventions, and constitutional protections.
9) They were unwelcomed to urban centers, except for being work force. But they came and changed the economy. Now they feel they are chased out due to the scare of spreading the virus.
10) If in the last week of March, 2020 trains were run to reach them back home, all of them would have returned safe and sound without going through huge hardships and also some of them affected by the virus. Every day 11,000 passenger trains and 23 million Indians travel, but for migrant labourers the government could not run trains.
11) The returnee migrants were clueless about their future. In another study of 915 respondents of Bihar the response to the question if the migrants have any recovery plan, some of the answers were very revealing. 1) 40% of the respondents said they had no idea what they were going to do; 2) 22% said they were going to work as daily labourers; 3) 17% hoped to engage in farming; 4) 15% said they would begin small business; 5) 3% hoped to return back to where they were working.[61]
12) Some returnee migrants were already contacted by their former employees to hire vehicle and come back to work. If not all some went back within weeks. If not the entire family at least individuals went back to the place they worked.

---

[60] Ibid. Aditi Thakur (et.al) p. 33.

[61] Priya Deshingkar, Sushil Kumar, Harendra Kumar Choubey & Dhananjay Kumar, *The Role of Migration and Remittances in Promoting Livelihoods in Bihar*, Overseas Development Institute, London , 2006. p. 15.

Some went after paddy transplantation. A substantial number of returnee migrants went back immediately because there was no livelihood back at home in Bihar and if they did not go and earn a living, they and their families would be forced to starve.

It is pertinent to note that many of the state governments set up portals for the returnee migrants to register themselves. This was done to identify all those who are returning and to isolate them for quarantine and also for future interventions. While the first objective was fulfilled, the second objective was thrown to the winds. No follow up in terms of self-employment with the support of the government, jobs under MNREGA, etc., were the hopes of the returnee migrants. But this only remained a propaganda.

Issues Related to Migrants

An UNESCO publication highlighted the plight of migrants in India. Despite the fact that approximately three out of every ten Indians are internal migrants, internal migration has been accorded very low priority by the government, and existing policies of the Indian state have failed in providing legal or social protection to this vulnerable group. This can be attributed in part to a serious data gap on the extent, nature and magnitude of internal migration. It also demanded for some responses as given below:[62]

1. **Documentation and Identity:** Proving their identity is one of the core issues impoverished migrants face when they arrive in a new place, a problem that can persist for years or even decades after they migrate. Identity documentation that is authenticated by the state is indispensable for ensuring that a person has a secure citizenship status and can benefit from the rights and protections that the state provides.
2. **Housing:** Migration and slums are inextricably linked, as labour demand in cities and the resulting rural to urban migration creates greater pressures to accommodate more people. In 2011, 68 million Indians lived in slums, comprising one quarter of the population of India's 19 cities

[62] UNESCO. Social Inclusion of Internal Migrants in India. 2013.

with more than 1 million residents. No effort is made to provide low-cost housing for migrants.

3. **Limited Access to Formal Financial Services:** Despite the economic imperatives that drive migration, migrant workers essentially remain an unbanked population. Since migrants do not possess permissible proofs of identity and residence, they fail to satisfy the Know Your Customer (KYC) norms as stipulated by the Indian banking regulations.
4. **Social Exclusion:** Irrespective of innumerable efforts to do away with caste and untouchability, migrants who mostly hail from lower socioeconomic strata are discriminated.
5. **Political Exclusion:** In a state of continuous drift, migrant workers are deprived of many opportunities to exercise their political rights. Because migrants are not entitled to vote outside of their place of origin, most are simply unable to cast their votes.

Rampant Exploitation: Migration flows are mediated by an elaborate chain of contractors and middlemen who perform the critical function of sourcing and recruiting workers and hugely benefit from the labour, vulnerability of the migrants. It is not that the common masses do not want to register through the government mechanisms the details needed to prove that they are labourers and or migrant labourers. Even if they want, the system does not work in favour of these marginalised.

For instance, if a labourer who is 30 to 40 kilo meters far from the district headquarters where he has to register himself as a labourer in the office of the labour officer, he has to leave a day's wages, he has spend the money for bus ticket, he has to take care of his food, etc. After all these if he reaches the office, if the office functions and if the officers are there and if the computer and internet works then he is lucky. If none of these work or not available, then he is at triple loss. Next time, he will not attempt to go to any office. He will discourage others too. But the government keeps on insisting that it would only recognise the labourers and migrants who are registered and not others. So in most cases, the labourers and migrants loose any benefit or compensation.

Let us take another example from the northeast of India. It was reported in December, 2011 that 50 lakh people are likely to migrate from the northeast in 5 years.[63] Exodus of people from northeast is at its peak and in the next five years, around 50 lakh people from the region are likely to migrate to other parts of the country for education and jobs, a study said. Attributing poor infrastructure for higher education in the region as the main reason for the exodus, the study conducted by New Delhi-based think tank 'North East Support Centre & Helpline' said, "Migration (from northeast) is at its peak now. 50 lakh people are expected to migrate in the next five years."

According to the research findings, exodus from the region has increased 12 times in the last five years with 414,850 people migrating in 2010. "Lack of employment opportunities, economic backwardness and socio-political unrest are other reasons for the exodus," the report said. Around 66% of the people migrate for higher studies, while the remaining 35% do so for employment opportunities, it said. According to estimates, currently over 2,75,000 students from the Northeast have migrated to other cities of the country, particularly Delhi and the NCR region.

Only 5% of the migrants return to their native state on completion of their studies, while those who work in government jobs and private sector stay there until they retire, the study said. The study warns that with the increase in migration, cases of racial discrimination and sexual violence against those from the region are going to increase. "The challenges of racial discrimination and sexual violence faced by Northeast communities in mega cities will also increase," the study said, adding that there has been a paradigm shift from racial discrimination to sexual violence and from sexual violence to human trafficking. Neither the people who are migrating, nor the community are in a position to address the issues of migration like this. The government which is supposed to address these as priority issue is silent. It is more interested in moving the local population out and hand over the resources to corporates.[64]

---

[63] Press Trust of India, Kolkata, December 26, 2011.

[64] For more on this, refer to Prakash Louis and Syeda Hameed. *Viewing Indian Polity from the Prism of Manipur, Northeast Conflict: A Compendium on Manipur Conflict and Crisis.* Manak Publications: New Delhi. 2024.

Ravi Srivastava and S. K. Sasikumar based on their studies highlighted the impacts and key issues on migration.[65]

- internal migration often involves longer working hours, poor living and working conditions, social isolation and poor access to basic amenities.
- while there seems to be some positive impact on incomes and investment, the major function of internal migration is to act as a 'safety valve' in poor areas.
- most migrant labourers in India are employed in the unorganised sector, where the lack of regulation compounds their vulnerability; they are largely ignored by government and NGO programmes.
- legislation regarding migrants fails because regulatory authorities are over-stretched; the state sees migrants as a low priority; and migrant workers have little support from civil society.
- international migrants have mainly come from Kerala, Tamil Nadu, Andhra Pradesh and Punjab, and have consisted of people with professional expertise of technical qualifications migrating to industrialised countries; and skilled and semi-skilled workers migrating to the Middle East.
- overseas migrants account for less than one per cent of the total workforce of India, so have little direct impact on the national labour market; however, the effects are significant in major sending regions such as Kerala, where there emigration has reduced unemployment.
- emittances are the main benefit of external migration, providing scarce foreign exchange and scope for higher levels of savings and investments.
- in Kerala, remittances made up 21 per cent of state income in the 1990s, and emigration appears to have increased the wealth of the state.[66]

---

[65] Ravi Srivastava and S. K. Sasikumar. An Overview of Migration in India, its Impacts and Key Issues. Regional Conference on Migration, Development and Pro-Poor Policy Choices in Asia. 2003.

[66] But the people also have paid and are paying heavy price. The study shows that nearly 1.5 million Keralites now live outside India. They send home more than Rs. 4,000 million a year by way of remittances. Three-quarters of a million former emigrants have

As we conclude this section, let us try to capture a glimpse of the deplorable state of migrants.

Issues Related to Migration

1. work and living conditions of most of these migrants are deplorable. These are from the vulnerable communities.
2. effect of migration on women if they migrate or not, children and aged.
3. educational – probability of children getting education is less.
4. poor health situation. Negative focus is now on Aids. But not on malaria, tb etc.
5. loss of citizenship. Place of origin and place of destination.

Why Migration

- 80% of the income is generated from migration in a tribal family.
- 65% of the population earn their livelihood of labouring when they go on migration.
- In a tribal family 4 to 5 members migrate for four to five months.
- 42% are women in migrant family.
- Some times earnings from migration become main source of livelihood for poor.
- Women are the worst sufferers during migration; the major problem they face is for fuel wood, drinking water and availability of toilets.
- Women are paid less wages than a male.

Many migrants travel long distances for work. This increases their vulnerability in a crisis situation that also makes it difficult for them to return home. This includes workers who are footloose and who migrate frequently without a regular or a single unique employer. The transportation facilities available to them tell a tale of misery and exploitation. In 2007, an overloaded truck met with an accident in Rajsamand, claiming about 86 lives. Rajasthan Government decided to launch a fortnight-long drive against overloading of buses and trucks

---

come back. They live mostly on savings, work experience, and skills acquired while abroad. More than a million families depend on an internal migrant's earnings for subsistence, children's education and other economic requirements. K. C. Zachariah, E. T. Mathew and S. Irudaya Rajan. Impact of Migration on Kerala's Economy and Society. IOM. October, 2008. With policy and political changes in many countries, more and more Keralites are going to return home to an economy which is more on consumption and less on production.

and the vehicles plying illegally on the national and State highways. Mr. Kataria, who presided over a high level meeting around the same time, said a recommendation would be made to the Chief Minister to provide 1,000 new buses to the State Road Transport Corporation, while the Transport Department would allow more private vehicles to ply on roads. Nothing really came out of it. In a similar accident in Bharatpur in June 2011, an overloaded bus carrying more than 120 passengers overturned (Reported in *The Hindu, Dainik Bhaskar*).

No one is punished and no compensation paid. Those who remained back in those families are left to cry their fate. Others have their mobility tied to a single employer/contractor. Contractors also act as intermediaries to augment labour migration to a particular region. Such migration through an intermediary could involve anyone from an informal contractor in one's kinship network to a more formal recruitment agency, and reduces the risk of unemployment. Increasingly, social networks have also emerged as a common medium and driver of migration (ILO 2020, p. 12).

To a careful reader of the reality of the distressed migrant labourer, it becomes clear that the state of the migrants is deplorable and devastating. It is they who are the authors of many things but they are nowhere in terms of dignity and right. Let us see what the Bible tells us about migration and the migrants.

3

Migration and Migrants in the Bible

The Bible, the sacred scripture of the Christians contains a collection of ancient stories, teachings, and poetry, presents a captivating viewpoint on migration and migrants. From the journeys of biblical figures to the movement of people of Yahweh, to the themes of suffering, human degradation as well as hospitality and justice, the Bible reveals a deep connection between faith and the human experience of displacement, movement and seeking a new home.

In the Old Testament, the Jewish people were deported, exiled, enslaved, scattered and dispersed. Recalling the migration of the Jewish people out of Egypt, Jesus, Mary, and Joseph themselves were refugees who fled into Egypt (Mt 2:15). In the Gospels, Jesus enters the world during his family's journey to be enrolled in their ancestral homeland (Lk 2:1-7), where they are denied lodging. The Holy Family flees to Egypt to avoid persecution by King Herod and, even after Herod's death, cannot return to Israel, but must settle in Nazareth for fear of Herod's son, Archelaus (Mt 2:13-15, 19-23).[67]

Since, the communities that believed in Yahuwah and the communities that believed in Messiah Jesus Christ, themselves were subjected to displacement, forced movement, wandering in the desert, being strangers in others land and finding the promised land, it was

[67] Justice for Immigrants. Scripture and Migration. USCCB. 2004. A diverse group of Catholic organizations with national networks joined the U.S. Catholic bishops' Justice for Immigrants Campaign (JFI) in an effort to unite and mobilize a growing network of Catholic institutions, individuals, and other persons of goodwill in support of immigration reform.

also aware of the sufferings and subjugation a person goes through. Thus we see that the Bible emphasizes the importance of caring for and treating migrants with compassion, justice, and hospitality. It calls for welcoming and protecting those who are displaced from their homes, regardless of their background or nationality. This call to care for migrants is present in both the Old and New Testaments, highlighting the shared humanity of all people and the sacred responsibility to welcome and protect the vulnerable.

Further, in the Old Testament, widows, orphans, and strangers or foreigners or sojourners are often referred to as the most vulnerable people. Many of these texts place a strong emphasis on their care and protection. God is portrayed as their defender, and the Israelites are commanded to show compassion and avoid exploiting them. This concern for the vulnerable is a recurring theme throughout the Old Testament, particularly in the legal and prophetic texts.

The Old Testament reiterates God's care for the poor over and over. The Church Fathers and other commenters on Sacred Scripture saw an important symbolism in these particular groups of suffering people. In Scripture, marriage is a symbol of fullness in the domestic life, whereas widowhood symbolizes loss and emptiness. Isaiah referred to Israel as a widow to show that God relieves suffering and redeems his people (Isaiah 54:4–5). In the Scripture, orphans symbolize the epitome of loss, defenselessness, and vulnerability. Their great need demands advocacy. They are separated from their parents—their source of provision and protection—and so God himself protects them. The sojourners of Scripture are those who are traveling and living far from their home. To be a stranger in the land is to physically endure the consequences of homelessness, exile, defenselessness, unfulfilled longing for one's home.[68]

This section highlights the biblical understanding of migration and migrants. But this is not a theoretical exercise. We are invited to reflect and act on this biblical truth, 'God provides for these groups out of his divine charity, but He uses his faithful people to provide this care.' If we fail in this responsibility, we fail God Himself/Herself.

[68] Derek Barr. Widows and Orphans and Sojourners. St. John Vianney Theological Seminary Lay Division. March 29, 2019.

From Abraham to the Promised Land

Abraham: The Prototypes of Migration are demonstrated in the faith journeys of our patriarchs and matriarchs – Abraham and Sarah, Isaac and Rebecca, Jacob and his wives with their children and, finally, the descendants of Jacob, after their 600 years of slavery returning through 40 years wandering in the wilderness to the Promised Land. The Bible tells how Terah left Ur of the Chaldeans with his son Abram, Abram's wife Sarai, and Lot, the son of Abram's deceased brother Haran. Their intention was to go to the land of Canaan (Gen 11:31), but they stopped in the city named Haran, and there Terah died. The reason for this migration was a period of dryness, which had affected the Middle East, starting around 2300 B.C. and reaching its peak around 1800 B.C. The wave of the migrants also conquered a few of the Canaanite city-kingdoms and turned them into fortified cities.[69] The biblical story of Abraham's journey to Canaan becomes a central theme in the Bible, highlighting the importance of migration and the divine purpose behind it. The journey represents a transformative experience, both for individuals and for the unfolding of God's plan. For, Abraham embarked on a journey from Ur to the Promised Land, guided by God's call (Gen 12:1-4). When Sarah died, Abraham was a sojourner, alien in the land of Hittites, he had to beg them to sell a piece of land to bury her (Gen 23:4). Thus, the migration, motivated by faith and obedience, set a precedent for many biblical figures who followed in his footsteps.

Patriarch Jacob's life is a story of migration. In the narrative Gen 27:46-36:43, Jacob, the son of Isaac and Rebekah, left his home in Canaan to flee from his brother Esau, whom he had deceived out of his birthright and blessing. His journey took him to Haran, where he worked for his uncle Laban for many years. This move was significant as it illustrated both physical migration and a transformation in Jacob's life, culminating in his eventual return to Canaan with his family and possessions. This return was marked by both reconciliation and confrontation, highlighting the complexities of his migrant experience. Jacob's story reflects themes of displacement, identity, and the search for belonging, which are common in many migration narratives.

---

[69] Issar, A.S. (2014). "From Shem the Son of Noah to Abraham Son of Terah", In: *Strike the Rock and There Shall Come Water. Springer Briefs in Geography*. Springer, Cham. https://doi.org/10.1007/978-3-319-01937-6_8 (accessed on 29th Jan. 2025).

Moses and the Exodus: A Defining Migration Story

The story of Exodus can indeed be interpreted as a profound migration narrative. The Israelites were enslaved in Egypt for several generations, facing harsh labour and oppression under Pharaoh.[70] When Jacob's family entered Egypt, though famine was the primary cause of their migration, it was voluntary with a dignified entry (Gen 46-47). But they were forced into servitude (loss of dignity) due to xenophobia (Ex 1:8-10). This situation reflects an involuntary migration, as they were forced into servitude in a foreign land. Their flight from oppression occurs under the leadership of Moses. This escape is initiated after a series of plagues that culminated in the Exodus, emphasizing the urgency and necessity of their departure. The ten plagues accompanied by tremendous pain, suffering and destruction points to the perseverance and struggle of the broken people.

The Israelites' journey to freedom is marked by significant challenges. They faced obstacles such as the Red Sea, which they miraculously crossed, and various hardships in the desert, including scarcity of food and water. This reflects the difficult realities many migrants face while seeking a better life or freedom from oppression. Again, the search for a homeland, which the Bible calls "the Promised Land" — a place of safety, security, and opportunity — takes them through the wilderness that lasted 40 years, symbolizing a challenging transition as they sought to establish a new identity and community.

During their journey, the Israelites received the Ten Commandments and other laws at Mount Sinai, which helped to establish their identity as a nation and their covenant with God. These aspects are crucial for migrants, as they often seek to maintain their cultural and spiritual identity in new settings. For the first time, the 'no people – slaves' become 'God's own inheritance and God's people.'[71] Eventually, the Israelites arrived at the borders of Canaan, where they prepared to settle. This moment can be seen as the culmination of their migration journey, where they were transformed from a group of oppressed people into a distinct community with a shared identity and purpose. Thus, the Exodus narrative serves not only as a historical

---

[70] According to Exo 12:40 Israelites were in Egypt for 430 years; Acts 7:6 it is 400 years.

[71] Exo 19:5; Dtr 7:6; 14:2; 26:18; in all these verses the term *segula* means possession/ inheritance.

and religious account but also as a powerful migration narrative that resonates deeply with themes of liberation, identity, and belonging.[72] It reflects the struggles and hopes of those seeking refuge and a new life, making it a timeless story that continues to inspire and resonate with diverse migrant experiences today.

Exile and Return of the Israelites as a Migration Narrative

The exile and return of the Israelites are a significant narrative in the history of the Jewish people and can be understood as a migration narrative with profound cultural, religious, and social implications. This story primarily revolves around the Babylonian Exile (586-538 BCE) and the subsequent return to Jerusalem, which is documented in various biblical texts, particularly in the books of 2 Kings, Jeremiah, Ezekiel, and Ezra-Nehemiah.

The Exile: The Migration Experience: Historically, the Babylonian Exile began when the Babylonian Empire, under King Nebuchadnezzar II, conquered the Kingdom of Judah. The elite, including priests, nobles, and skilled workers, were forcibly taken to Babylon. This act of displacement can be seen as a migration experience, where a significant portion of the population was uprooted and forced out from their own homeland. In Babylon, the exiled Israelites faced the challenge of maintaining their identity in a foreign land. They adapted to new cultural norms while striving to preserve their religious practices and communal bonds. This period saw the development of new forms of worship and the compilation of texts that would later become part of the Hebrew Bible. The experience of exile had profound psychological effects on the Israelites. Themes of loss of homeland, longing for the same, and the search for meaning permeated their writings. The Psalms, particularly Psalm 137, express deep sorrow and yearning for Jerusalem, encapsulating the emotional weight of exile.[73]

---

[72] It is very unfortunate that Israel of today has been trying to destroy Palestine and has been waging war against Palestine forgetting its own history.

[73] Psalm 137 is a deeply mournful lament expressing the pain and longing of the Jewish people during their exile in Babylon, vividly describing their sorrow at being forced to leave their homeland and the destruction of Jerusalem, with a particularly poignant image of hanging their harps on the willow trees by the rivers of Babylon, signifying their inability to sing joyful songs in captivity; the psalm concludes with a strong plea for God to bring retribution upon their enemies, especially the Edomites who had gleefully participated in the destruction of Jerusalem.

The Return: The Migration Back: The return began in 538 BCE when Cyrus the Great of Persia conquered Babylon and issued a decree allowing the exiled people to return to their homelands. This marked a significant moment in the migration narrative, as it provided the opportunity for the Israelites to return to Jerusalem and rebuild their temple. The return was not merely a physical journey but also a spiritual and communal restoration. The returned exiles faced numerous challenges, including opposition from local populations, resource scarcity, and the task of rebuilding the temple and the walls of Jerusalem. The books of Ezra and Nehemiah describe these efforts, highlighting the importance of community organization and religious reform.[74]

The return to Jerusalem was a pivotal moment for the Israelites, as it allowed them to re-establish their religious practices and cultural identity. The rebuilding of the temple symbolized a renewed covenant with God and a restoration of their national identity. This period also saw the emergence of new religious leadership and the solidification of Jewish law.

Thus, the narrative of exile and return resonates with broader themes of migration, displacement, and identity. It reflects the struggles faced by displaced peoples throughout history and the resilience required to maintain cultural identity in the face of adversity. The exile and return are central to Jewish theology, symbolizing themes of sin, punishment, redemption, and hope. The narrative has been interpreted as a metaphor for spiritual exile and the longing for divine presence. The story of the Israelites' exile and return has influenced various migration narratives in religious and secular contexts. It serves as a powerful reminder of the complexities of migration, the search for belonging, and the enduring human spirit.

---

[74] In Ezra 4:1-5, when the "enemies of Judah and Benjamin" hear about the rebuilding of the temple, they approach the Jewish leaders with a seemingly helpful offer to join the construction, claiming to worship the same God; however, Zerubbabel and the leaders firmly refuse, stating that only the Israelites should build the temple as per King Cyrus' command; this rejection then leads to the surrounding people actively hindering the construction by discouraging and frightening the Jewish people, even bribing officials to obstruct their efforts throughout the reigns of Cyrus and Darius. In Nehemiah 4 and 6:1-13 describe Nehemiah's efforts to rebuild the walls of Jerusalem after the Israelites returned from exile in Babylon. Nehemiah encouraged the people to work together and be vigilant, and they kept guard around the wall day and night.

The Lord's Concern for Migrants: Deuteronomy 10:17-19

Deuteronomy 10:17-19 highlights the importance of showing concern and care for migrants, a timeless message that resonates even today. The passage emphasizes that God loves the migrant, providing for their needs and showing them justice. **This biblical call for compassion towards migrants is a powerful reminder for believers to uphold the dignity and rights of those who are vulnerable and marginalized in society.** The message from Deuteronomy calls upon individuals to extend hospitality and kindness to migrants, recognizing their inherent worth and the hardships they may face. It emphasizes the need to treat migrants with respect and fairness, reflecting the divine command to love one's neighbour as oneself. This moral imperative transcends time and culture, guiding believers to act with empathy and compassion towards those who are strangers in a foreign land.

In a world marked by increasing migration and displacement, the principles outlined in Deuteronomy 10:17-19 hold particular relevance. As societies grapple with issues of immigration and refugee crises, the biblical injunction to care for migrants serves as a guiding light for policies and attitudes towards newcomers, that is, foreigners, immigrants or interstate workers. It challenges individuals and communities to look beyond borders and differences, recognizing the shared humanity and dignity of all people. Drawing from scholarly articles, books, and reputable websites, it becomes evident that the concern for migrants is deeply rooted in ethical and religious traditions across various cultures and faiths. By engaging with diverse sources, we can enrich our understanding of the importance of compassion and hospitality towards migrants from different perspectives.

Welcoming the Foreigner: Leviticus 19:33-34

Understanding the historical context of Leviticus is crucial for comprehending its treatment of migrants, particularly in passages such as Leviticus 19:33-34. The text emerges within a milieu where Israel is steering its identity, having recently exited slavery in Egypt, thus emphasizing empathy toward the stranger or migrant. This empathetic call is deeply rooted in the collective memory of the Israelites as sojourners, highlighting their own experiences of vulnerability and oppression. The dual portrayals of the stranger, as seen in the motif of the *gēr* (sojourner) versus the *nēkār* (foreigner), reveal a complex societal relationship marked by both compassion and fear. In this framework, texts like Deuteronomy 10:17-19 articulate God's love for the stranger, while other narratives illuminate the historical underpinnings of social separation inherent in a foundational document supporting settler-colonial ideologies.

The ethical implications of Leviticus 19:33-34 extend beyond mere adherence to ancient laws, inviting a contemporary examination of our obligations toward migrants. The text's directive to love the stranger emphasizes a universal principle of hospitality that transcends cultural and temporal boundaries. This imperative reflects the theological foundations discussed by Tavanti, who argues that true hospitality is grounded in justice and respect for the dignity of others, regardless of their origins. Moreover, the concept of Ubuntu, which embodies interdependence and communal identity, supports seamlessly with the biblical mandate to treat migrants with compassion and solidarity. Such ethical constructs urge individuals and communities to reject xenophobia and embrace those on the margins, reinforcing that our commitment to uphold the dignity of every person is intertwined with our shared humanity. Ultimately, Leviticus serves as a profound call for ethical engagement in our diverse societies.

Leviticus 19:33-34 presents a profound ethical directive that resonates with contemporary discussions on migration and social justice. By emphasizing the need to treat migrants with the same compassion and respect afforded to one's own community, the text challenges societal norms that often marginalize vulnerable populations. This scriptural mandate not only advocates for equitable treatment but also emphasizes the larger moral obligation to recognize the shared humanity between natives and migrants. In an era marked by rising nationalism and xenophobia, the message of inclusivity found in these verses serves as a vital reminder of the responsibilities that come with cohabiting a diverse society. Ultimately, the principles outlined in Leviticus invite us to engage in self-reflection and foster a culture of empathy, urging individuals and communities alike to embrace their roles as stewards of justice and equality in a world increasingly distinguished by its plurality.

Ruth and Naomi: Migrants Seeking Refuge

The story of Ruth and Naomi is a powerful narrative that vibrates with themes of migration, refuge, and resilience. In the biblical book of Ruth, we encounter two women who find themselves in a precarious situation, forced to leave their homeland in search of a better future. Ruth and Naomi's (it is only a return migration for Naomi (homecoming) whereas Ruth is a stranger (*nokri*)) journey as migrants seeking refuge offers valuable insights into the challenges faced by displaced individuals throughout history. As the narrative unfolds, we see how Ruth and Naomi's bond transcends familial ties, becoming a source of strength and support in the face of adversity. Despite the hardships they encounter, including poverty and discrimination, the two women remain steadfast in their commitment to each other. Ruth's unwavering loyalty to Naomi, expressed through her famous declaration, "Where you go, I will go" (Ruth 1:16), stresses the power of solidarity in times of crisis.

Their story also highlights the importance of community and mutual aid in times of need. When Ruth and Naomi arrive in Bethlehem, they are welcomed by the local community, who provide them with food and shelter. This display of compassion and empathy serves as a reminder that hospitality and generosity can make a significant difference in the lives of migrants and refugees. Moreover, Ruth and Naomi's narrative challenges traditional notions of identity and belonging. As foreigners in a new land, they traverse complex social dynamics and cultural norms, ultimately challenging the boundaries of inclusion and exclusion. **Through their resilience and determination, Ruth and Naomi demonstrate that belonging is not limited to one's place of origin but is rather rooted in the bonds of love and companionship.**

Thus, the story of Ruth and Naomi offers a timeless lesson on the power of solidarity, compassion, and resilience in the face of displacement. By examining their journey as migrants seeking refuge, we are reminded of the enduring relevance of their experiences and the universal quest for dignity and belonging. The themes of intermarriage between locals and foreigners and their role in the salvation history is an added element within this narrative.

Jesus as a Migrant: God Migrating to Humanity

Throughout history, Jesus Christ has been depicted as a figure of compassion, love, and sacrifice. One aspect of his life that is often overlooked is his experience as a migrant. Jesus, like many individuals today, was forced to seek refuge in a foreign land due to political persecution and violence. By understanding Jesus as a migrant, we can gain a deeper appreciation for his teachings on love, acceptance, and the treatment of others. One cannot overlook the profound symbolism that surrounds His status as a migrant. The idea of God migrating to humanity through the person of Jesus is a central tenet of Christian theology, highlighting the deep connection between God and His creation (Jn 1:14; Phil 2:6-8).

This concept, rooted in the belief that Jesus left the divine realm to enter into the human experience, carries significant implications for understanding the nature of God and His relationship with humanity. **The notion of Jesus as a migrant, challenges conventional notions of power and authority, presenting a vision of God that is intimately involved in the lives of ordinary people.** By choosing to take on human form and experience the joys and struggles of human existence, Jesus demonstrates a radical solidarity with those on the margins of society. This act of migration embodies a profound act of humility and love, illustrating God's commitment to walking alongside His creation in the midst of their struggles.

Moreover, the story of Jesus as a migrant accentuates the universal nature of God's love and grace. **By crossing boundaries and embracing diversity, Jesus reveals a vision of inclusivity that transcends cultural, social, and political divides.** His willingness to take on the identity of a migrant echoes a broader message of compassion and empathy towards those who are marginalized and oppressed. In conclusion, **Jesus as a migrant represents a powerful symbol of God's presence and activity in the world.** Through His migration to humanity, Jesus reveals a God who is intimately connected to His creation, willing to enter into the messiness and complexity of human life. This image of God as a migrant challenges us to reexamine our own conceptions of power, authority, and privilege, inviting us to embrace a vision of love and justice that crosses all boundaries.

New Testament: Migration and the Kingdom of God

The New Testament presents a unique perspective on migration and the Kingdom of God, shedding light on the interactions between these two themes. On the one hand, migration, the movement of people from one place to another, has been a constant feature of human history and is reflected in various passages of the New Testament. The concept of the Kingdom of God, on the other hand, refers to the reign of God over all creation, emphasizing justice, peace, and righteousness. By examining how migration is portrayed in the New Testament in relation to the Kingdom of God, we can gain insights into the intersection of these two important aspects.

Migration in the New Testament is often associated with themes of journey, displacement, and seeking refuge. For example, the story of Jesus' birth in Bethlehem, a result of a census that required Joseph and Mary to travel from Nazareth (Lk 2:1-5), highlights the idea of forced migration due to external circumstances. Additionally, the flight of the Holy Family to Egypt to escape King Herod's persecution (Mt 2:13-15) demonstrates the vulnerability and challenges faced by migrants seeking safety and security.

In the context of the Kingdom of God, migration can be viewed as a reflection of the universal reach of God's reign. The New Testament emphasizes the inclusivity of the Kingdom, welcoming all people, regardless of their background or status. This perspective links with the teachings of Jesus, who preached love, compassion, and hospitality towards strangers and foreigners. Moreover, the early Christian community, shaped by the message of the Kingdom of God, embraced diversity and unity among believers from different cultures and traditions.

Jesus' encounters with the actual foreigners like the Centurian in Mt 8:5-13, Phoenician woman in Mk 7:24-29, the Samaritan woman Jn 4, and Jesus as a stranger in Mt 25:31-46 and Lk 24:1-33, the appointment of foreigners (Greeks) as deacons in Acts 6:1-7, and the ECC as a real migrant community (Acts 8:1-4) highlight the proactive stand taken by Jesus to converse, communicate and ensure co-habitation in a common home, created by God the Father and mother. The Acts of the Apostles further strengthens this collective sense of all human beings and the need to proactively move out of borders and barriers to reach out to the frontiers.

Overall, the New Testament provides a nuanced understanding of migration in relation to the Kingdom of God, highlighting the interconnectedness of these themes in shaping the Christian worldview. By exploring the biblical narratives and teachings on migration, we can glean valuable insights into the ethical, social, and theological implications of human movement and its implications for realizing the Kingdom of God on earth.

Citizens with the Saints: Ephesians 2:11-22

The passage Ephesians 2:11-22 presents a rich tapestry of theological concepts that echo deeply with the contemporary experience of migrants. Ephesians was written during a time when the early Christian community contended with significant transitions. The divide between Jewish and Gentile believers was a pressing issue. This division is central to understanding the message of Ephesians 2:11-22, where Paul calls for unity among different groups. Migrants today often confront similar divisions in society. They may feel alienated and unwelcome as they crisscross through complex political and social landscapes. The Apostle Paul's exhortation to transcend these divisions can offer encouragement and hope to those who find themselves on the margins of society.

The opening verse of this passage alludes to the historical context of circumcision, a critical marker of Jewish identity. Paul identifies the Gentiles as those who were previously "far off," (2:13, 17) emphasizing the separation caused by cultural and religious boundaries. Migrants today may resound with this sense of alienation. Many face obstacles that stem from entrenched societal norms that define who belongs and who does not. This barrier can take many forms, from legal restrictions to social ostracism. Paul's words serve as a reminder that the boundaries we erect can often be overcome through acts of inclusion and acceptance.

Moreover, within the text, Paul emphasizes the role of Christ as the unifier. In Ephesians 2:14, Paul states that Christ has "broken down the dividing wall" that separates humanity. For migrants, this serves as a powerful metaphor for integration within host societies. The current global landscape highlights how communities can be fractured by fear and misunderstanding. Nonetheless, Christ's role as a reconciler encourages individuals and churches to foster environments of acceptance rather than exclusion.

Another critical aspect of Ephesians 2:11-22 is its emphasis on the new identity formed within the body of Christ. The passage culminates in the assertion that all believers are "members of the household of God" (2:19). In the context of migration, this notion affirms that one's identity transcends nationality or ethnicity. Migrants often struggle for recognition and legitimacy in societies that may prioritize local identities. Paul's assertion that we are "fellow citizens" provides reassurance. It emphasizes a collective identity rooted in faith rather than division based on societal constructs.

A well-reasoned analysis of Ephesians 2:11-22 also prompts us to consider what lies ahead. The continued rise in globalization will inevitably lead to increased migration, whether for economic, social, or environmental reasons. In the light of this, the message of Ephesians can function as a guiding principle for future responses. There is an opportunity for communities to more fully embody the call to inclusivity and acceptance that Paul espouses. Innovative community programs that seek to integrate migrants, celebrate multiculturalism, and address systemic injustices can emerge from a thorough reflection on these biblical principles. Thus, the implications of Ephesians 2:11-22 resonate powerfully within the context of contemporary migration.

This passage challenges the entrenched divisions that often characterize societal structures. Through the lens of a migrant's experience, we can find affirmation in the message of unity, collective identity, and the need for hospitality. As societies continue to face the complexities of migration, the teachings of the New Testament serve as a vital foundation for advocating for a more inclusive and compassionate world. Future developments in this area will depend on how communities choose to embrace these lessons and work towards fostering belonging for all people, reflecting the unity desired in the body of Christ.

Pauline Understanding of Migrants

St. Paul addresses the concept of migration primarily through the lens of community, identity, and divine purpose. The Apostle Paul, a prominent figure in early Christianity, frequently engaged with diverse communities, many of whom were composed of migrants. In his letters, Paul emphasized the idea that in Christ, there is neither Jew nor Gentile, neither slave nor free, nor male and female (Galatians 3:28). This declaration highlights a radical inclusion that serves as a foundational aspect of his teaching. For Paul, the membership in the Christian community transcends cultural, ethnic, and social barriers, highlighting an important dimension of how migrants are viewed in the context of faith.

The implications of Paul's teachings on community are significant when reflecting on the experiences of modern migrants. The early church itself was born out of a context of diaspora. Paul's missionary journeys often took him to regions populated by believers who were not originally from those areas. This historical context demonstrates that migration is not a new phenomenon; rather, it has been a part of human existence and spiritual history. Migrants, as viewed through Pauline theology, are integral members of the Christian body, bringing their unique backgrounds and experiences to enrich the community.

In examining various perspectives surrounding the Pauline understanding of migrants, the audit of contemporary socio-political contexts is crucial. The rise of nationalism and xenophobia in recent years has placed immense challenges on migrants worldwide. Paul's theological framework can offer a counter-narrative to such divisive ideologies. His letters often advocate for compassion, hospitality, and the calling of Christians to embrace those who are different. For instance, Hebrews 13:2 encourages believers not to neglect showing hospitality to strangers, thereby illuminating the ethical obligations that arise from a Pauline worldview. This perspective fosters an ethos of welcome and care, encouraging communities to rally around those who find themselves in vulnerable situations.

Recent scholarship emphasizes the role of the church in advocating for migrants' rights and championing their dignity.[75] This advocacy lines up closely with Pauline teachings, which encourage active engagement with societal injustices. Moreover, contemporary events have illustrated the urgency of applying Pauline theology to

---

[75] Andrew F. Walls, *The Missionary Movement in Christian History: Studies in the Transmission of Faith,* Maryknoll, New York: Orbis Books, 1996; Sugirtharajah, R. S. (ed.), The Postcolonial Biblical Reader, Oxford: Blackwell, 2006.

migration issues. The Syrian, Palestinian and Ukrainian refugee crisis, for instance, has mobilized churches and religious organizations to respond to the humanitarian needs of migrants. Initiatives aimed at providing shelter, food, and legal assistance are often rooted in the instructive elements of Pauline theology. This makes parallel with a deeper understanding of what it means to be a follower of Christ: to live out love, mercy, and grace towards those in need. The involvement of faith communities in this context reflects Paul's vision of a community of believers who thwart barriers and embody Christ-like compassion.

Looking ahead, the Pauline understanding of migrants is poised to influence future discussions on immigration policy, social justice, and community building. As the world continues to wrestle with the complexities of migration in an increasingly interconnected society, there is a growing necessity to return to the teachings of Pauline thought. Dialogues surrounding migration must consider ethical imperatives, as well as scriptural foundations, urging communities to re-evaluate their responses to migrants with an emphasis on dignity and inclusion. In conclusion, Pauline understanding of migrants offers rich theological insights that challenge contemporary attitudes towards migration.

By promoting an inclusive community that transcends ethnic and social boundaries, Paul's teachings inspire believers to engage with the realities faced by migrants today. The influence of influential thinkers and the practical responses of faith communities further highlight the applicability of Pauline thought in contemporary migration discourse. As society evolves, so too must the interpretations of these teachings, creating a framework that not only acknowledges the struggles of migrants but actively seeks to empower them within the larger community.

Migrants in the Book of Revelation

In the book of Revelation, the concept of migrants emerges as a recurring theme that holds significant theological implications. The text portrays a vivid imagery of people moving through different spaces and realms, symbolizing a spiritual journey towards salvation and redemption. These migrants are not merely physical beings but also represent the souls seeking refuge in the promises of God. One of the prominent instances of migrants in Revelation can be found in the vision of the New Jerusalem. In Rev 21:2, John sees the holy city coming down out of heaven, adorned as a bride for her husband. This image conveys the idea of a divine migration, where the heavenly realm descends to earth, signalling the ultimate reunion of God with his people. The migrants in this context are the believers who eagerly await the fulfilment of God's promises and the establishment of the new, eternal kingdom.

Furthermore, Revelation depicts the ultimate destination of these migrants as the presence of God himself. Revelation 7:15-17 describes how the faithful will dwell in the presence of God, serving him day and night in his temple. This vision reinforces the idea that the journey of migrants in Revelation is not aimless but holds a specific goal of communing with God for eternity. Moreover, the concept of migrants in Revelation also highlights the eschatological tension between the earthly and heavenly realms. As believers journey through a world filled with tribulations and temptations, they are reminded of their ultimate citizenship in heaven (Philippians 3:20). This tension puts emphasis on the transient nature of earthly life and urges believers to live as sojourners and exiles, eagerly anticipating their true home in God's eternal kingdom.

Thus, migrants in the book of Revelation serve as powerful symbols of the spiritual journey towards salvation and communion with God. The imagery of migration conveys the themes of redemption, hope, and the ultimate fulfilment of God's promises. As believers go through the complexities of life, they are encouraged to keep their eyes fixed on the heavenly destination where God's presence awaits them.

Thus, we see that even in the harsh stories of migration, God is present, revealing himself. Abraham stepped out in faith to respond to God's call (Gn 12:1). He and Sarah extended bounteous hospitality to three strangers who were actually a manifestation of the Lord, and this became a paradigm for the response to strangers of Abraham's descendants. The grace of God even broke through situations of sin in the forced migration of the children of Jacob: Joseph, sold into slavery, eventually became the saviour of his family (Gn 37:45)–a type of Jesus, who, betrayed by a friend for thirty pieces of silver, saves the human family.

The key events in the history of the Chosen People of enslavement by the Egyptians and of liberation by God led to commandments regarding strangers (Ex 23:9; Lv 19:33). Israel's conduct with the stranger is both an imitation of God and the primary, specific Old Testament manifestation of the great commandment to love one's neighbour: "For the Lord, your God, is the . . . Lord of lords, the great God, mighty and awesome, ... who executes justice for the orphan and widow, and befriends the alien, feeding and clothing him. So you, too, must befriend the alien, for you were once aliens yourselves in the land of Egypt" (Dt 10:17-19). For the Israelites, these injunctions were not only personal exhortations: the welcome and care of the alien were structured into their gleaning and tithing laws (Lv 19:9-10; Dt 14:28-29).

Recalling the migration of the Chosen People from Egypt, Jesus, Mary, and Joseph themselves were refugees in Egypt: "Out of Egypt I called my son" (Mt 2:15). From this account the Holy Family has become a figure with whom Christian migrants and refugees throughout the ages can identify, giving them hope and courage in hard times.

Taken together, the Bible, with its diverse narratives and powerful themes, offers a lens through which we can understand the experience of migration and its enduring impact on humanity. From the journeys of individuals to the teachings on justice and compassion, the Bible highlights the universal human experience of seeking a new home and the importance of welcoming and supporting migrants. The ongoing debate surrounding migration demonstrates the enduring relevance of these ancient texts in addressing modern challenges. Scholars continue to explore the intersection of biblical interpretation, migration, and social justice, drawing on both traditional and innovative approaches to understanding these complex issues.

The Holy Spirit has been present throughout the history of the Church to work against injustice, division, and oppression and to bring about respect for individual human rights, unity of races and cultures, and the incorporation of the marginalized into full life in the Church. In modern times, one of the ways this work of the Spirit has been manifested is through Catholic social teaching, in particular the teachings on human dignity and the principle of solidarity.

The Bible thus is full of references to migration and migrants. It continues to invite us to know, understand and accept the reality of migration and to accompany and assist the migrants, especially the distressed labour migrants. As true Christians we are called to meditate, pray over and assist those in need. If we fail to do this, then our sacrifice may not be accepted by God. Amos reiterates this in the Bible, "I hate, I reject your festivals; I don't enjoy your joyous assemblies. If you bring me your entirely burned offerings and gifts of food— I won't be pleased; I won't even look at your offerings of well-fed animals. Take away the noise of your songs; I won't listen to the melody of your harps. But let justice roll down like waters, and righteousness like an ever-flowing stream." (Amos 5: 22-24).

Reverend Dr. Martin Luther King, Jr. reiterated the need to convert our religiosity into concern for the other, especially the marginalised. "The church must be reminded that it is not the master or the servant of the state, but rather the conscience of the state. It must be the guide and the critic of the state, and never its tool. If the church does not recapture its prophetic zeal, it will become an irrelevant social club without moral or spiritual authority." The Old Testament of the Bible repeatedly presents this prophetic call of the prophets who stood by the marginalised and migrants.

4

Migration in Christian Theologising

We judge ourselves as a community of faith by the way we treat the most vulnerable among us. The treatment of migrants challenges the consciences of elected officials, policymakers, enforcement officers, residents of border communities, and providers of legal aid and social services, many of whom share our Catholic faith.

The theological[76] implications of migration, particularly within a Christian context, emphasize God's love and desire to cross over barriers, highlighting the dignity of the human person, especially migrants, and the importance of welcoming the "other". Here below we are presenting a more detailed exploration of these theological implications:

• God's Migration and Incarnation

A key theological concept is that God, in Jesus Christ, "migrated" into the world, taking on human form and experiencing the "far country" of human suffering and brokenness. This demonstrates God's love and desire to be present with humanity, even in its most vulnerable states.

---

[76] When we term this section, theological it does not limit to viewing migration from the perspective of theology. It is more from the point of view of theologising which means what is stated and communicated is not fixed and final but evolves and evolves based on the praxis of text and context. Hence, the theological approach from this perspective encompasses theologising, missiology, ecclesiology, spirituality, hermeneutics, pastoral cycle, etc.

• Jesus as a Migrant and Refugee

The Gospel of Matthew recounts Jesus's family fleeing political persecution and becoming refugees in Egypt, further emphasizing the divine taking on the narrative of the most vulnerable among us. Thus, Jesus symoblises the displaced, the migrants and refugees.

• Crossing Divides

A theology of migration emphasizes crossing over the nonhuman-human divide, highlighting the inherent dignity of all people, especially migrants who are often marginalized. It also crosses the divine-human divide, showing God's grace and initiative in reaching out to those in need. God migrates to become human to live the life of human beings.

• The Encounter with the "Other"

Migration inevitably involves encountering the "other," and a theological perspective emphasizes the importance of integration and understanding between migrants and host communities. Since both are children of God, there cannot be differences among them.

• Biblical Narrative

The Bible itself contains numerous narratives of migration, including the Israelites' journey out of Egypt and their search for a home, highlighting the theme of migration as a search for a place where God's people can find blessings and worship him.

• Remembering the Past

The concept of "Remember that you were a migrant in Egypt" (Exodus 22:20; Leviticus 19:34) is a powerful reminder of the Israelites' experience of migration and serves as a call to compassion and justice for migrants.

• Practical Theology

The theological implications of migration extend to practical issues such as liturgy, worship, spirituality, livelihood, health care, and education, as well as how churches can better serve migrant communities.

• Ethical Considerations

Some ethical considerations on migration include reciprocity, the duty to protect, equality in fundamental rights, and the renunciation of complete conformity. Migrants also have fundamental rights, since they are covered under the right to be human.

• Ecclesiological Considerations

The Church is called to respond to this reality of the migrants in its midst in a pastoral and missionary way. This has already been happening in practice and theology throughout history of the Pilgrim Church, but perhaps more intensely in the last 150 years when the Holy See institutionalized this concern for the whole Church.[77]

• Missiological Considerations

There is a very urgent need to take seriously the implications of migration on marriage and family life. The social, spiritual and moral implications need urgent assessment by all. Husbands separated from wives, and children from parents are a direct consequences of contract labour migration, showing signs of breakdown of both marriages and families.[78]

Various efforts have been made by different agencies, institutions, forums, seminaries, etc., to theologise on the hard realities of migrants. Migration being a contemporary reality which hits anyone who dares to observe, understand and respond, theologising helps in this. Theologising on migration is in a sense continuation in the line of biblical writing. Let us explore some of the salient features of theologising of migration.

From a theological perspective, Groody uses the word 'migrant' to refer primarily to those who 'are poor, vulnerable, and marginalized, especially economic migrants, forced migrants or refugees, internally displaced people, and victims of human trafficking' (2022:26). Groody's usage is a reminder that many migrants today may be identified as those whom Jesus called the 'least of these' in Matt 25:40.[79]

---

[77] *Rev. Fr. Michael A. BLUME, S.V.D.,. Towards an Ecclesiology of Migration.* Undersecretary, Pontifical Council for the Pastoral Care of Migrations and Itinerant People. December, 2002.

[78] Jonathan Y. Tan. *Migration in Asia and Its Missiological Implications: Insights from the Migration Theology of the Federation of Asians Bishops' Conferences* (FABC)

[79] *Ilsup Ahn.* Migration and Christian Theology. St. Andews Encyclopaedia of Theology. February, 2024. We have extensively used this article of Ilsup Ahn in our presentation.

As an academic discipline, migration theology is hermeneutically established as a theological reflection on various phenomena of human migration. For instance, Catholic theologian Peter Phan summarizes this hermeneutic approach with three steps. The first is a socio-political and cultural analysis of migration. **It is crucial to note that 'a theology of migration must be deeply rooted in the flesh-and-blood stories of migrants themselves as human beings whose dignity and rights have often been trampled upon' (Phan 2016: 855). The second step, which he calls 'hermeneutical mediation', follows the first 'socio-analytic' step. This step involves the provision of proper theological meaning to the life stories of migrants, sociological, historical, and legal data, and theories of migration.**[80]

The stories of migration in the Old and New Testaments, the teachings of the church on migration, and the history of the movements of Christians throughout history become important theological sources to interpret those socio-analytic data. The last step of migration theology is 'practical mediation'. Phan argues that the theological understanding of migration should not remain at the level of rhetoric but should be translated into concrete actions with and for migrants.[81]

What, then, constitutes the theology of migration? How does migration theology differ from other studies of migration, such as social scientific studies of migration? In answering these questions, this article incorporates a phenomenological approach as a theological method. From this perspective, there are three key aspects that are indispensable in establishing a theology of migration: the experience of movement, the journey of faith, and the encounter with the other(s).

First, the experience of movement. Since migration is not possible without the experience of movement, all migration theologies address humanity's varied experiences of movement. Unlike social scientific studies of migration, which largely focus on the spatial phenomenon of migration (moving from one place to another), migration theology offers the distinctive perspective that migrants can experience movement not only as a spatial event but also as a

---

[80] Peter C. Phan. 'Deus Migrator—God the Migrant: Migration of Theology and Theology of Migration', *Theological Studies* 77, no. 4: 855. 2016.

[81] Ibid. 856.

progression in time. Through migration, humanity gets closer to 'the end of the age' (Matt 28:20).

The second aspect is the journey of faith. Unlike the social scientific descriptions of migration that explain the phenomenon of human migration as a result of 'push factors' and 'pull factors', many migration stories in the Bible portray the phenomenon of migration as a result of the migrant's response to God's calling. Groody thus writes, 'migration is inextricably connected to the journey of faith and often functions as a root metaphor for the search for a deeper knowledge of God, the hope for a better life, and the path of salvation' (Groody 2022: 66). As will be seen below, the theological meaning of various biblical narratives of human migration cannot be understood without considering the 'faith factor'.

The last aspect of a migration theology is the inevitable fact of all human migration, i.e., the encounter with the other(s). When someone migrates to a new land or territory, often far away from her or his own native land, that person inevitably encounters the people of the land who commonly regard him or her as a stranger or an alien. Migration is a proven way to create social 'others' in any hosting society, and it can potentially entail social unrest and dissension, as well as societal growth and integration. From a theological perspective, how to integrate migrant people and hosting citizens thus becomes an indispensable theological issue. This entry explores these ***three key aspects of a migration theology by interfacing them with the three persons of God: the journey of faith – God the Father; the experience of movement – God the Son; the encounter with the other – God the Holy Spirit.*** Before doing so, however, it is important to examine what the Bible says about human migration.

God and Migration

Theology is speaking about God. As Catholic theologian Peter Phan writes, 'theology is *logos* about *theos*, a human discourse about God that is made possible and authorized by God's own speech to humanity, that is, God's self-revelation in history' (2016: 858). Migration theology is then speaking about God concerning humanity's diverse experiences of migration. There are roughly two ways of speaking about God in the field of migration theology. One is by way of referring to 'who God is' whereas the other is by way of alluding to 'what God does.

The following section examines how these two different approaches enhance and expand theological understandings of the phenomenon of human migration.

'Who God is' and Migration

From a critical perspective, speaking about 'who God is' is an impossible project because – in Karl Rahner's terms – God is the ineffable Absolute Mystery. There is an inherent *agnosis* (non-knowledge) in human *gnosis* (knowledge) of God, and 'our speech about God, even the most learned, is nothing but a stammering, by means of analogies, to describe who God is' (Phan 2016: 859). Despite this intrinsic deficiency of human language about God, Phan argues that some of these metaphors, images, and analogies to speak of God are 'authorized', that is, used and licensed by the Bible, and therefore should not be discarded without cause. Phan goes on to say:

It is in this context that a theology of migration can refer to God, I suggest, as *Deus Migrator* (God the Migrant). Of course, the threefold movement of affirmation-negation-transcendence in God-talk must also be applied there: God *is*, is *not*, and is *infinitely* a migrant. With this caution in mind, we can explore how the Christian God can be thought of as the ***Deus Migrator*, 'God the Migrant' or 'Migratory God' or 'God-on-the-Move.'** Even though the term 'migrant' is not used of God in the Bible, there are hints suggesting that God possesses the characteristics commonly associated with migration and migrants (Phan 2016: 859).

Ilsup Ahn goes on to raise this question, how is the theological statement that God is 'the Primordial Migrant' possible? Why does Phan argue that God is *Deus Migrator*? Phan answers the question by reinterpreting the theological doctrine of God's **creation**. Phan begins by saying that there is an indispensable element of movement in God's creation, and a migration theology can be developed based on this basis. Phan shows how migration and creation can be interlinked by pointing out the necessary component of 'crossing the border' in God's creation. He describes this necessary component as follows: 'In creating that which is other than Godself, God crosses the border between Absolute Spirit and finite matter, migrating from eternity to temporality, from omnipotence into weakness' (2016: 860).

Phan's migration theology is established through his theological imagination of God's creation, as well as the phenomenological analysis of the migration experience. This theology culminates in the statement that 'in the creative act, God experiences for the first time the precarious, marginalized, threatened, and endangered condition of the migrant' (2016: 860).

In answer to the question of what the theological statement that God is *Deus Migrator* has to do with humanity. Phan emphasizes that we should be reminded how God created human beings in God's own image. If God is understood as the *Deus Migrator*, migration is then considered to be an important theological theme that characterizes who humans are and what we should do. Migrants become the *imago Dei*, created in the image and likeness of God who is the 'Primordial Migrant.' Phan calls attention to the theological significance of his statement: What is distinctive and unique about the migrant is that he or she is the *imago Dei migratoris*, the privileged, visible, and public face of the God who chooses, freely and out of love, to migrate from the safety of God's eternal home to the strange and risky land of the human family, in which God is a foreigner needing embrace, protection, and love (Phan 2016: 861).

Phan's theological idea, that migrants are quintessentially the *imago Dei*, is especially significant when considering that the human rights of many migrants such as refugees and undocumented migrants are often ignored or even denied by the state or hosting societies, leaving them in politically and economically vulnerable positions. From the perspective of the *Deus Migrator*, all human beings created in God's image come to have the ontological ground of human rights. Other Christian theologians such as Daniel Groody, Lisa Sowle Cahill, and Mary Catherine Hilkert all agree with Phan regarding the theological significance of *imago Dei* related to migrants.

For example, Daniel Groody writes, 'defining all human beings in terms of *imago Dei* provides a very different starting point for the discourse on migration and creates a very different trajectory for the discussion.'[82] Cahill and Hilkert, respectively, also note the importance of the Christian idea of the image of God (Cahill 1980; Hilkert 1995).

[82] Daniel G. Groody. 2009. 'Crossing the Divide: Foundations of a Theology of Migration and Refugees', *Theological Studies* 70, no. 3: 638–667. 2009.

As Groody summarizes: 'The image of God is the primary Christian category or symbol of an interpretation of personal value', and 'this symbol grounds further claims to human rights and gives rise to justice' (Groody 2009: 644).

Although theological language such as *Deus Migrator* and *imago Dei* is not commonly circulated and is often ignored in the public discourse, these ideas may still indirectly impact society, especially regarding the protection and promotion of human rights and dignity of migrants. For instance, inspired by a theology of migration, Christian believers could initiate or participate in social movements to change peoples' views on migrants by advocating for the removal of such dehumanizing terms as 'illegals' or 'illegal immigrants' or 'encroachers' from the public discourse.

'What God Does' and Migration

In the Western theological tradition, there are roughly two ways of doing theology: apophatic (or negative) theology and cataphatic (or positive) theology. While the former focuses on the infinite qualitative difference between humanity and divinity, rendering it impossible to identify God by any positive terms, the latter emphasizes the relationality between humanity and divinity, making it possible to achieve a certain positive knowledge of God by measures such as analogy. From the cataphatic approach to theology, speaking of 'who God is' is then possible. Apophatic theology, however, finds it difficult to say positively who God is. Regarding the nature of God, apophatic theology can speak of 'who God is' only negatively, because any positive identification of God may be liable to idolatry. From the perspective of apophatic theology, the close relationality and even similarity between humanity and divinity may lead us to perceive God based on our own self-understanding. Therefore, there is a higher chance that cataphatic theology may become 'ontotheology.'

Although the idea of apophatic theology is not widely shared by scholars within the community of migration theology, this article incorporates its theological explorations here with the purpose of expanding the theological imagination on the migration of people. How, then, does apophatic theology start to talk about God? Catherine Keller answers this question by exploring Gregory of Nyssa's (332–395 CE) apophatic theological works, especially his *The Life of Moses*, in which Gregory uncovers the apophatic source of theology in the story of Moses' intimate encounter with God in the cloud on Mount Sinai. Keller then captures the key aspect of apophatic theology by distinguishing *knowing that* from *knowing what*: 'We know that he is, but admit we are unable to understand his Being.'[83]

According to Keller, Gregory is right when he develops the distinction between 'the unknown *essence* of God' and the 'relationally trusted *existence*'. Regarding how this perspectival shift from the essence of God to the trusted existence of God is possible, Keller agrees with Gregory, who answers the question by holding that this shift is possible through seeing what God does: 'For us God comes to be known as existing by means of his activities bestowing only faith, not the knowledge of what he is' (cited in Keller 2015: 61).

Jean-Luc Marion also explicates Gregory's theological insight by prioritizing the phenomenon of 'giving' over 'Being/being'. According to Marion, then, apophatic theology is possible because giving precedes Being/being. He recapitulates this core element of apophatic theology as follows: 'The gift crosses Being/being. *The gift delivers Being/being*' (1995: 101, original emphasis). In a similar vein, he also writes: 'Because God does not fall within the domain of Being, he comes to us in and as a gift.'[84]

This leads to the question of what connection there is between apophatic theology and migration. What theological significance could we draw from apophatic theology regarding the matter of human migration? One of the key theological inspirations from apophatic theology is a new theological insight that the global phenomenon of migration can be viewed in terms of what Kathryn Tanner calls the 'economy of grace.'[85] The origin of this new economy lies in God's apophatic love of giving, and there is nothing that can prevent it from its establishment.

Stephen Webb writes, 'The theory of giving helps us understand how grace works by creating its own kind of economy, quite different

[83] Catherine Keller. *Cloud of the Impossible: Negative Theology and Planetary Entanglement*. Columbia University Press: New York. 2015, p. 61.

[84] Jean-Luc Marion. *God Without Being*. University of Chicago Press: Chicago. 1995.

[85] Kathryn Tanner. 'Economy of Grace', Word & World. 2010. 30, no. 2: p. 174.

from the economics of exchange that pervades the modern spirit.'[86] Regarding migration, an important theological insight from the apophatically-inspired economy of grace is that 'the global migration of people should be recontextualized in God's divine economy of grace, as part of God's apophatic unfolding gift-giving love' (Ahn 2019: 57). In this new perspective of the economy of grace, migrants – especially those who are commonly labelled as 'illegal' immigrants – may become the gift of God.

Further, some theologians and church leaders have begun to identify these migrants as God's gift. Rowan Williams, in a public lecture delivered in London sponsored by the Council for Assisting Refugee Academics, proclaimed that migrants should be regarded as a 'gift' (Ahn 2019: 57). Arguing against Lord Carey of Clifton – who claimed in *The Times* newspaper that migration threatens 'the very ethos or DNA of our nation' (10 September 2008) – Williams emphasized that migrants 'help us see who we are'. He then went on to say, the vocal anxieties we hear from some quarters about the survival of British identity in the face of migrants and refugees betrays a lack of proper confidence in the capacity and the commitment of our society both to learn and to teach.[87]

In a similar spirit, Archbishop of Colorado Samuel J. Aquila states that Dreamers (undocumented immigrants who came to the US as children and in many cases identify themselves as American) are a tremendous gift (Ahn 2019: 58). Across the Pacific in the Philippines, Cardinal Luis Antonio Tagle also argues that Christians should approach the immigration crisis not as 'migration and the refugee problem', but as 'migrants and refugees as Sacred Gift', adding: 'This requires a shift from viewing them as a problem in need of solutions to situating them within the horizon of gift and opportunities' (Ahn 2019: 58). In an increasingly globalized society that is administered by the neoliberal economy of contract, exchange, and scarcity, Christian communities across the globe should reorganize their social ministries, especially for migrants and refugees, to become

[86] Stephen H. Webb. *The Gifting God: A Trinitarian Ethics of Excess*. Oxford University Press: New York. 1996, p. 10.

[87] Rugh Gledhill. 'Archbishop Asks Christians to View Migrants as a Gift', *The Times*. 24. 14 May. 2010.

the primary care and advocacy agency to receive them as the gift of mysterious and unknowable God.

Christ and Migration

There is an intrinsic relationship between the story of Jesus 'the Nazarene' and the experience of migration. As briefly mentioned above, Jesus' family was not only forced to migrate from their home due to violent political persecution but their return from Egypt was also marked with displacement, since they could not go back to Bethlehem because of Archelaus' despotic reign (Alfaro 2022: 67). To engage in this one has to explore the theological significance of the salvific ministry of Christ Jesus with regard to the experience of migration. In so doing we need to focus on such key theological themes as incarnation, crucifixion, salvation, and the kingdom of God.

Incarnation as Migration of the Word

From a phenomenological perspective, Jesus' incarnation is quintessentially a phenomenon of migration. According to John's Gospel (1:14), the Word became flesh. This means that without supposing the aspect of movement – the movement from high above to here below, from heaven to earth, from divinity to humanity – incarnation cannot be conceived. If incarnation takes a central position in Christian theology, so does migration. Highlighting this essential relationship between the theology of incarnation and the phenomenon of migration, Groody writes: No aspect of a theology of migration is more fundamental, nor more challenging in its implications than the incarnation. Through Jesus, God enters into the broken and sinful territory of the human condition in order to help men and women, lost in their earthly sojourn, find their way back home to God.[88]

Drawing from various studies, Groody goes on to highlight three key theological aspects that Jesus' incarnation signifies in regard to the phenomenon of migration.[89]

First, the incarnation of the Word in Christ Jesus means that 'for God, there are no borders that cannot be crossed, neither within himself nor in the created world' (Groody 2009: 650). The incarnation

[88] Daniel G. Groody. 'Crossing the Divide: Foundations of a Theology of Migration and Refugees', *Theological Studies* 70, no. 3: 638–667, 2009.

[89] *Ilsup Ahn.* Migration and Christian Theology. St. Andrews Encyclopaedia of Theology. February, 2024.

is a 'border-crossing event', and at the centre of this event lies God's unfathomable love of humankind, out of which God empties Godself so that God can more fully identify with humans, entering completely into our vulnerable condition and accompanying us in a profound act of divine-human solidarity (2009: 652). As Groody points out, 'even as human beings erect barriers of every sort, God walls off no one from the divine embrace' (2009: 650).

Second, divine migration is unlike human migration. Human migration tends towards an upward mobility and greater realization of human dignity and wellness. Divine migration, realized in the incarnation of the Word in Christ, tends toward a 'downward mobility' that is even willing to undergo the worst human indignities and sufferings. Groody thus writes that although 'Scripture depicts the movement of a people toward a promised land, God's movement is just the opposite: it is an immersion into those territories of human life that are deprived of life and prosperity' (2009: 650). This downward movement is so radical that God ultimately becomes one of the lowly and the strangers, not just reaching out to or living among humanity but identifying with them: 'God's identification with humanity is so total that in Christ he not only reaches out to the stranger but becomes the stranger' (2009: 650–651).

In a similar yet more radical manner, Miguel De La Torre contends that 'Jesus, a colonized man, was an undocumented alien, a victim of political circumstances beyond his comprehension or control' (2016: 155). According to De La Torre, the radicalism of the incarnation for Christians is not so much that the Creator of the universe became a frail human, but rather that God chose to become undocumented, fleeing the oppressive consequences of the empire of the time.[90]

Third, the incarnation of the Word in Christ may also 'offend'. It can particularly offend those who regard themselves as the guardians of the society, establishing law and maintaining order, and as the defenders of their world, their social norms, and their religious ideals. The incarnation moves people beyond a narrower, more self-serving identity into a greater identification with those considered 'other' in society, particularly those like migrants and refugees who

[90] Miguel A. De La Torre. 2009. *Trails of Hope and Terror: Testimonies on Immigration.* Maryknoll, NY: Orbis. 2009. p. 155.

are poor and thus regarded insignificant. Therefore, it is more likely to offend. In this respect, Groody writes, it challenges especially those who exclude on the basis of superficial notions of private property, legal status, and personal or even national rights without any social, moral, or divine reference point, or any regard for the exigencies of distributive, contributive, and restorative justice that flow as a natural consequence from divine gratuity (Groody 2009: 652).

Christ and the Crucified Lord of all Migrants

According to the gospels, Jesus' border-crossing incarnation ultimately leads him to his violent death on the cross. Kanan Kitani captures it as follows: A marginal person throughout his life, Jesus also died as such. His violent death on the cross was a direct result of his border-crossing and ministry at the margins which posed a serious threat to the interests of those occupying the economic, political, and religious centre.[91]

This leads to the questions of what Jesus' crucifixion has to do with those who are on the move at the margins of society, and what theological significance can be discovered in the event of Jesus' crucifixion as we develop a theology of migration in an age of migration. Christian theologian Gioacchino Campese answers these questions by demonstrating that many migrants, especially those undocumented and unauthorized, are indeed what Ignacio Ellacuría (1993) and Jon Sobrino (1994) call the **'crucified people'.**

Ellacuría draws an engaging parallel between the figure of the Suffering Servant of Yahweh – found in Second Isaiah – Jesus, and the 'crucified peoples', identified as the collective body of the poor, insignificant, and oppressed majorities of the world (Campese 2008: 284).

The paralleling commonalities include these features: They are chosen by God; they suffer for historical reasons; they are rejected and considered sinners even if they are not responsible for what they are suffering; they accept carrying the sins of those who are really responsible for their suffering; and finally, precisely because of their

---

[91] Kanan Kitani. Jesus the Paradigmatic Migrant', in *Christian Theology in the Age of Migration: Implications for World Christianity*. Edited by Peter C. Phan. New York: Lexington Books. 2020, p. 141.

willingness to carry the burden of sin, they become the 'light of the nations'[92] (Campese 2008: 283).

One of the key hallmarks of the crucified peoples is that 'they are victims of an institutionalized violence, of a violent system that, because of its ability to cover-up, often goes unrecognized and unchallenged' (Campese 2008: 291). In this respect, Campese argues that many undocumented migrants who died at the US-Mexico borders due to controversial US immigration laws and policies should be referred to as 'the crucified people'. Campese calls these people '***crucified immigrants***'. He then writes, 'The lives of these crucified immigrants are the concrete manifestation of the incarnation of the Crucified Christ in history' (2008: 292).

The core of Christian theology lies in the belief that the crucifixion of Christ is not only about God's participation in human suffering and death, but ultimately it is also about the salvation of people. This leads theologians to consider how the 'salvific power of crucifixion' can be discovered in the theology of 'crucified people', and how those crucified immigrants may offer salvific power. Campese engages with these questions by focusing on theological ideals and moral values that enable 'new life in the midst of death' (2008: 292). He illustrates these ideals and values as follows: They [crucified immigrants] also reveal the values that these immigrants carry: courage in the midst of apparently insurmountable obstacles; faith that recognizes in the Crucified Christ a faithful God who understands and accompanies them, and suffers with them; hope in a better future and a new life because God is good; solidarity with those who suffer; a sense of community; hospitality in a world that is suspicious about strangers; willingness to sacrifice for the sake of their families; and so on (Campese 2008: 292).

From the theology of crucified people,[93] then, the US-Mexico border and the Mediterranean Sea become the modern-day 'Golgotha',

---

[92] Ibid. 283.

[93] It is pertinent to note that usually Christian theology in many places, contexts, situations is more a pacifist theology or ideology which supports the status quo. This theology presents Jesus as a mild and soft Christ. At times, there is also a victorious theology which projects Christ and Christianity to be a very victorious one. In these theologies there is no room for 'the Suffering Servant of Yahweh'. The theology presented here keeping the lives and the struggles of the migrants is directly related to the crucifixion of Jesus and in them the crucifixion of the migrants.

illustrating a theological truth that 'God's grace and salvation can be found in the most unlikely places' (Campese 2008: 293).

Salvific Migration and Nearing the Kingdom of God

The sections above have examined how 'crucified people' at the US-Mexico border may be identified as today's Crucified Christ. According to Ahn, a more holistic theology of migration is possible only when one seriously engages in the reality of 'suffering' to which many migrants are vulnerable. Ahn asks what the theological nature of this suffering is, and what theological commonality there is between the suffering of many migrants and the suffering of Crucified Christ. To begin, Ahn identifies the suffering of many migrants (especially of undocumented immigrants) as 'destructive suffering' by adopting Michael Stoeber's distinction between 'transformative suffering' and 'destructive suffering' (Stoeber 2003: 429). Ahn then argues that 'the mounting destructive suffering of many migrant people is deeply interlocked with what is commonly known as "terror," especially the type of state terror' (Ahn 2019:26).

In studying the relationship between the destructive suffering of migrants and what David Tombs calls state terror, that is, terror administered by the state, Ahn argues that many countries adopt state terror as a political strategy. For example, the Trump administration's family separation policy against unauthorized migrants in a militaristic and criminalizing fashion (2019: 27). Many migrants and refugees, especially 'illegal' migrants or what is called undocumented migrants fall victim to destructive suffering because of skewed geopolitical politics and an unjust neoliberal global economy, as well as due to the 'state terror' of the countries of destination (Ahn 2019: 29).

Ahn then argues that Jesus himself also fell victim to state terror in the form of crucifixion, yet there is an important theological significance to the state terror that targeted Jesus: its purpose was to deter Jesus and his followers from migrating to a new theopolitical statehood called 'the Kingdom of God'. According to Ahn, then, crucifixion is quintessentially interlocked with the idea of migration, in that migration is theologically conceived as an indispensable process to come near and enter the Kingdom of God. The state terror of Golgotha is also theologically conceived as a political measure to prevent this salvific vision of migration from being carried out.

The suffering of many migrants is then theologically interconnected with the suffering of Crucified Christ because of the existence of state terror and the violated vision of migration.

According to Ahn, a new theology of migration is possible because Jesus' crucifixion further changes the nature of migration itself. Due to Jesus' vision of the Kingdom of God, migration is theologically envisaged as an essential aspect of the Kingdom of God. In other words, migration is no longer regarded solely as a personal, socio-political, or socio-economic issue: 'migration allows all nations, all tribes, and all people to interact with each other across all borders rendering it possible to create a new unity, solidarity, and brotherhood and sisterhood amid differences and otherness' (Ahn 2019: 35).

Since this conducive social effect of migration refers to the eschatological vision of the Kingdom of God described in Rev 7:9, people's migration itself becomes a key theological matter. The author of Revelation portrays this eschatological vision of the Kingdom of God as follows: After this, I looked and there was a great multitude that no one could count, from every nation, from all tribes and peoples and languages, standing before the throne and before the Lamb, robed in white, with palm branches in their hands (Rev 7:9).

From the perspective of migration theology, Jesus' resurrection is deeply entangled with the imagery of migration, because the resurrection of Christ signifies that even state terror cannot deter people from migrating to the Kingdom of God. In sum, the suffering, crucifixion, and resurrection of Jesus, as well as his central message of the Kingdom of God, become the Christological foundation of migration theology.

The Holy Spirit and Migration

As Sam George and Godfrey Harold put it, 'migration is one of the mega-themes of the Biblical narratives' (2021: 1).[94] Migration is also one of the mega-themes that characterize God's divine nature. The earliest story that reveals God's migratory nature is Gen 1:2, which reads, 'the earth was a formless void and darkness covered the face of the deep, while a wind from God swept over the face of the waters' (NRSV). Other versions (such as KJV or NIV) change the 'wind from

[94] Sam George and Godfrey Harold. 'Motus Dei (The Move of God): A Theology and Missiology for a Moving World', *Pharos Journal of Theology*. 2021. 102: 1.

God' to 'the Spirit (*Ruach*) of God'. Indeed, even before God spoke creation commands in Gen 1:3, God was on the move hovering above the surface of the earth. George and Harold observe that the hovering image of the Spirit of God (Gen 1:2) may be compared to the image of an eagle hovering over its nest (Deut 32:10; 2021: 2).

Since the movement of the Spirit of God over the formless, empty, and dark earth is sequentially entailed by God's creation of the ordered, abundant, and luminous earth, it can be said that the work of the migrating Spirit of God is aligned with creative, formative, and conducive nature, rather than divisive, destructive, and chaotic quality. This section examines how the Holy Spirit involves the various aspects of migration. As will be seen, the divine work of the Holy Spirit is essential in developing a more holistic theology of migration.

The Holy Spirit and the Empowerment of all Migrants

In the creation narrative in Genesis, the Spirit of God or the divine breath is not only transcendent over the creation (1:2) but also immanent within it.[95] Gen 1:30 narrates that all living creatures have been constituted by God's (Elohim's) 'breath of life'. The infusion of the breath of life to human beings is particularly noticeable because they were personally visited by the creator God: 'The Lord God formed man from the dust of the ground, and breathed into his nostrils the breath of life, and the man became a living being' (Gen 2:7).

If the infused breath of life originates in the Spirit of God, which was on the move hovering above the surface of the earth, one can infer that all living creatures – especially human beings – are originally meant to migrate. In other words, migration is the ontological DNA of human beings. It is therefore not too much to say that to be alive is to be able to migrate, and, in a similar manner, that the essential hallmark of resurrection will be the resumption of migration.

The next questions to ask are what the Holy Spirit does in the history of human migration, and how the work of the Holy Spirit regarding the global phenomenon of migration should be understood. Amos Yong notes that 'the Spirit is at work not just at the level

---

[95] Amos Yong. *Who Is the Holy Spirit? A Walk with the Apostles*. Brewster, MA: Paraclete Press. 2011.

of the individual but also at the level of society and its various political and economic structures' (Yong 2011: x). Adopting Yong's pneumatological vision – 'the work of the Spirit is to redeem and transform our world as a whole along with all of its interconnected parts, systems, and structures' (2011: x) – enables the development of a new pneumatological theology of migration, distinguished from the old paradigm of the individualistic, spiritualistic, and ecclesiocentric approaches.

Yong argues that there is an important theological connection between the Pentecost and the Abrahamic-Mosaic covenant: Since the Day of Pentecost was the traditional Feast of Weeks which occurred fifty days after the Feast of Passover (Lev 23:15–21; Deut 16:9–12) and Jews celebrated the wheat harvest as symbolic of the renewal of the Mosaic covenant, the Pentecostal experience would have a theological connection with the Mosaic covenant (Ahn 2019: 69).

This has theological significance regarding the phenomenon of human migration. The core of the promise made to Abraham was the establishment of a new nation and the eventual blessing of all the nations (Gen 12:2; 22:18). Pentecost has to do with the fulfilment of this promise: 'In the Pentecost event, linguistic, ethnic, cultural, and national barriers between Israel and the Gentiles are overcome, making clear the universal scope of God's promises' (Yong 2011: 12).

The phenomenon of *glossolalia* (speaking in tongues) at the Pentecost event is important because it signifies a theological vision, that the work of the Holy Spirit is to include and embrace all ethnic, cultural, linguistic, and religious others in the progression toward the Kingdom of God. Since the encounter with others cannot be conceived without peoples' migration, migration is integrated and enfolded into the all-encompassing work of the Holy Spirit. Ahn thus writes, 'Since the event of the Pentecost in Acts 2, migration has historically been a major conduit through which the Kingdom of God on earth has been continuously extended beyond all borders and boundaries' (2019: 71).

In two ways, the Holy Spirit works specifically in humanity's migratory journey toward the Kingdom of God: the empowerment of those on the move and the reconciliation between migrants and hosts. Most biblical scholars and theologians agree that the Spirit of God is indispensably interlinked with power. For instance, in his study of Pauline pneumatology, Gordon D. Fee writes that '[t]he single most notable characteristic of the Spirit of God is his power.' going on to say: The Spirit of God, therefore, meant the effective working of the power of God. It is probably fair to say that even though the two words (spirit and power) are not coterminous, the presence of the one (spirit) always implies the presence of the other power.[96]

Regarding the power of the Holy Spirit, there is a critical theological paradox: the Spirit of God is experienced not in an occasion in which believers feel powerful but in which they feel their weakness and helplessness. James Dunn writes, in connection with Rom 8:26–27, that it is an 'astonishing feature of Paul's pneumatology' that the power of Spirit is experienced in human weakness (1998: 438). Fee also argues in the same manner that the relationship between the Spirit as God's empowering presence and the theme of weakness is an important one in Paul's theology. Fee, however, goes further, clarifying what Paul meant by 'weakness'. He distinguishes the weakness in the sense of 'life *in* the flesh' and the weakness in the sense of 'life according to the flesh.'

One can then ask how the Pauline notion of the power of the Spirit in human weakness relates to the case of human migration. Given that a countless number of migrants are socially, economically, culturally, and psychologically marginalized, discriminated against, and even systemically oppressed due to their otherness, the Pauline notion of the power of the Holy Spirit in human weakness seems to perfectly apply to many cases of migration, especially to unauthorized migrants. Indeed, for many of these, 'the power of the Holy Spirit is the only hope they cannot but depend on in the midst of their tribulations and weaknesses' (Ahn 2019: 75).

In a more specific way, Groody also holds that 'the suffering they [migrants] experience is an important starting point for a discussion about their spirituality' (Groody 2002: 32). According to Groody, moral conversion from powerlessness to empowerment begins when migrants realize that they have 'something to say, something to offer, and something to contribute' (2002: 98). As a result of God's empowerment, when migrants begin to realize that they are active instruments in the coming of God's Kingdom, they no longer

[96] Gordon D. Fee. 1994. *God's Empowering Presence: The Holy Spirit in the Letters of Paul*. Peabody, MA: Hendrickson Publishers. 1994, p. 906-7.

see themselves as immigrants but as 'children of God with a divine mission to accomplish' (2002: 101).

The Holy Spirit and the Works of Hospitality

According to May Ling Tan-Chow, the Holy Spirit initiated a pneumatic movement in the early church by demonstrating an extraordinary kind of inclusiveness and hospitality: 'Pentecost is a decisive revelation of the radical hospitality of God – the Father's open house and also the opening up of human persons for filial perichoretic existence with the triune God.' As testified by the apostles, the hallmark of the Pentecostal Spirit was the equal regard and universal acceptance of all, transcending without being hindered by any borders and boundaries.

According to Tan-Chow: Subsequent outpourings of the Spirit upon the Samaritans (Acts 8:14–17), the Gentiles represented by Cornelius and his household (Acts 10:44), and the disciples of John the Baptist in Ephesus (Acts 19:1–7) are indicative that boundaries are no longer impregnable, but made permeable by the universal and ecumenical sweep of the Spirit.[97]

Peter sums it up in Acts 10:34: 'I truly understand that God shows no partiality, but in every nation, anyone who fears him and does what is right is acceptable to him.' Ahn points out that there is an unequivocal connection between this newly established culture of hospitality enabled by the Pentecost and the covenantal hospitality offered to unknown visitors by Abraham and Sarah (Gen 18:1–15). The demonstration of hospitality is an unmistakable sign of the presence of the Spirit, especially on the part of the host.

It is not an exaggeration to say that 'migration is quintessentially a theological event of the covenantal-pneumatological progression that encompasses both migrant people and hosting citizens as the agents of *missio Spiritus*' (Ahn 2019: 73). Equal regard for all and radical hospitality are particularly needed in the contemporary world which witnesses the rising number of unauthorized migrants and various types of refugees. It seems evident that if these hosts in destination countries are not willing to show the spirit of hospitality then many migrants will suffer, and more heightened walls and fortified barriers will appear not only on state borders but also in human relations.

---

[97] May Ling Tan-Chow. *Pentecostal Theology for the Twenty-First Century: Engaging with Multi-Faith Singapore*. Hampshire: Ashgate. 2007, p. 31-35.

Consideration of the theological importance of the practice of radical hospitality in 'an age of migration' leads to exploration of diverse theological-ethical perspectives on hospitality, and to questions such as: what is the Christian theological-ethical understanding of hospitality, and what makes Christian hospitality distinguished from other types?

From its origins, Christian hospitality focuses on the inclusion and acceptance of those regarded as the 'least of these'. According to Amy Oden, although hospitality is largely known as the welcoming of strangers, '***its meaning within the Christian biblical and historical traditions has focused on receiving the alien and extending one's resources to them***' (2001: 14). In the same vein, Christine Pohl argues that, compared to its Greek and Roman contemporaries, Christian hospitality was distinguished due to its ethos that 'offers a generous welcome to the "least" without concern for advantage or benefit to the host.'[98]

The contemporary Roman society also practiced hospitality by establishing the law of hospitality (*ius hospitii*). Unlike that of early Christianity, however, the Roman *ius hospitii* emphasized formal reciprocal obligations between the givers of hospitality and its receivers, and 'the tradition emphasized the worthiness and goodness of recipients rather than their need' (Pohl 1999: 18). Regarding the theological focus on the 'least of these', as Kristin Heyer warns, it is especially important not to treat migrants as passive beneficiaries of hospitality: '***Considering migrants as passive beneficiaries or burden fails to appreciate their agency and contributions.***'[99]

By referring to this original distinctiveness of radical hospitality, Christian ethicists such as Luke Bretherton develop a Christian cosmopolitan duty of care to refugees. Drawing on Giorgio Agamben, Bretherton identifies refugees as 'bare life'. He then goes on to argue that 'the involvement of churches with refugees should be characterized as the hallowing of bare life'. As he points out: 'The hollowing of bare life is intrinsic to the command to hallow the name

---

[98] Amy G. Oden. 'And You Welcomed Me: A Source Book on Hospitality in Early Christianity', Nashville, T. N.: Abingdon Press. 2001, p. 16.

[99] Kristin E. Heyer. 2010. 'Social Sin and Immigration: Good Fences Make Bad Neighbours', *Theological Studies* 71: 410–436. 2010.

of God.'[100] This leads to the question of what is the theological ground of Christian radical hospitality, and why does Christian hospitality particularly focus on refugees, strangers, foreigners, and even enemies.

Arthur Sutherland answers this by pointing out that, although Christians were once both strangers and enemies to God, they now have been brought into a relationship with God through an act of divine hospitality.[101] Sutherland's remarks are a reminder of some key verses of the Hebrew Bible, in which God commands the Israelites to remember that they were once aliens in the land of Egypt (Exod 22: 21; 23:9).

The second ***distinctive feature of Christian radical hospitality lies in its non-conformist or even resistant attitude to the discriminatory or oppressive ordinances of secular governance*** toward vulnerable migrant people. It is critical to recognize that hospitality has both 'spiritual' and 'social' dimensions. Spiritually, believers are on their way to what Augustine calls the heavenly city (*Civitas Dei*), yet socially they remain in a particular social, political, economic, or cultural context. Many contemporary migrants are greatly affected by the unjust structural formations of hosting societies, whether as a result of a neo-liberalized global economy or hostile political governance, which Kristin Heyer calls **'social sin'** (2010).

British theologian Anna Rowlands describes the hostile social dimension as follows: 1) intensification in the use of cruel and draconian powers of detention and forced expulsion by the state; 2) use of legislative power to remove welfare support and legal provision in order to deter future asylum claimants; 3) new practices of displacement of the responsibilities of the sovereign state onto private actors, and into offshore and inter-territorial spaces[102] (Rowlands 2012: 184).

---

[100] Luke Bretherton. 2006. 'The Duty of Care to Refugees, Christian Cosmopolitanism, and the Hallowing of Bare Life', *Studies in Christian Ethics* 19, no. 1. 2006. p. 55.

[101] Arthur Sutherland. *I Was a Stranger: A Christian Theology of Hospitality*. Nashville, TN: Abingdon Press. 2006, p. 26.

[102] Anna Rowlands. 2012. 'The State Made Flesh: Catholic Social Teaching and the Challenge of UK Asylum Seeking', *New Blackfriars* 93: 175–192. 2012, p. 184.

The consideration of this hostile social dimension clearly shows why the practice of hospitality needs to be a non-conformist or even resistant act. It should be also noted that the church adopted this radical trait from its beginning. According to Amy Oden, because of the political and social oppression they experienced, the early Christians were able to identify themselves with exiles and refugees, and this rendered them more radical in terms of providing hospitality to unwanted or unwelcome people: Because Christians were at times under threat from civil authorities, the act of harbouring refugees who were brothers and sisters in Christ became imperative. Sheltering strangers was essential to the survival of Christianity in a hostile empire (Oden 2001: 38).

One of the great temptations for the contemporary church is a social pressure to conform to what pope had called 'the growing dichotomy between the spiritual and social dimensions of Christian belief and life and here hospitality.' The Catholic Social Teachings pointed out repeatedly the false dichotomy created by some between faith and practice. Spiritual awakening to hospitality is necessary for the church's practice of radical hospitality; its spiritualization, however, is likely to lead the church to be complicit in social sin.

The final distinctive aspect of Christian radical hospitality is that it can be regarded as 'scandalous' due to the boundless or ad hoc nature of its scope and practice. Thomas Reynolds writes: 'Christians are called to hospitality. Yet this is no easy matter, for welcoming the stranger requires becoming vulnerable.' Reynolds illustrates a particular case in which a church community decided to cover its sanctuary's cross as it hosted a Jewish funeral.

Reflecting on this case from a theological perspective, Reynolds arrives at the conclusion that 'hospitality is not a matter of regulations and procedural codes, a law to be applied univocally' (2006: 201). Instead, he holds: 'Hospitality is a work of the Spirit, the divine figure who works between boundaries to join together in solidarity what was estranged.'[103] Similar 'scandalous' demonstrations of radical hospitality are found in the New Testament – Cornelius' call for Peter followed by Peter's vision in Acts 10 and Jesus' meeting with a Samaritan woman in John 4. As these two cases illustrate, spirit-filled

---

[103] Thomas Reynolds. 'Welcoming Without Reserve? A Case in Christian Hospitality', *Theology Today* 63: 191–202. 2006.

hospitality ultimately brings in the redemption of people despite its seemingly scandalous nature.

The question for the contemporary church is how to revive this quintessential ecclesial virtue of radical hospitality in the age of migration. As an example, Tan-Chow points to the Pentecostal revival of Azusa Street from 1906 to 1915, which was characteristically distinguished by 'all-embracing inclusiveness': 'What makes the Azusa event special and significant is the recovery of an experience of the living presence and power of God in the persona of the Holy Spirit that transcends all barriers' (2007: 46). Tan-Chow especially focuses on what the Pentecostal movement leader William J. Seymour was experiencing. According to Tan-Chow, disillusioned by white Pentecostals who continued to mistreat their Black fellow believers, Seymour realized that 'the surest sign of the Spirit's Pentecostal presence' was 'not tongue speaking but the dissolution of racial barriers' (2007: 47).

Tan-Chow goes on, saying, 'Seymour saw the outpouring of the Spirit as the divine event to bring into existence a church that is characterized by an "***all-embracing inclusiveness***"' (2007: 47). The following section therefore investigates the church's ecclesial role and responsibility related to this characterization, considering the rising global phenomenon of human migration. The expectation for the church's role and responsibility concerning the crisis of global migration is high and urgent.

The Church and Migration

It was seen above that Christian theology is born out of migration; in a similar manner, the church is born with migration. Ulrich Schmiedel thus writes: '***There would be no church without migration***' (2020: 156). He concurs with Peter Phan's claim that migration is a 'marker of church, both historically and systemically. Church is always already on the move.'[104] If the church is always on the move as a migratory community heading toward the kingdom of God, there will be a constant event of encountering others in the church, because the encounter with others is a necessary component of all migrations. The 'other' here does

[104] Ulrich Schmiedel. 'Coalitional Church: Ecclesiology in the Age of Migration', in *Christian Theology in the Age of Migration: Implications for World Christianity*. Edited by Peter C. Phan. New York: Lexington Books. 2020.

not always mean 'other peoples'; it could include new ideas, unfamiliar cultures, foreign languages, different lifestyles, or unconventional theologies.

Susanna Snyder conceptualizes the four types of encounters in which the church and faith-based organizations are called to engage (2012). First, encounters of grassroots service. These encounters have 'to do with ***the pastoral care of individuals and represent the "cuddlesome" face of religion valued by governments***. They are person-centred and rooted in the activities of befriending, listening, visiting and service provision' (S.Snyder 36).

Second, encounters with power structures. This 'designates activities of lobbying, campaigning, advocacy and transforming attitudes in relation to asylum aimed at the established population—and particularly people or structures with power'. Snyder clarifies the notion of power by explaining: 'Powers' indicates both people with authority on asylum matters in the UK and the systems, institutions, and structures which influence the experiences of those seeking sanctuary. These include governmental departments, politicians, the civil service, the media, local authorities, key public and corporate figures, and think tanks (S.Snyder 39-40).

Third, encounters in worship. This 'refers to engagement with people seeking sanctuary in the context of Christian liturgy and prayer. Such encounters take different forms', including worship services and special services (S. Synder 43).

Fourth, encounters in theology. This indicates 'engagement with people seeking sanctuary through theological reflection. These encounters are manifest in the choice of biblical verses for project tag lines, the worship resources mentioned above, and a growing body of academic work.'[105] (S. Synder 43).

Now we will explore the different roles and responsibilities of the church in conjunction with the rising crisis of global migration. This includes focus on two areas: the church's caring ministry for vulnerable migrants and the church's engagement in promoting social justice for oppressed migrants.

---

[105] Susanna Snyder. *Asylum-Seeking, Migration and Church.* Ashgate Publishing: Burlington, VT. 2012.

The Church on the Move and the Caring Community of all Migrants

As Gemma Tulud Cruz points out, 'International migration[106] is a reality that touches nearly all corners of the globe today largely due to the structures and processes of globalization.' The age of migration overlaps with the age of globalization. The key features of globalization are thus closely connected with the rising phenomenon of international migration. Globalization has divided the world into 'First World' or Global North countries and 'Third World' or Global South countries, entailing an enormous wealth gap between them. The ever-widening wealth gap becomes the 'push' factor in countries in the Global South and the corresponding 'pull' factor in the Global North countries, and these 'push' and 'pull' factors played a major role in the global phenomenon of human migration.

As Cruz observes, 'For many people, especially those from the Global South suffering from calamities caused by human and natural disasters, migration is the best, if not the only way, out of poverty and death-dealing conditions.'[107] ***The church's caring and advocating ministries are contextualized in this changing global setting***.

Many migrants in an age of globalization share certain commonalities as 'needed but not wanted' people. For instance, Cruz (189) describes three key features of contemporary cross-border labour migrants in the Asia Pacific region. First, migration of people occurs primarily under temporary (contractual) migration regimes and for low-skilled work. Second, migrants are highly gendered depending on the types of work they would be engaged in. Third, unauthorized migration of people occurs in parallel with authorized migration. By default, many low-skilled migrants constitute the underclass in their destination countries. As a result, they are commonly confined to vulnerable positions in society and then become easy targets for exploitation and abuse by various actors in the process of migration. The church's caring ministry is then geared toward assisting these migrants. As seen above, the moral and pastoral imperative to care for

---

[106] Though Gemma talks of international migration, the same can be said of internal migration.

[107] Gemma Tulud Cruz. 2013. 'A New Way of Being Christian: The Contribution of Migrants to the Church', in *Contemporary Issues of Migration and Theology*. Edited by Elaine Padilla and Peter C. Phan. New York: Palgrave-Macmillan. 2013.

these migrants is not only biblically grounded but also ecclesiastically approved in Christian tradition.

For instance, *Gaudium et Spes*, one of the four constitutions resulting from the Second Vatical Council, stipulates it as follows: When workers come from another country or district and contribute to the economic advancement of a nation or region by their labour, all discrimination as regards wages and working conditions must be carefully avoided. All the people, moreover, above all the public authorities, must treat them not as mere tools of production but as persons, and must help them (194).

Kristin Heyer exemplifies the church's caring ministry for migrants by visiting and interviewing with the Kino Border Initiative. According to her, 'the Kino Border Initiative's origin and approach embody essential values for ecclesial responses to migration' (Heyer 2016: 84). ***Established in partnership with Jesuit Refugee Services, the bordering dioceses and Jesuit provinces, and the Missionary Sisters of the Eucharist, the Kino Border Initiative is devoted to three goals***: (1) offering humanitarian assistance to deported migrants on the Mexican side of the border; (2) educating and forming communities on the US side; and (3) supporting research and advocacy on migrant abuses and immigration policy (2016: 84).

The church's pastoral caring ministry for migrants is an ecclesial practice of transforming 'xenophobia' into 'xenophilia' on a societal as well as on an individual level, on the understanding that xenophobia is theologically unwarranted and opposed to God's plan for humanity.

Therefore, as Luis N. Rivera-Pagán writes, ***in times of increasing economic and political globalization xenophilia should be the duty and vocation of the church, as a faith affirmation not only of believers' common humanity but also of those vulnerable beings living in the shadows and margins of their societies.***[108] Concurring with this, Cruz writes, 'In an economically globalized world that feeds on the discrimination, exploitation, and abuse of migrant workers, the churches are challenged to serve as a counterforce for harmony, an institution for transformation, and a home for all' (2021: 201).

---

[108] Luis N. Rivera-Pagán. 'Xenophilia or Xenophobia: Toward a Theology of Migration', in *Migration and Public Discourse in World Christianity*. Edited by Afe Adogame, Raimundo C. Barreto, and Wanderley Pereira da Rosa. Minneapolis: Fortress Press. 2019.

The Church of Migration and the Politics of Hope

The church's social justice work and initiatives also make a big difference to the livelihood of many migrants, in addition to its pastoral ministry (Cruz 2021: 197). Cruz outlines 'three discernible forms' of the church's justice ministry for migrants. ***The first is public and academic research that not only helps in understanding the experience of migrant workers but also in determining effective pastoral solutions.*** Researchers' contribution to the promotion of justice, human rights, and dignity is critical, in that their research helps both the public and policymakers have a better understanding of what is really going on in many instances of the migration crisis.

The second form of justice-oriented social ministry is '***political advocacy***.' Some examples of this advocacy ministry include church leaders' calling for action and ecclesial organizations' involvement in lobbying. For instance, 'Filipino bishop Ruperto Santos called for action against maid auctions in Saudi Arabia and accountability on the part of placement agencies, especially those who send minor-aged domestic workers' (Cruz 2021: 197). Meanwhile, 'Australian Catholic Religious Against Trafficking in Humans (ACRATH) was at the forefront of lobbying the Australian government for the work payment of the twenty-two seasonal workers from Vanuatu' (2021: 197).

The third form of the church's social ministry for migrants relates to ***practical services that try to address causes of suffering***. Cruz introduces the 'Safe Migration' project of Caritas Asia and Caritas Luxembourg in Chittagong, and Cox's Bazar in Bangladesh, as examples. These projects 'support people who want to go abroad and work by educating them about the risks of unsafe and unauthorized migration' (Cruz 2021: 197).

If this can be further extended, Ulrich Schmiedel's concept of a 'coalitional church' refers to an ecclesial model for the church's social engagement in justice for both migrants and citizens: a coalitional church is open to coalitions with religious and with nonreligious partners for the sake of the other. Openness to otherness, then, is the central criterion of the coalitions which it enters. In these coalitions, it is not concerned with saving its identity, but with saving its alterity – the other (Schmiedel 2020: 162).

The Sanctuary Movement of the 1980s in the US is an excellent example of the social ministry of a coalitional church, especially concerning the reception of 'undesirable aliens.' According to researchers, at the peak of its movement up to 600 churches and secondary sanctuary groups joined the movement across the country, declaring themselves official 'sanctuaries' (Chinchilla, Hamilton and Loucky 2009: 106). There are two distinct aspects of the Sanctuary Movement. First, the movement had a significant social impact on the American public, a rare thing for the church to achieve in a secular society. The idea of 'sanctuary' itself spread out and affected other civil institutions including schools and colleges, cities and states, and even other religious organizations (Ahn 2019: 95). Second, the movement exemplified the church's spirit of resistance against structural injustice that victimizes the marginalized and the disenfranchised.

In responding to the rising number of 'unauthorized' and 'undesirable' migrants in the contemporary world, ***the Christian church across the globe can also acknowledge that, as the body of Christ, its central mission is to provide unconditional care for those in dire need***. The church should stand in solidarity with the voiceless, not only to protect their God-given human rights and dignity but also to promote justice against structural injustice by initiating or joining a coalitional ministry.

As Victor Carmona and Robert Heimburger point out, the church's solidarity work will likely have to face the secular 'populism' (especially, they believe, 'right-wing' populism) that 'furthers the perception of immigrants as a threat' (Carmona and Heimburger 2022: 40). Against this challenge, as demonstrated by Catholic and Anglican churches in the US and the UK, the church faces the challenge of continuing to confront populist immigrant policies directly and indirectly, in light of scripture[109] (Carmona and Heimburger 2022: 43).

Without hope, no one can live a meaningful human life; this is even more so for those who are in hopeless situations due to systemic and structural reasons. The church can be the place where these

---

[109] Victor Carmona and Robert Heimburger. 'The Border, Brexit, and the Church: US Roman Catholic and Church of England Bishops' Teaching on Migration, 2015–2019', Journal of Moral Theology 11. 2022.

people find hope. In this respect, the church's engagement in all types of coalitional activities for 'the least of these' can be called a 'politics of hope.' From the perspective of a migration theology, the church becomes itself when it engages in the coalitional politics of hope, globally as well as locally, in the age of migration.

A Note on Theology, Migration and Theology of Migration

Daneil O. Groody writing on the theme, 'A Theology of Migration: A new method for understanding a God on the Move,'[110] if one migrates from the comfort of one's room, library and ideas about God in search of insight among the vulnerable of the world, the living "texts" of the poor and the challenge of the living God, then one can encounter the theology of "the crucified peoples of today," as the theologian Ignacio Ellacuría, S.J., described them.

As theology in general becomes more professionalized, theologians can lose touch with the pastoral life of the church, causing the task of faith seeking understanding to degenerate into a career in which understanding seeks recognition. When this happens theologians can spend much time answering questions that no one is asking and speaking in a language few understand, while ignoring pressing issues that affect the human community and offering little guidance or nourishment for this journey to a better homeland.

Theological reflection can be short-circuited when inner walls leave Christians short of a life-giving message because of sterile intellectualism, lobotomized fundamentalism, obsessive rubricism, privatized pietism or frenetic activism. What Native American elders said of the pilgrimage of life could also be said of theological understanding: the long journey of human life moves from the head to the heart and back to the head again. It is a journey.

While it shares much with other theological approaches, my method involves the study of the written word (printed texts), attentiveness to the spoken word (living texts), engagement with the marginal word (crucified texts), and understanding of the contemporary word (cultural texts), expressed at times through multiple media or the visual word (symbolic texts). All of these texts are an integral part of the task of theology, serving the evangelizing

[110] Daniel O. Groody. *A Theology of Migration: A New Method for Understanding a God on the Move.* America: The Jesuit Review. February 07, 2011.

mission of the church in its proclamation of the incarnate Word (the revealed text).

Theological method should be based on the Incarnation, the belief that God migrated to humanity so all of us in turn could migrate back to God. Broadly considered, these elements are woven together in a process that involves 1) immersion in the world, especially into the life of the poor; 2) "interfluence," or the ways in which the lived experience of Christian faith and the deposit of Christian tradition mutually influence each other; and 3) an interpretation of life that seeks to deepen our relationship with God and each other. This method is not just about retrieval and application, nor the gathering of new information for human formation. Rather it is a vision of life that leads to transformation and the construction of a new imagination.

A Migrant God for a Migrant People

A theology of migration is based on the truth that God in Jesus Christ so loved the world that he left his homeland and migrated into the far distant territory of humanity's sinful and broken existence. There he laid down his life on a cross so that we could be reconciled with God and migrate back to our homeland, where there is peace, harmony, justice and life. God's love in Jesus is so boundless that it cannot be walled in or contained by human attempts to constrict it. God always crosses over the divisions we create in order to help us find a right relationship with God and each other.

First, a theology of migration crosses over the nonhuman-human divide and so brings out the dignity of the human person, especially those who, like migrants, are treated like insects, dogs or slaves. Second, it crosses the divine-human divide, and thus helps us see the utter gratuity of God, who moved from his homeland with a love that could not be limited by legal or political policies and reached out to those whose lives are most threatened—the sinner, the tax collector, the prostitute, the outsider and the poor. Third, it crosses the human-human divide, as is revealed in Jesus' ability to cross racial, religious, political, economic and social barriers to foster a vision of human solidarity that highlights our interconnection as one family of God. Fourth, it crosses the country-kingdom divide, where we begin to see beyond national identities in recognition that the Christian's true citizenship is in heaven; our true calling is to cross borders as agents of God's reconciliation.

Speaking about the Desert Ordeal, Daniel G. Groody[111] highlights the plight of the migrants in Mexico-US border, which could be said of any situation in the world today. "We are migrating not because we want to but because we have to," said Mario. "My family at home depends on me. I'm already dead in Mexico, and getting to the U.S. gives us the hope of living, even though I may die."

Amid these contentious debates, much has been written about the social, political, economic, and cultural dimensions of immigration. But surprisingly very little has been written from a theological perspective, even less from the vantage point of the immigrants themselves. This is all the more intriguing because from the holy family's flight into Egypt to the missionary activity of the Church, the very identity of the People of God is inextricably intertwined with stories of movement, risk, and hospitality.

Broken Borders, Crossing Borders, Beyond Borders: God's Migration

Scriptures and the CST state that human beings are created in God's image and likeness (Gen 1:26-27). ***But the common denominator around the world among all who migrate is their experience of dehumanization***. Against this the ultimate measuring point of Gods image and likeness to examine how well the most vulnerable and the migrants are faring. For us the Christians the Imago Dei insists that we see immigrants not as problems to be solved but people to be healed and empowered.

In the incarnation God migrates to the human race and, as Karl Barth notes, makes his way into the "far country." **This far country is one of human discord and disorder, a place of division and dissension, a territory marked by death and the demeaning treatment of human beings.** The Gospel of Matthew says God in Jesus not only takes on human flesh and migrates into our world but actually becomes a refugee himself when he and his family flee political persecution and es-cape into Egypt (Matt 2:13-15). The

[111] Daniel G. Groody. *Dying to Live: Theology, Migration, and the Human Journey.* Yale University. 2008.

divine takes on not just any human narrative but that of the most vulnerable among us.

The mission of the Church is to proclaim a God of life and make our world more human by building up, in Pope Paul VI's words, the "civilization of love." In imitation of Jesus, it seeks to make real the practice of table fellowship. The significance of Jesus' table fellowship with sinners and social outcasts is that he crosses over the human borders that divide one human being from another. If the incarnation is about God crossing over the divine-human divide, the mission of the Church is to cross the human-human divide. It is fundamentally a mission of reconciliation, a realization that the borders that define countries may have some proximate value but are not ultimately those that define the body of Christ.

Daniel G. Groody goes on to argue that theology offers not just more information but a new imagination, one that reflects at its core what it means to be human before God and to live together in community. In seeking to overcome all that divides us in order to reconcile us in all our relationships, Christian discipleship reminds us that the more difficult walls to cross are the ones that exist in the hearts of each of us. Unable to cross this divide by ourselves, Christian faith rests ultimately in the one who migrated from heaven to earth, and through his death and resurrection, passed over from death to life. From a Christian perspective, the true aliens are not those who lack political documentation but those who have so disconnected themselves from their neighbour in need that they fail to see in the eyes of the stranger a mirror of themselves, the image of Christ (Matt 25:31-46), and the call to human solidarity.

Let us conclude this section by highlighting some of the central points of Christian theologising of migration. God, in Jesus Christ, "migrated" into the world, taking on human form and experiencing human suffering and brokenness. This demonstrates God's love and desire to be present with humanity, even in its most vulnerable states. Jesus who migrated to be with human beings knows the lives and struggles of the migrants. If incarnation takes a central position in Christian theology, so does migration. Through Jesus, God enters into the broken and sinful territory of the human condition in order to help men and women, lost in their earthly sojourn, find their way back home to God.

Christian theology while focusing on the lives and the struggles of the marginalised and the migrants unearths a parallel between the figure of the Suffering Servant of Yahweh and the 'crucified peoples', identified as the collective body of the poor, the marginalised, the migrants and the refugees. Hence, a theology of migration must be deeply rooted in the flesh and-blood stories of migrants themselves as human beings whose dignity and rights have often been trampled upon but whose side God takes.

A theology of migration reiterates the fact that for God, there are no borders that cannot be crossed, neither within himself nor in the created world. In this sense, migration is no longer regarded solely as a personal, socio-political, or socio-economic issue. It is a theological and religious issue. Because, migration allows all nations, all tribes, and all people to interact with each other across all borders rendering it possible to create a new unity, solidarity, and brotherhood and sisterhood amid differences and otherness. It is in this sense every Christian is demanded to welcome, protect and promote the rights and dignity of migrants.

Considering migrants as passive beneficiaries or burden fails to appreciate their agency and contributions. We are not asked to do charity for the migrants. May Day celebration alone is not enough. But we are invited to reflect and act on this fact that the distinctive feature of Christian radical hospitality lies in its non-conformist or even resistant attitude to the discriminatory or oppressive ordinances of secular governance. Finally, this needs to be affirmed that the Christian church across the globe can also acknowledge that, as the body of Christ, its central mission is to provide unconditional care for those in dire need and those in margins cum periphery

5

Socio-Economic and Political Factors and Implications of Distressed Migration

Migration takes place due to various social, cultural, economic, political, ecological, religious, regional reasons. These are the factors which induce or motivate or propel migration of persons, especially labourers from one place to another. Further, while labourers in general move from their source location to destination location to enhance their earning, distressed labourers are forced to migrate for sheer existential mechanism. In most cases, it is their need to keep themselves and their families at the survival which compels them to migrate. But even this cannot be placed under neat category. Migration in India today like in most parts of the world takes place in various forms, shapes, dynamisms, routes, levels.

Previous Census reports of India show that employment-induced out-migration is a common feature of several states like Bihar, Jharkhand, Uttar Pradesh, Assam, West Bengal, Madhya Pradesh, Odisha, Chhattisgarh and north eastern states. But this does not mean that the southern, and western states are not under the spell of migration. From some of the southern states, better off people migrate to USA, Canada and European countries to make their life even better. The labour class and service class from here move to gulf countries to earn better income. This creates vacuum in these states. Now the migrants from north and northeast India are filling up this gap.

Studies highlight this fact that Kolkata experienced in-migration since the time it started to experience growth, as it was the capital of the British in India till 1911. People migrated to the city not only from the nearby states like Bihar, Orissa and Assam but also from distant states like Punjab, Tamil Nadu and Kerala. A large number of Nepalese, Chinese and Bangladeshis (after the partition of 1947) have also migrated to the city.[112] Kolkata was the only metropolitan city in eastern India with enormous employment opportunities in the industrial sector.

The extensive migratory movements of citizens in India are indicative of some major developments taking place in the country. 1) there is a break through with demographic growth by way of containing mortality rates in the low-income states. This break though would result in declining in land-mass ratios, compelling people to migrate. 2) opening up of a vast internal labour market provides employment to those who are disguisedly unemployed in the hinterland. The terms and condition on which they find employment or take up residence in their host states or destination are matters of abiding concern. 3) what are the consequences of these is something that are not studied.

Any study or response to migrants should go at length to narrate the scale of intensity of deprivation faced by the migrant workers with special reference to a number of parameters or indicators or variables like social origins, backgrounds, age, gender, skill content, linguistic and cultural roots, community associations, assets, wages, working conditions, housing, health care, etc. These potentially draw attention to their social, financial, cultural, political and psychological vulnerabilities in different regions of India.

The National Commission for Enterprises in the Unorganised Sector (NCEUS) of India, using secondary and macro-data, established a nexus of poverty, vulnerability, type of employment and social status of workers. Because of these reasons, these workers tend to undertake the riskiest, lowest paying and most hazardous jobs, with clear patterns of segmentation by caste and gender. To this one can also add class, religion, region, etc. This signifies how social inequalities are replicated in the segmentation of the labour markets. Interestingly, social inequalities are replicated in the education system and the education system reproduces inequalities. This also

---

[112] UNICEF (2014). *Children of Migrant Poor in Kolkata: A Study on Human Development Perspectives*. Kolkata, India: Institute of Social Sciences.

impacts migration because those who are better educated and English speaking migrate for better economic opportunities, while the distressed labourers move to survival migration.

Factors of Migration: *Push Factors*: those that force the individual to move voluntarily, and in many cases, they are forced because the individuals risk something if they stay. Poor economic activity and lack of job opportunities are strong push factors. Conflict, draught, famine, flood or forceful displacements are also factors. Discriminatory social, cultural and economic factors can lead to intolerance. The push factors are poverty, lack of work opportunities, unemployment and underdevelopment, poor economic condition, lack of opportunities, exhaustion of natural resources and natural calamities, scarcity of cultivated land, inequitable land distribution, low agricultural productivity etc.

***Pull Factors*:** those that attract the individual or group to leave their home for better economic opportunities, more jobs, higher wages and better life and facilities. Pull factors mostly seen in the common examples of better job opportunities, higher wages, and improved living conditions. These factors can also include access to quality education, healthcare, and a higher standard of living. Given the opportunity if there is the possibilities of climbing up in the ladder or social mobility, there are people who would opt for this. At times, the urban attraction and facilities also draw people to urban centres.[113]

Often both pull and push factors operate. Better-off migrants are 'pulled' towards better job prospects, while the poor are 'pushed' to find jobs: 'push' and 'pull' migration are twin children of inequality in the same sort of village; but they are also sources of new inequality.

Both the push and pull factors can be based on economic, social, educational, political, cultural, religious, environmental, locational, physical, age, sex, etc. Examining migration, especially distressed migration under the purview of push and pull factors also has its own

[113] To give an example. While working among the domestic working girls who migrate to Delhi, it was realised that those who go home for holidays, dress up well, have expensive bags, their mannerism is different, their families have additional income, etc. In the last two decades, the smart phone also has become a point of attraction. If we look at the boys, we can see that jeans pants and mobile appear to be the attracting aspect to urban centres. The possibilities of having drinks also is an added pull factor. We are not denigrating their desire to possess these. But stating as a matter of fact.

limitations. Since, not any single factor but multiple factors in most cases work together to move people as migrants.

Migration Patterns in India

1. Rural-rural: it is the movement of people from one rural area to other rural place in search of a better job. Ex. An agricultural labourer moves during the harvesting season.
2. Rural-Urban: it is the movement of people from the countryside to the city. This happens due to urban growth attracting people for job.
3. Urban-Urban: it is the movement of a person or group of people moving from one urban area to another urban area. Ex. Specialised job seeker moves for these purposes. For instance, those who got professional studies and training in IT sector move to IT hubs like Bengaluru, Chennai, Hyderabad, Pune, Mumbai, etc.
4. Urban-Rural it is the opposite movement of rural-urban that people move from urban to rural areas for any kind of purposes.

Like elsewhere, in India too, migration patterns are diverse, encompassing intra-state, inter-state, and international movements. But in terms of numbers it is internal migration which is dominant.

Types of Migration

Voluntary migration is based on a person's free will, initiative and desire to live in a better place and to improve their financial status, among other factors.

Involuntary migration is based on a person being forced out of their home due to certain unfavourable economic, social, environmental and political situations.

Reluctant migration is when a person is put in a situation that encourages relocation or movement outside their place of residence.

Forced migration is when a person is unable to return home or undergoes a legal procedure to qualify as a refugee in the host country or is forced to leave their home due to a conflict or development but does not cross any boundaries – internally displaced persons, known as IDPs.

Seasonal migration related to agricultural labourers and other informal sector workers who often migrate seasonally, particularly for sowing and harvesting. Also refers to those who during lean season in their own agricultural cycle migrate and return back to carry out their agricultural occupation. Various studies had highlighted this fact that the sugar belt of Maharashtra gets seasonal migrants to harvest sugar cane fields. The harvesting season starts in October and ends in March. The migrant workers come here from draught prone tribal belts.[114] Seasonal migration from the state consisted of 88% male migrants. Additionally, the study finds that 80% of workers migrate alone while the rest move with their families.[115]

Circular migration means the movement of migrants between their place of origin and destination periodically without permanent relocation. It is also known as repeat or return migration, refers to the temporary and repetitive movement of individuals between a home country and a destination country, often for employment purposes. This pattern of migration can be either cross-country or within a country, like rural-urban movement. It's a cyclical process where people leave their home area, work elsewhere, and eventually return, often to repeat the cycle.[116]

Permanent migration from the village to the city is desired in a context where it offers better work and education opportunities. In particular, young people aspire to have a firm foothold in the city to access new opportunities in urban India. This is coveted even more in the context of decline of agriculture and lack of employment in rural areas. At the same time, permanent migration also requires substantial resources that only a few can afford.

Temporary migrants, on the other hand, 'difficult work and working conditions during their stay outside progressively reduce their capacity and desire to undertake such journeys.'

Step migration: Migration initiating from a small settlement and moving to a larger one in the urban hierarchy over the years. This includes a pattern of closer, not too destabilizing migrations from a person's place of origin to an ensuing destination, such as movement

[114] For more on this refer to Saroj Shinde. "Our Poverty has No Shame; the Stomach has No Shame, so We Migrate Seasonally": Women Sugarcane Cutters from Maharashtra, India". Caste/ A Global Journal on Social Exclusion. 30th October, 2023.

[115] Seasonal Migrations of Marginalized (Tribal) Communities in Madhya Pradesh & Rajasthan. Humanitarian Foresight Think Tank. September, 2016.

[116] P. Deshingkar and J. Farrington. *Circular Migration and Multi-locational Livelihood Strategies in Rural India.* Oxford University Press: New Delhi. 2009.

from a farm to a village, then to a town and subsequently to a suburb (if applicable) and finally into a city. This category also includes the movement of people from a smaller to a bigger city.

Return migration: Return migration, on the other hand, refers to a one-time migration and return after an extended stay outside the host territory. The voluntary movements of immigrants back to their place of origin. This is also known as circular migration.

Chain migration: Migration of families at different stages of the life cycle from one location to the next, who subsequently bring people from their home location to this new place. In theory, a chain of people constantly moves from place to place, supported by those who migrated before them. A series of migrations within a family or defined group of people. A chain migration often begins with one family member who sends money to bring other family members to the new location. Chain migration results in migration fields—the clustering of people from a specific region into certain neighbourhoods or small towns.

Vulnerability of Migrants

Distressed migrants as stated above, refers to the fact that the labourer is vulnerable where his original village or residence is. Due to this vulnerability or because of vulnerability, labour in distress moves to elsewhere to eke out a living. It is a fact that there too, he is in distress. These are the facts for this. They have meagre personal assets and suffer a range of deprivations in the destination areas. In the source areas, migration has both negative and positive consequences for migrants and their families. Whether agricultural or non-agricultural sector the labourers are involved they live in deplorable conditions. These people experience vulnerabilities in origin, transit and destination.

Vulnerability of migrants to human rights violations is the result of multiple and intersecting forms of discrimination, inequality and structural and societal dynamics that lead to diminished and unequal levels of power and enjoyment of rights. As shown in the diagram below (Ojasvi Goyal. 2019), the vulnerabilities suffered by the distressed labour migrants are social, economic, physical, political and financial. Each of these aspects reinforce on the other and make vulnerabilities even stronger that each generation gets sucked into this system of exploitation and oppression and not able to liberate itself.

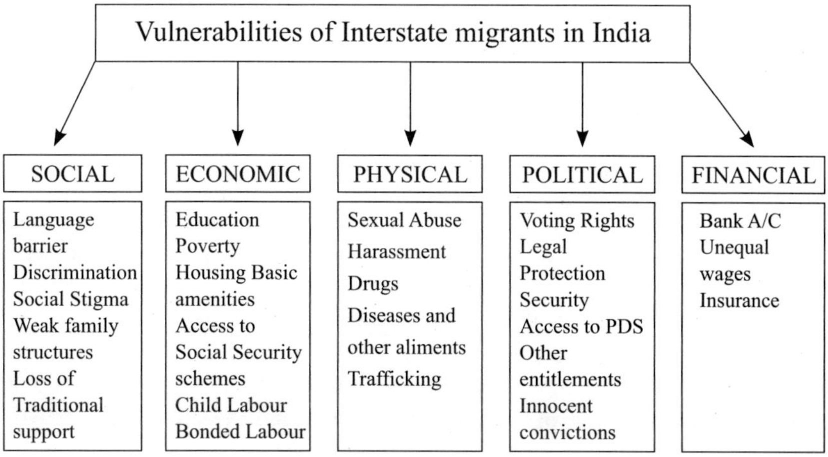

Interestingly, the Aadhaar Card, which was supposed to be an ID card for all including the migrants remains a dream. the UIDAI claims that on the basis of the UID card, which will contain information on the individual's biometric details and her/his state, poor individuals, including migrants, will receive an "identity". Moreover, on that basis, they will be able to claim financial inclusion and various other entitlements. These claims are important since the UIDAI claims to resolve in one stroke three issues central to migrants' social protection – providing them with identity, claim to an entitlement, and an actual entitlement. However, it seems to us that the claims made by the UIDAI on behalf of, or for, migrants, are not well grounded.[117]

Constitutional and Legislative Frame Work for Migrant Labourers in India

Every migrant migrates with the intention to earn a living and to live with human dignity in a healthy environment. The Constitution of India guarantees many rights to the migrants which in some cases are in addition to what is provided to all the citizens. Some of them are as follows:

Article	Rights Guaranteed Under the Constitution of India
21	Rights to human dignity to live in a healthy environment is covered under this article.

[117] Ravi Srivastava. Vulnerable Internal Migrants in India and Portability of Social Security and Entitlements. Institute of Human Development: New Delhi. 2020.

38	The State to promote the welfare of the people by securing and protecting as effectively as it may a social order in which justice, social, economic and political and strive to minimize the inequalities in income, and endeavour to eliminate inequalities in status, facilities and opportunities, not only amongst individuals but also amongst groups of people residing in different areas.
39 (e)	The State shall direct its policy towards securing the health and strength of workers, men and women; and the children of tender age will not be abused; the citizens should not be forced by economic necessity to enter avocations unsuited to their age or strength.
39 (f)	The State shall direct its policy towards securing that children are given opportunities and facilities to develop in a healthy manner and in condition of freedom and dignity and the childhood and youth are protected against exploitation and against moral and material abandonment.

Even a cursory glance at the legal framework for the protection of the rights of labourers and migrants is not lacking in India as elsewhere. But the implementation of these legislations is found wanting. The primary legislation governing inter-state migration in India is the Inter-State Migrant Workmen (Regulation of Employment and Conditions of Service) Act, 1979. This law regulates the employment of migrant workers and ensures they receive fair wages, suitable working conditions, and access to welfare measures like accommodation and medical facilities. Additionally, the Emigration Act, 1983 addresses the emigration of Indian workers for overseas employment, ensuring their welfare and protection.

A Number of legislative provisions exist in India to secure the rights of the migrant labour and workers as follows:

Sl. No.	Legislation	Objective
1.	Workmen's Compensation Act, 1923	To provide compensation for injury by accident for the payment by certain classes of employers to their workmen.
2.	Payment of Wages Act, 1936	To regulate the payment of wages to certain classes of employed persons.
3.	Minimum Wages Act, 1948	To provide compensation for fixing minimum rates of wages in certain employments.
4.	Immoral Traffic (Prevention) Act, 1956	To provide compensation for the prevention of immoral traffic.

5.	Contract Labour (Regulation and Abolition) Act, 1970	To regulate the employment of contract labour in certain establishments and to provide for its abolition in certain circumstances and for matters connected therewith.
6.	Contract Labour (Regulation and Abolition) Rules, 1971	Rules were formulated to implement the acts so that there is no ambiguity.
7.	Bonded Labour System (Abolition) Act, 1978	To provide for the abolition of bonded labour system with a view to preventing the economic and physical exploitation of the weaker sections of the people.
8.	Equal Remuneration Act, 1978	To provide for the payment of equal remuneration to men and women workers and for the prevention of discrimination, on the ground of sex, against women in the matter of employment.
9.	Inter-State Migrant Workmen (Regulation of employment and Conditions of Service) Act, 1979	To regulate the employment of inter-state migrant workmen and to Provide for their conditions of service.
10.	Emigration Act, 1983	An Act to consolidate and amend the law relating to emigration of citizens of India.
11.	Child Labour (Prohibition & Regulation) Act, 1986	An Act to prohibit the engagement of children in certain employments and to regulate the conditions of work of children in certain other employments.
12.	Building and Other Construction Workers' Welfare Cess Act, 1996	An Act to provide for the levy and collection of a cess on the cost of construction incurred by employers with a view to augmenting the resources of the Building and Other Construction Workers' Welfare Boards constituted under the Building and Other Construction Workers (Regulation of Employment and Conditions of Service) Act, 1996.
13.	Building and Other Construction Workers (Regulation of Employment and Conditions of Service) Act, 1996	To regulate the employment and conditions of service of building and other construction workers and to provide for their safety, health and welfare measures.
14.	Unorganised Workers Social Security Act, 2008	To provide for the social security and welfare of unorganised workers.

While these acts are supposed to address the issues of the labourers and migrants, in reality, they do not. Under the Article 15 of the Constitution, it categorically states that no individual shall be discriminated on the grounds of religion, race, caste, sex or place of birth which is applicable to the migrants as well. But these are there to be violated and not implemented. While the state and central governments of India have failed in their duty to uphold the rights of the labourers and migrants, an international organisation like the ILO has come out with policy frameworks to attend to the rights of the labourers and migrants.[118] Thus, it can be stated that there are no dearth of constitutional and legislative framework. But the lack of implementation is the issue that needs to be addressed.

The Inter-State Migrant Workmen Act, 1979, mandates the host state to protect migrant workers and safe guard their rights such as wage equality with local labourers, the provision of suitable residential accommodation and free medical facilities, protective clothing and suitable conditions of work. However, host governments are generally infamous for their hostility towards migrant workers. Too often, migrants cannot claim rights guaranteed by the Constitution and laws on account of the migrant-native divide which is embedded in the politics of internal migration in India.[119]

Migrants are seen as a law and order problem: Migrants are perceived to be a 'law and order problem', and views like the one below, by a police officer are common. We have asked firms employing migrant labourers to submit their details. Our data collection would convey a strong message to them that if they are involved in any kind of anti-social activities, they will be traced... (Karthick 2012).

Anju Bala[120] addressing the issue of causes and consequences of migration highlights the following facts: The pull factors of better job facilities, good salary, and more income, medical and educational facilities are attracting the rural people to move to the cities (Kundu, 2012) [5]. The push factors of no job facilities, low salary, less

---

[118] ILO. Road map for developing a policy framework for the inclusion of internal migrant workers in India. ILO: New Delhi. 2020.

[119] Amrita Dutta. *Continuity and Change: Migration and Development in India*. The Case of Bihar. PhD. Thesis. 2019.

[120] Anju Bala. Migration in India: Causes and Consequences. International Journal of Advanced Educational Research. Volume 2; Issue 4; July 2017.

income, drought, less medical and education compel people towards cities.

People migrate in large number from rural to urban areas in search of employment in industries, trade, transport and services. The rural areas do not provide employment to all the people living there. Even the small-scale and cottage industries of the villages fail to provide employment to the entire rural community. About 10.22 per cent of migrants migrated for employment in 2011.

Due to lack of educational facilities in rural areas, people migrate to the urban areas for higher education. Many of them settle down in the cities for earning a livelihood after completing their education. In 2011 census, about 1.77 percent people migrated for education.

Political disturbances and interethnic conflicts drive people away from their homes. Large number of people have migrated out of Jammu and Kashmir, Assam, northeast, central India during the last few decades due to disturbed political conditions there. People also migrate on a short-term basis in search of better opportunities for recreation, health care facilities, etc.

Millions of people migrated from their far-off villages to the big cities of Kolkata, Mumbai or Delhi. The appalling living conditions like slums, lack of safe water, absence of sanitation, overcrowding with the attendant increase in crime, insecurity for women, sexual abuse and exposure to frequent epidemics and AIDs are the immediate outcome of this population shift.

Strands of Thoughts Regarding Migration

There are various strands of thoughts regarding migration. One strand is that migration from rural Bihar may be understood as a response to rising labour demand in distant urban markets elsewhere in India. It is argued under this that increasing migration has been accompanied by a change in the pattern of income in rural areas between 1999 and 2011. Remittances have become very important, particularly for those in the bottom income quintiles. The local non-farm sector also emerges important, but income from this sector remains concentrated in the upper income quintiles.[121]

[121] Amrita Dutta. *Continuity and Change: Migration and Development in India.* The Case of Bihar. PhD. Thesis. 2019.

Overall, there has been a decline in agriculture in the context of the growth of the rural non-farm sector, and the thesis provides evidence of this decoupling of agriculture from the 'rural'. These aforementioned changes have occurred in a context where migration continues to be male-dominated and circular. Most migrants eventually return to the village to retire, and permanent migration, of the kind that entails relocation of the entire household from the village to the city is very limited. From this point of view, migration emerges as a source area household livelihood strategy.

There is another trend that upholds migration with development. Economic discourses may overstate the importance of income in migrant welfare and thus negate migrant experiences and subjectivities – a critical component of well-being. To do justice to the migrants, it is important to incorporate migrant's subjectivities and emotions for a more comprehensive and nuanced analysis of rural-urban migration in academic and policy discourses.

Even in enumerating migrants there are biases. For instance, the Census uses two distinct criteria to define migration: first, migration by place of birth, and second, migration by place of last residence. Census does not collect data on temporary and short-term migration, seasonal and circular migration and the NSSO uses a cut-off point of 6 months to define short-term migration. In these kinds of data collection, there are possibilities of missing out some important data.

On the other hand, micro-studies often tend to focus on temporary and precarious migration streams and thus report much higher incidence of migration than the official datasets. It is of little surprise, therefore, that estimates of internal migrants in India vary widely and are fraught with methodological and other concerns. It is in this context that the Working Group on Migration advised that differences regarding the extent of migration need to be addressed carefully and institutionally if the issue of migration is to be addressed in an evidence-informed manner (GoI 2017).

Bihar, has a long history of male outmigration. However, recent decades have witnessed a rapid rise in the incidence of migration, and changes in its pattern; migration streams have become longer-term and over time migration destinations have predominantly shifted from rural to urban areas.[122]

In the post-liberalisation period, there has been a growing recognition that migrants are clearly important actors in an economic sense. Yet, there remains an underlying disconnect between urbanisation and migration in the state's discourse – while urbanisation is clearly desirable, often, **the state's view on migration remains ambivalent**. As one of the official stated, 'We cannot provide employment here in Bihar and hence we are neither telling the people to go or not to go'. On the whole, migration from rural Bihar has become more differentiated by education and caste, and there seems to be some shift towards pull factors, though push factors continue to remain important.

There are also preferred destinations for migration. For example, the national capital region of Delhi too became a favoured destination among migrant workers. In 2009, 28 per cent of all migrant workers from Bihar worked in Delhi (Rodgers et.al. 2013).[123] Migrants moved into non-agricultural work such as rickshaw pulling, building and construction work, carpentry, masonry and casual work in the informal sector.[124]

The type work one has been doing in the village and the type of village one gets or opts for also plays a major role in deciding to remain or to move. For upper castes, doing manual wage work in their villages continues to be a taboo as it is against the ritual hierarchy of caste. Many people thus prefer to work outside to be able to undertake a variety of work and access diverse occupations (Karan 2003). At the same time, many lower castes are averse to work in the village on account of the history of feudal exploitation and subsequent caste tension, strife, and violence in Bihar. From their perspective, migration has provided a route to 'work with dignity and freedom' (Deshingkar,

---

[122] G. Rodgers, A. Datta, J. Rodgers, S. K. Mishra and A. N. Sharma (2013) *The Challenge of Inclusive Development in Rural Bihar*. New Delhi: Institute for Human Development and Manak Publications.

[123] Rodgers, G., A. Datta, J. Rodgers, S. K. Mishra and A. N. Sharma (2013) *The Challenge of Inclusive Development in Rural Bihar.* New Delhi: Institute for Human Development and Manak Publications.

[124] Karan, A. (2003) 'Migration from Rural Bihar', in G. Iyer (ed.) *Migrant Labour and Human Rights in India,* pp. 102-139. New Delhi: Kanishka.

Kumar, Choubey and Kumar 2006), and increased migration may be an important agent of change in rural Bihar (A. N. Sharma 2005).

Historically speaking, the Royal Commission on Labour in India (RCLI) pointed out that: The city, as such, has no attraction for him and, when he leaves the village, he has seldom an ambition beyond that of securing the necessities of life. Few industrial workers would remain in industry if they could secure sufficient food and clothing in the village; they are pushed, not pulled, to the city (RCLI 1931: 11). But over time, this scenario has changed and continues to change.

With time, however, the migration-industrialisation-development nexus gave way to the industrialisation-development nexus, and the policy discourse in newly independent India became increasingly silent about labour migration. The key input labourers in general and migrants in particular were forgotten. Symbolic gestures were exhibited on May Day.

Complications were expected to arise in the movement of large numbers of workers, and it was felt that 'bringing gainful work to the doors of people in distress may be a better way of dealing with their problems' (GOI 1956). Thus emerged a fundamental contradiction in the state's discourse in early plan documents – that industrialisation was necessary for development, but migration was not desirable. That trend continues even today.

This contradiction made way for another paradox. Given that rural urban migration was inextricably linked with urbanisation, the discourse on urbanisation became entangled with difficulties related to migration. The perception that migration is a 'problem' emerges in the state's narrative time and again, as we will discuss in the course of this chapter. This is clearly pointed out in the Third Plan (1961-66), where, while urbanisation itself was considered an important aspect of the process of economic and social development, the Plan argued that urbanisation was, closely connected with many other problems such as migration from villages to towns, levels of living in rural and urban areas, relative costs of providing economic and social services in towns of varying size, provision of housing for different sections of the population, provision of facilities like water supply, sanitation, transport and power, pattern of economic development.[125]

---

[125] Third Five Year Plan. Chapter 33, Housing and Urban and Rural Planning. 1961.

The industrialisation project failed to significantly transfer labour from rural to urban areas, and the expected urban migration associated with large scale industrial employment did not materialise. On the other hand, successive droughts in the mid-1960s triggered distress migration from the rural areas; migration from villages to towns in search of employment ex-acerbated during the drought period (GOI 1970).[126] The drought of 1965-67 was a landmark in several ways. First, it changed the industrialisation development narrative, and shifted the policy focus to agriculture. Second, technological innovation in agriculture, and the adoption of high yielding varieties of seeds with assured inputs of irrigation and chemical fertilisers culminated in the Green Revolution.

The first National Commission on Labour was set up in 1966[127] with the mandate to examine all aspects of labour problems. The Commission endorsed rural works programmes, laying an emphasis on labour-intensive schemes such as road building, minor irrigation, soil conservation, area development programmes, irrigation, flood control and rural electrification. This was expected to expand non-farm rural employment and absorb under-employed workers in the agricultural sector (NCL 1969). The Commission also noted that the Inter State Migrant Workmen Act was ineffective because the state labour departments were reluctant to cooperate with the originating states' labour departments. For the labour depart-ment officials, the contractors, owners of enterprises are more lucrative than the labourers from whom they will not get any favour.

The Act was not enforced effectively and migrant workers were largely ignorant about their rights under the Act. Even if they were aware of the act, they have no bargaining power to get the act enacted in their favour. On the contrary, if the labourers raise their voice and protest against the exploitation they are subjected to, they can be booked and put behind bar. The police, the administration, the factory owners and the politicians can go to a ridiculous level to book

[126] Datta et.al (2012).

[127] One correction is called for. The first Labor Commission in India was the Royal Commission on Labour in India (RCLI) in 1931. But the first Commission for Labour in independent India was set up in 1961.

the labourers in one of the most draconian laws like the Unlawful Activities Prevention Act (UAPA).[128]

In addition, the trade unions were not interested in the plight of migrant workers. Three actors – government officials of origin state, government officials of destination states and trade unions were not interested in the migrant labourers issue. Trade unions were not happy with migrant labourers since the migrant labourers are informal and cannot be unionised. Also, a sense that the migrants take away the jobs of the local labourers by accepting to work for lower wages. Thus, the migrants reduce the bargaining power of the union members.

The Green Revolution contributed to pockets of high growth, and large-scale employment of migrant labour. The National Commission on Rural Labour (NCRL) estimated that 40 per cent of agricultural workers were migrants. The Commission also noted that these migrant agricultural workers lived and worked in precarious conditions, and their problems were severe; they had long hours of backbreaking work in the fields, they had no housing facilities, and mostly lived on the farms where they worked, and often, their payments were delayed and de faulted. The Commission argued that agriculture of prosperous states like Punjab depends on migrant workers and therefore, they should legitimately mete out fair treatment, ensure fair housing, adequate wages and social security benefits for them (NCRL 1991; NCL 2002).

The Sixth Five Year Plan discussed welfare activities and dormitory housing in destination areas for migrant workers, and recommended the constitution of Migrant Welfare Boards and Migrant Welfare Cells in all states – a pertinent recommendation which did not materialise as envisaged even after 60 years.[129]

State documents in the period emphasise the importance of rural-urban linkages, and acknowledge that rural areas, rural workers and rural resources have contributed to urban growth and development, thus indicating the state's persistent urban bias. Take, for instance the following paragraph from the Ninth Five Year Plan (1997-2002): The rural hinterland has played a critical role in sustaining urbanisation. This is reflected in the indicators of sources of primary inputs,

---

[128] Prakash Louis. Fr. Stan Swamy: An Anti-National or A Martyr? Masihi Sahitya Sansthan: New Delhi. 2022.

[129] GoI 1981.

competitively priced labour for urban economic activities, primary funds as reflected in comparative urban and rural credit-deposit ratios and markets for urban pockets.... effective urban strategies and programmes cannot be developed in isolation of those living in rural areas.[130]

It is also a fact that in the post-liberalisation period, migration for work substantially increased, and there has been a growing recognition that migrants are clearly important actors in an economic sense. There has also been an acknowledgment of the positive role of the rural worker in urban development, but there remains an underlying disconnect between urbanisation and migration in the state's discourse – while urbanisation is clearly desirable, often, the state's view on migration was ambivalent. Since, the migrant labourers, especially the distressed migrant labourers do not constitute a bargaining power, the governments do not bother about them or their welfare. At the most, they become a point of reference in the election manifestos.

Land can contribute in both the ways: Land is another variable that is linked to migration. It is a fixed factor in agricultural production, and in this context, the practice of agricultural operations may hold people back in the village and reduce the tendency to migrate. On the other hand, land ownership can have a wealth effect, and can offer collateral or cushion to facilitate migration. There are no neat categories in this discussion. In some regions, land degradation, low productivity, and lack of irrigation can force people to seek better opportunities elsewhere. For instance, Gaya district of Bihar is one of the draught prone areas. Hence, lots of people, especially from the Mahadalit communities migrate to eke out a living.

There are also regions in India where areas with high land value or access to profitable agricultural markets can attract migrants. For instance, from 1970s to 2000 lots of labour migrants from Bihar and UP moved to Haryana and Punjab to earn a living in the green revolution of agriculture. Again, people from Bihar moved to Raipur of Chhattisgarh once it became a separate state and since the land price was low then, purchased land and settled there. In both cases land can become push factor as well as pull factor.

---

[130] Ninth Five Year Plan, Volume II, Chapter 3.7 Housing, Urban Development, Water Supply and Civic Amenities. 1997.

Driving Forces Behind the Migration of Unskilled Workers: According to a study conducted by the International Institute for Environment and Development (IIED) in the year 2021, climate change and related events such as drought and flood combined with the socio-economic and socio-political factors increase the vulnerability of households and in turn, motivate people to migrate. It was seen that education too played a significant role, as people who only had primary and secondary education migrated more than people with higher education. Seasonal migration increased due to low yields in agriculture and fishing, forcing people to move in search of livelihood in the off-seasons. Migration is further compounded by a lack of opportunities for the unskilled labourers in their hometowns. This lack of opportunities is due to the seasonal nature of jobs as well as low levels of education amongst the labourers. In such a scenario, better employment opportunities in the manufacturing sector in urban areas present themselves as lucrative to the labourers. They provide opportunities to work, save and buy assets back home and thus exit from inter-generational poverty.[131]

The Plight of the Unskilled Migrants in the Destination States: Article 19(1)(e) of the Constitution of India guarantees all Indian citizens the right to reside and settle in any part of the territory of India, subject to reasonable restrictions. The poor implementation of the Inter-State Migrant Workmen (Regulation of Employment and Conditions of Service) Act (ISMW), 1979 which deals with the protection of inter-state migrant workers, has led to their marginalization. The ISMW Act gives interstate migrant workers some safeguards. Contractors that hire migrants must: (i) be licenced; (ii) register migrant employees with the government; and (iii) arrange for the worker to be provided with a passbook that documents their identity. The law also specifies the salaries and benefits that the contractor must give (such as lodging, free medical care, and protective clothing).

The Standing Committee on Labour reported in December 2011 that worker registration under the ISMW Act was low and that the Act's provisions were poorly implemented. According to the report, the union government has not taken any real and fruitful steps to

[131] Ritu Bharadwaj, Somnath Hazra, Mohan Reddy, Shouvik Das and Daljeet Kaur. *Connecting Dots: Climate Change,* Migration and Social Protection. IIED. 2021.

ensure that contractors and employers register the people they employ and hence labourers are not able to obtain benefits under the Act (Iyer, Gopal. 2020).

The inadequate supply of affordable housing (including rental and ownership), near places of work is also a huge issue in urban areas. This results in the proliferation of slums with poor water and sanitation facilities and unhygienic living conditions, affecting the health and productivity of these workers in the long term. The children of migrant workers face accessibility issues in school, and absenteeism due to clashes between academic season and the seasonal migration cycle. This disruption in academic life eventually leads to their dropout as they are unable to cope with the pressure (Faetanini & Tankha, 2013).

Waste picking is one of the occupation that absorbs many migrants. Waste pickers are not legally permitted by state municipalities to collect, segregate and sell waste from garbage dumps across the country, and they are deemed to be committing theft under the Indian Penal Code, 1860. Supriya Routh,[132] found that most waste pickers who were interviewed for a study in 2011 had been taken into police custody at least once in their lives and had been booked for petty cases. Due to a strong lobby that advocates that privatisation of garbage collection is cheaper and more efficient, the waste pickers are displaced now by local and multinational operators.

Political Ecosystem Dealing with Unskilled Migration:[133] Politicians in the destination states tend to ignore the concerns of the migrant workers and only pay heed to such workers who permanently reside in their constituency. This is primarily because migrant workers have no voting rights in the destination states and thus do not form part of the constituency of the politicians, whose main agenda is to get re-elected. In the case of rural migrants within the state who can vote in the local elections, the lack of information regarding the voting process, the complex procedure of voter registration by providing necessary residency proof, and other identity documents limit their

---

[132] Supriya Routh. *Enhancing Capabilities Through Labour Law: Informal Workers in India.* Routledge: New Delhi. 2016.

[133] Pankhuri Jain, Keerthi Priya Yerramalla and Vyoma Dadhich. Economics and Politics of Internal Migration among Unskilled Workers in India. International Journal of Policy Sciences and Law. Volume 2, Issue 3. 2022.

electoral participation. This belief about migrants' propensity for low turnout in the electoral process disincentivizes the politicians to consider them as vote banks and perpetuates the discrimination in the allocation of scarce resources they already face.

The manifestation of negligence toward migrants was brought out in a study[134] wherein the local councillors received letters from residents requesting a call back to address their concerns. The residents were more likely to receive the call from the councillor than the migrants and registered migrants more than the unregistered migrants. Additionally, the politicians might be channelizing their constituents, i.e., residents' cultural and economic issues concerning the migrants, and becoming unresponsive towards the migrants. Finally, the politicians might themselves be prejudiced against the migrant workers.

This was clear during the first lockdown where approximately 10 million migrant workers were left to fend for themselves due to administrative negligence. The workers reportedly walked for miles together, with no access to food, water and transport facilities during their journey back home with some of them even losing their lives. When the same issue was raised in Parliament, the government cited a lack of data regarding the same and evaded a reply. This is reflective of the broader administrative attitude towards migrant workers. Local elites harbour disdain towards migrant workers due to the differences in the language, creed, and culture. While they might tolerate the ones who are ethnically similar to them, the ones who are ethnically dissimilar are completely unwelcome (Gaikwad & Nellis, 2017).

The "Sons of the Soil" argument is wielded when there is high unemployment among the local populace. However, the study (Bhavnani & Lacina, 2015) refutes the above argument. They found that the alignment of the native population with the central government determines the extent to which the natives' grievances are addressed. The native populations aligned with the Central government are provided with more resources to address their grievances. In such cases, states resort to police intimidation and bureaucratic discrimination to exercise control over the migrants, preventing them

[134] Gaikward, Nikhar and Gareth Nellis. *The Majority-Minority Divide in Attitudes toward Internal Migration: Evidence from Mumbai*. American Journal of Political Science. Volume 61, Issue 2, April, 2017.

from gaining access to more resources without any impunity. On the other hand, the natives who are not politically aligned, are provided fewer resources by the Central government and enjoy lesser impunity. Hence, they cannot resort to official channels to discriminate against the migrants and nativism is more likely to manifest in riots against the migrant workers.

Employers of the Migrant Workers

Hiring unskilled workers at lower wages can add innumerable benefits to the company's growth in terms of increased output at lower costs. However, employers suffer from commitment issues on the side of the workers as there are no signed contracts. The unskilled workers are mobile and switch jobs frequently and thus, provide no form of security to the employers in terms of long-term performance. On the other side, jobs such as cleaning, and driving which do not require a specific skill set pose a troublesome situation for the migrant workers as this allows employers to hire and fire the workers at will as employees are seen as dispensable and easily replaceable.

The Interest of the Contractors, Middlemen, Agents: The contractors benefit from commissions in exchange for cheap unskilled labour to employers. According to (Mazumdar et al., 2013), the workers recruited through unregulated labour contractors suffer violence, inhumane treatment, and harassment by contractors. However, they incur losses if there are sudden labour shortages due to unforeseen reasons, e.g. the COVID-19 crisis. Due to the mobile nature of migrant workers, contractors must also ensure that labour works efficiently as per expectations and maintain labour supply.

***Administrative and Political System*:** Migrants themselves and those who assist them are aware of the fact that the migrants are looked as 'outsiders' by the local people, administration and govt and as a burden on systems and resources at the destination. But the companies, factories, construction proprietors want them. Migrants' right to the city is denied on the political defense of the 'sons of the soil' theory, which aims to create vote banks along ethnic, linguistic and religious lines. Exclusion and discrimination against migrants take place through political and administrative process, market mechanism and socio-economic processes, causing a gulf between the migrants and locals.[135]

The Consequences in an Hostile Situation

Consequently, some of the issues they may face are listed as follows:

- The migrant workers face onerous requirements of producing documentary proofs to access essential services. In the case of the Public Distribution System (PDS),[136] though the National Food Security Act, 2013 applies to all irrespective of their domicile, the migrants registered in the origin states lose their benefits when they move to the destination states. This is also evident in the access to formal financial services.
- The waiving of local address proofs under Know Your Customer (KYC) norms by the Reserve Bank of India (RBI) for migrant workers is followed in its breach by many banks. The migrants still rely on informal networks to send money to their families back home. There is always the possibility of getting cheated.
- The lack of access to proper healthcare exacerbates their vulnerability. Inaccessibility arises from the expensive private care, the opportunity cost of the labour wages lost while seeking treatment, and language barriers. The government's recent scheme Ayushman Bharat tried to address this issue with the portability feature, wherein the beneficiaries can benefit anywhere.
- Lack of identity card of the local place where the migrant is residing and or working leads to many problems. Some organisations have given ID cards from their end which is helpful in many situations. For example, the Bengaluru Archdiocese distributes ID card which some banks accept to open the bank account. Also helpful when identity of oneself has to be communicated to the police.

---

[135] M. Faetanini and R. Tankha. *Social inclusion of Internal Migration in India.* UNESCO: Delhi. 2013.

[136] The present government of India has been proclaiming from roof tops that it is moving towards 'One Nation, One Ration Card'. But in reality there is no political will to implement this announcement. Instead, the government is busy planning for 'One Nation, One Election'.

Gendered Migration[137] – Place and Role of Women

Gendered migration refers to the ways in which migration patterns and experiences are shaped by gender norms, roles, and power dynamics. It recognizes that migration affects women and men differently, influencing who migrates, why they migrate, their access to opportunities, and their vulnerabilities. Understanding gendered migration is crucial for developing effective policies and programs that address the unique needs and challenges faced by migrants of all genders. Gender norms can influence why individuals choose to migrate, with some migrating for economic reasons, while others may be fleeing violence or seeking family reunification.

Richard Gonsales goes on to state another aspect of gendered migration. There has been a propensity to view internal migration as essentially a male activity. Since migration is associated with the ideas of aspiration and progress which ae chiefly a male prerogative, women's issue are overlooked with women as residual or dependents in the process of migration. Therefore, it is important to center on the narratives of migrant women and adopt an intersectional approach to gendered migration.

Among all the works or employments possible and or available for women, domestic work seems to be the most feasible form of employment for women. Their own involvement in their house leaves them with little avenues to explore option other than domestic work. Moreover, motherhood ties them to their infant which proves to be constraint for them. The world of domesticity is all they have to explore. Domestic work though pushed to the margins and seen as outside the ambit of capitalism, is actually located at the heart of capitalism or market economy. The traditional social arrangement granted the public sphere to men and private to women and projected the home as an enclave outside the forces of the market.[138]

Most of these domestic workers get paid a meagre amount of Rs. 2,000.00 only. If they manage to get 3 to 4 households to work as domestic help, then they make some money. If not, they and their

---

[137] Richard Gonsalves. *Cityscape for Young Migrant Women: A Reflection on Intra Domestic Workers in Bangalore.*

[138] Vast number of women and migrant women can get only an occupation of this type. In terms of caste and ethnicity, more Dalit and Tribal women are forced to take up this work, since this may be the only employment they get.

family become vulnerable. It is also significant to note that during the covid, most of these domestic workers lost their jobs due to fear of infection and or the female head of the household had the facility to work from home. This imposes double disadvantage to these women.

The gender-wise trend line has taken only 50 years to show a drastic change. Between 1961 and 2011, the percentage of female in-migration to Kolkata has increased from around 21 to 43 per cent. Even so, the number of male migrants still occupies a higher position in comparison to the female migrants in Kolkata city.[139] This goes to indicate that there is more movement of women and also migration of people as a family.

This is also possible that migration has the possibility of autonomy of women who migrate. But does it empower and enable women in any way or do they remain entrapped in the patriarchal arrangements has to be studied and understood. Migration, in certain contexts, can contribute to women's autonomy, but it's also a complex and potentially risky process. When women migrate to seek better economic opportunities or escape patriarchal structures, they may gain independence and agency, particularly within the household and labour market. However, migration can also expose women to exploitation, trafficking, and gender-based violence, especially if they lack documentation or take dangerous routes.

Successful urban migration can bring significant changes for the lives of women migrants and their families. The experience can empower women and provide a new autonomy to develop self-esteem and capacities. Research shows that women's authority and value improve, while traditional roles and norms are challenged. Women often build on their new assertiveness, skills, and expertise and venture into small businesses.

In addition, women migrants tend to remit a higher share of their earnings than male migrants, even though the total amount is smaller as women earn lower wages than men. Remittances of women tend to have a higher impact on their family's well-being than those of men, as funds are more frequently directed to health care and education.[140]

---

139 Sumita Roy and Gopa Samanta. *Informal Laborers in Kolkata City: Migration from Undivided Bihar and Uttar Pradesh.* Space and Culture, India 2020.

140 Cities Alliance. Migration, Gender, and Women's Empowerment. UNDP.

One of the reasons while male migration is higher than female migration is the living cost in the urban areas is quite high with respect to rural areas which resist them to migrate with their family.

Lastly, it needs to be highlighted that migration results in huge cost, at times, even with life. The article titled, 'graveyard of inter-state migrant workers on Gujarat's Alang Beach: An inquiry into how migrant workers constitute **a community of fate**" by Gopal Krishna traces the journey of migrant workers from villages in Gorakhpur, Uttar Pradesh, to the ship-breaking yards of Aland beach, Bhavnagar, Gujarat. The global economy has marginalised the workers so much that migrant workers continue to come to work in the graveyard of foreign ships undertaking dangerous and hazardous jobs, which ends up being their own graveyard.[141]

Social Impact of Migrant Families[142]

1) Decline in joint family system: due to migration the joint family converted to nuclear families. This is a general feature notices in most of the slums.
2) Landlessness: migrant from rural to urban areas are detached from land and agriculture.
3) Joblessness being displaced they lose their means of livelihood. Creation of new jobs or alternative sources of income for them becomes very difficult since the migrants do not possess any skill or required skill to earn a living. Those who were owners of some means of production now have become daily wage earners.
4) Increase in workers looking for jobs.
5) Homelessness; loss of house and shelter remains a permanent feature for most of the migrants.
6) Food insecurity: migration increases the risk of chronic food insecurity. In urban areas everything has to be purchased.

---

[141] Gopal Krishna. *Graveyard of Inter-state Migrant Workers on Gujarat's Alang Beach: An Inquiry into How Migrant Workers Constitute a Community of Fate. Labour Migration in the Post-Liberalization Era.* Edited by Denzil F. and P.O. Martin. CISRS: New Delhi. 2019.

[142] Notan Bhusan Kar. *Impact of Globalisation on Urban Slum Dwellers-Migrants from Rural Areas: A Social Case Study of Barasat Town*, North 24-Parganas District, West Bengal. Denzil & Martin edited book. CISRS: New Delhi. 2019.

7) loss of access to common property: those moving to urban areas loose access common properties like water bodies, groves, grazing land, etc. so deprived of wood as fuel and other minor products.
8) social disintegration: migration dismantles family systems, kinship groups, livelihood and often scatters cultural identity of the people. Social, community and family networks that help people to cope with poverty through exchange of food and clothing, mutual help with farming, building houses and caring children are disrupted.
9) Increased morbidity and mortality: loss of ancestral and homestead land, less access to health care facilities, the psychological trauma caused thereby and the food insecurity together often leads to serious diseases.

Thus it can be stated that the migrants live a life of deprivation and dislocation, and therefore disentitled and disenfranchised. They are perhaps the most faceless, voiceless and invisible group in a city's populace. They are excluded and exploited by all. Within these exploited migrants, those from rural areas, those from the Dalit, Tribal, most backward castes and minorities are doubly exploited and excluded due to the already prevalent caste, class, religious background. Women are further discriminated and exploited. This is the fate of children too.

When the 'protector' state is in a mood to recede and the market is on the rampage, it is quite natural that the powerless and voiceless people who live on the margins would find themselves more vulnerable. Being a part of the neo-liberal market the marginalised with minimal control over material and human resources and cultural capital are engaged in fierce survival battle as dominant sections with much greater control over resources not only do not give them much economic and socio-political space but often intrude into whatever small space they occupy. The state with its administrative apparatus denies access to resources for the marginalised and enables the dominant to flourish.[143]

[143] Saikat Roy. Income Generation, Livelihood and Statelessness: An analysis of the Current situation of Tea Garden Workers of North Bengal. These tea garden workers were also brought by the British colonisers from former Chotanagpur and what is now Jharkhand around the year 1841.

6

The Catholic Church's Social Teaching on Migrants

"The church's social teaching is not only a doctrine but a way of life... the church's teaching itself is a kind of worship, a place where all people are called to labour to bring about a better social order" (Saint John Paul II. 1991). These words of Saint John Paul II rightly capture the context, content, objectives and the outcome of the Catholic Social Teachings.

Social encyclicals or Catholic Social Teachings (CST) or the Social Teachings of the Church (STC) the Social Doctrines of the Church (SDC) are the Church's institutional response to the social problems of a given time period. The social teaching of the church is a rich heritage of ethical reflections and insights on the social, economic and political questions of our contemporary world.

Pope Leo XIII, who wrote the first encyclical '*Rerum Novarum* On the Conditions of Labour' in 1891 stated, "The church has never failed to speak the words that are hers with regard to questions concerning the life in society."

Major Themes of the Social Teachings of the Church

1. Human Dignity, 2. Community and Common Good, 3. Rights and Responsibilities, 4. Option for and with the Poor and Vulnerable, 5. Participation in Common Destiny, 6. Dignity of Work and Workers, 7. Economic Justice to All, 8. Care of God's Creation, 9. The Virtue of Solidarity, 10. Role of Government, 11. Promotion of Peace, 12. Place

and Role of Women, 13. Integral Development, 14. Place and Role of Youth, 15. Place and Role of Laity.

Underlying in all these Encyclicals is the Christian View of the Human Person.[144]

- Each of us is made in God's image
- Each human being has tremendous dignity
- Each human being is a child of God
- We are special in God's eyes
- We have rights and responsibilities
- We have a spiritual nature
- God made us for himself
- We possess freedom; we must use it responsibly
- We are social beings
- We image God best when we love one another
- God made us co-creators with him
- We are wounded by sin and inclined to evil and error
- Jesus has much to reveal to us about who we are and how we should treat each other
- We are saved through Jesus' passion, death and resurrection
- We are to be compassionate like Jesus

CST came about due to this realisation of the Church that it is a pastoral priority for it to respond to the issues of development, governance, peace, justice and rights. Through the CST, the Church wants to present principles for reflection, criteria for judgment and directives for action leading to integral liberation through solidarity. To actualize it, the Church started Caritas in the early 1950s as the charity, development, relief and rehabilitation organ of the universal Church.

This split between the faith which many profess and their daily lives deserves to be counted among the more serious errors of our age. Long since, the Prophets of the Old Testament fought vehemently against this scandal and even more so did Jesus Christ Himself in the New Testament threatened it with grave punishments. Therefore, let there be no false opposition between professional and social activities on the one part, and religious life on the other. Christians who neglect

---

[144] Prakash Louis. *Catholic Social Teachings: Towards a Catholic Faith in Action.* Indian Social Institute: New Delhi. 2019.

their temporal duties, jeopardizes their eternal salvation (The Church in the Modern World #43).

The popes demanded that the social doctrines should be put into practice. It is not enough merely to formulate a social doctrine. It must be translated into reality. And this is particularly true of the Church's social doctrine, the light of which is Truth, Justice its objective, and Love its driving force (*Mater et Magistra* #226).

The Catholic Church's social teaching on migrants, articulated in papal documents and writings over the last century, emphasizes migrants' dignity, the need for solidarity, and nations' moral responsibility to welcome and protect those in need. The Church bases its teachings on migrants on foundational biblical traditions while firmly establishing them within Catholic doctrinal principles. The Church develops its migration practices through a lengthy tradition of theological analysis and pastoral support that aims to meet migrants' needs in a setting of religious belief and social fairness.

The Historical Context of Catholic Social Teachings on Migrants

The Catholic Church has maintained its historical involvement in migrant care through its longstanding traditions of hospitality and charity. Throughout history, the Church has offered refuge to strangers, starting with the early Christians who protected persecuted people and continuing to medieval monasteries that provided safe havens for displaced persons. The Church's approach to migration formalized its teachings through papal encyclicals, as early as in 1891 by Pope Leo XIII's, *Rerum Novarum* and in 1963 by Pope Leo XIII's *Pacem in Terris*. While the documents did not focus exclusively on migration, it highlighted key principles relevant to migrants and refugees, which defined migrant rights and responsibilities while advocating for social systems to uphold their dignity.

The Catholic Church has a long history of grappling with issues related to migration and refugees, drawing on its rich tradition to shape its views and responses. Tradition is pivotal in guiding Catholic perspectives on migrants, as it provides a framework rooted in moral teachings and ethical principles. One key aspect of Catholic tradition that informs its views on migrants is the concept of solidarity. Solidarity is a fundamental principle in Catholic social teaching, emphasizing the interconnectedness of all human beings and the duty to support and care for one another. This principle is often invoked in discussions about migration, as it calls on Catholics to show compassion and hospitality towards migrants and refugees in need. The tradition of solidarity underscores the importance of welcoming the stranger and providing assistance to those who are marginalized or vulnerable.

In addition to solidarity, the Catholic tradition also illuminates the dignity of every human person. Central to Catholic teaching is the belief that all individuals are created in the image and likeness of God, and therefore possess inherent worth and dignity. This understanding informs Catholic views on migrants, compelling believers to treat migrants with respect and to advocate for their rights and well-being. The tradition of upholding human dignity compels Catholics to oppose discrimination, exploitation, and mistreatment of migrants, and to work towards a more just and inclusive society. Furthermore, the Catholic tradition of social justice shapes the Church's response to migration.

Social justice calls for the promotion of a more equitable distribution of natural resources and welfare or economic opportunities, and the protection of the rights of the most vulnerable members of society grounded on the principles of Universal Destination of Goods, Subsidiarity and Solidarity. In the context of migration, this tradition calls on Catholics to address the root causes of migration, such as poverty, war, violence, and persecution, and to work towards creating a more just and peaceful world where all individuals can thrive.

Encyclicals from Popes

Rerum Novarum, an encyclical written in 1891 by Pope Leo XIII, does not explicitly mention migrant workers.[145] Still, it addresses broader issues related to labour, workers' rights, and the responsibilities of employers in the context of the Industrial Revolution. The encyclical focuses the dignity of work and the just treatment of all workers, which can apply to migrant workers as part of the labour force. It points indirectly to the rights of workers who migrate to find better opportunities, advocating for their fair treatment and protection

---

[145] https://www.vatican.va/content/leo-xiii/en/encyclicals/documents/hf_l-xiii_enc_15051891_rerum-novarum.html.

from exploitation while also acknowledging the potential benefits of migration for both sending and receiving countries; essentially viewing migration as a means to alleviate poverty in overpopulated areas and provide labourers in regions with shortages of workers but with a strong emphasis on ensuring humane conditions for migrants.

Exsul Familia[146] is a term that refers to the concept of an exiled family, often used in discussions surrounding immigration, family reunification, and humanitarian crises. This document (1952) is the first one in the Church to **explicitly** state that migrants have the right to migrate and to live with dignity. It was written in response to mass migrations that occurred before and after World War II and draws on Pope Leo XIII's *Rerum Novarum* to present emigration as a natural human right, justifying it on the grounds of the Universal Destination of Goods.[147] Pope Pius XII established that the local diocesan bishop has primary responsibility for the pastoral care of migrants. It recounts Pius XII's lobbying efforts to encourage nations with more land and fewer people to open their borders to migrants and highlights the struggles and challenges faced by families who are displaced from their home countries due to conflict, persecution, or other extreme circumstances.

The document in the very introduction says, "The *émigré* Holy Family of Nazareth, fleeing into Egypt, is the archetype of every refugee family. Jesus, Mary and Joseph, living in exile in Egypt to escape the fury of an evil king, are, for all times and all places, the models and protectors of every migrant, alien and refugee of whatever kind who, whether compelled by fear of persecution or by want, is forced to leave his native land, his beloved parents and relatives, his close friends, and to seek a foreign soil."[148]

Populorum Progressio written in 1967 in the historical context of decolonization, the encyclical addresses emerging nations' struggles,

---

[146] *Exsul Familia* is an apostolic constitution by Pope Pius XII on migration, released on August 1, 1952; please refer to https://www.papalencyclicals.net/pius12/p12exsul.htm (accessed on 11.03.2025).

[147] The **Universal Destination of Goods**, is a core principle of Catholic social teaching, asserts that the earth's resources are meant for the benefit of all people, not just a select few, and that private property rights must be balanced with the needs of the poor and marginalized.

[148] *Exsul Familia* #1.

hinting at migration from former colonies.[149] It critiques neocolonial economic structures that perpetuate dependency and displacement. It focuses on equitable global development, emphasizing solidarity between nations. While it does not explicitly focus on migrants, its principles provide a foundational framework for understanding migration through the lens of Catholic social teaching. The document argues that the underdevelopment as a cause of displacement, urging wealthy nations to address poverty and inequality.

By promoting fair economic systems (# 48), it indirectly addresses migration's root causes, advocating for development that allows people to thrive in their homelands. The topic of migrants is, indirectly, addressed by emphasizing the need for fair treatment and protection of migrant workers, highlighting the ethical concerns surrounding migration, particularly when driven by poverty and lack of opportunities in their home countries (# 67), and calling for international cooperation to ensure dignified conditions for migrant populations (# 69); essentially advocating for the rights and welfare of migrants within the broader context of global development.

Pacem in Terris (Peace on Earth) is a document issued by Pope John XXIII in 1963. In this the Pope says "Every human being has the right to freedom of movement and of residence within the confines of his own state. When there are just reasons in favor of it, he must be permitted to emigrate to other countries and to take up residence there. The fact that he is a citizen of a particular state does not deprive him of membership in the human family, nor of citizenship in that universal society, the worldwide fellowship of man."

In 1965, at the conclusion of the Second Vatican Council, Pope John XXIII, said in **Gaudium et Spes (The Church in the Modern World),** "The joys and hopes, the sorrows and anxieties of the women and men of this age, especially those who are poor or in any way oppressed, these are the joys and hopes, the sorrows and anxieties of the followers of Christ."

Octogesima Adveniens is an Apostolic Letter written by Pope Paul VI on May 14, 1971, to mark the eightieth anniversary of the

[149] Populorum progressio is an encyclical written by Pope Paul VI on the topic of "the development of peoples"; Refer to https://www.vatican.va/content/paul-vi/en/encyclicals/documents/hf_p-vi_enc_26031967_populorum.html. (accessed on 11.03.2025).

encyclical Rerum Novarum.[150] This letter Call for Action discusses themes related to social justice and the role of laypeople in the Church. The document draws attention to the rapid urbanization and the displacement of people, often forcing them into marginalized conditions. Migrants, particularly those moving to cities for economic survival, face similar struggles. Pope Paul VI calls for equitable urban development and policies that protect human dignity, indirectly addressing systemic issues affecting migrants.

It underlines the plight of marginalized groups and urges Christians to practice solidarity. Migrants, often excluded socially and economically, are included in this call. The letter advocates for inclusive communities that reject discrimination—a principle applicable to welcoming migrants (# 17). The text critiques unjust political and economic structures that perpetuate inequality. Migrants frequently encounter exploitative labour practices, inadequate legal protections, and xenophobia. It asserts structural reforms to uphold rights, aligning with later Church teachings on migrant rights (#23).

Pope Paul VI acknowledges the tension between individuals' hopes for a better life and systemic barriers. Migrants often embody this duality, seeking opportunity while facing exclusion. The document's emphasis on hope and collective responsibility resonates with migrant advocacy.

Laborem Exercens is an encyclical written by Pope John Paul II in 1981, on human work. It is part of the larger body of Catholic social teaching, which traces its origin to Pope Leo XIII's 1891 encyclical *Rerum Novarum*. In this encyclical, the Pope singles out the dignity of work and the rights of workers, acknowledging the difficulties faced by migrants who leave their homes seeking better opportunities. It accentuates the dignity of work and the fundamental rights of workers, which echoes deeply in the context of migration. It advocates for the acknowledgment of labour as a means of human fulfilment and social participation, giving importance to the plight of migrants who often face exploitation and lack of recognition for their contributions. In the migration discourse, the encyclical calls for a more humane approach that respects migrant workers' rights, promotes social justice, and

150 https://www.vatican.va/content/paul-vi/en/apost_letters/documents/hf_p-vi_apl_19710514_octogesima-adveniens.html. (accessed on 11.03.2025).

fosters integration, thereby affirming their intrinsic dignity and the essential role they play in society. (#23).[151]

Erga Migrantes Caritas Christi[152] is the Instruction from the Pontifical Council for the Pastoral Care of Migrants and Itinerant People in 2004 about how to care for migrants and refugees. The document was approved by Pope John Paul II. From the perspective of the theological foundation, the document highlights that the Church's pastoral care for migrants is rooted in the love of Christ (#1). It underlines the importance of acknowledging and protecting the rights of migrants, including their right to migrate and their right to live a dignified life, free from exploitation and discrimination (#03, 06, 21,27, 30, 86). The document speaks of the necessity of providing comprehensive pastoral care that addresses not only the spiritual needs but also the social, economic, and cultural challenges faced by migrants (Part II & III). It promotes that Christians are called to treat migrants with compassion and respect, recognizing their dignity as human beings created in the image of God (#12).

The Church is invited to accompany migrants at all stages of their journey, offering support and solidarity (# 41). This includes outreach, integration, and assistance in understanding and navigating local customs and laws (# 42-43). The Church is urged to work in collaboration with governments, civil society, and other organizations to better serve the needs of migrants and to advocate for just policies (# 33, 87). The document accents on the importance of integrating migrants into receiving communities while also respecting their cultural identities and contributions. It calls for a two-way process that benefits both migrants and host societies (# 34, 36).

It also articulates on the formation of migrant communities that can support one another and promote understanding between diverse groups. As part of an ecclesial exhortation the document urges the Church and its members to engage actively in the pastoral care of migrants, reflecting on the biblical themes of hospitality and welcoming the stranger, calling for raising awareness among local

---

[151] Refer to https://www.vatican.va/content/john-paul-ii/en/encyclicals/documents/hf_jp-ii_enc_14091981_laborem-exercens.html. (accessed on 11.03.2025).

[152] https://www.vatican.va/roman_curia/pontifical_councils/migrants/documents/rc_pc_migrants_doc_20040514_erga-migrantes-caritas-christi_en.html (accessed on 14.04.2025).

congregations and communities about the realities and contributions of migrants to foster an environment of mutual respect and understanding (Part. IV). As a conclusion, it should be noted that the document challenges the Church to be a sign of hope and unity for migrants, ensuring that they are not only received materially but also spiritually. It highlights Christian hospitality, justice, and solidarity, reminding the faithful that welcoming migrants is an essential expression of Christ's love.

Archbishop Agostino Marchetto, the secretary to the Pontifical Council for the Pastoral Care of Migrants and Itinerant People,[153] in a series of explanatory notes has articulated expansively the meaning and implications of the papal document, "*Erga Migrantes Caritas Christi.*"[154] The Council has issued several important documents addressing the pastoral, social, and ethical aspects of migration.[155] This Pontifical Council serves a crucial role within the Catholic Church, focusing on the spiritual and practical needs of migrants and itinerant communities. It responds to the growing complexities of migration, its mission aligns with the teachings of Blessed Scalabrini,[156] who illuminated three key functions: religious support, social assistance, and cultural identity preservation. The council's work is informed by these principles, advocating for just migration policies while fostering integration within local communities. Through this holistic approach, it aims not only to preserve the faith but also to safeguard migrants' rights during their transition into new environments.

[153] In 1914 Pope Pius X created the Consistorial Congregation's Office for the Spiritual Care of Emigrants, focusing on Catholic migrants leaving Europe. In 1967 Pope Paul VI created the Pontifical Commission for the Pastoral Care of Migration and Tourism, which later evolved into the Pontifical Council. In 1988 Pope John Paul II elevated it to a full Pontifical Council under *Pastor Bonus*, expanding its mandate to all itinerant people, including refugees, seafarers, and nomads. In 2017 Pope Francis merged it into the Dicastery for Promoting Integral Human Development, centralizing Vatican efforts on migration, justice, and social concerns.

[154] https://www.vatican.va/roman_curia/pontifical_councils/migrants/pom2006_101/rc_pc_migrants_pom101_the-challenge-migr.html (accessed on 24.03.2025).

[155] "*De Pastorali Migratorum Cura*" (Apostolic Constitution), 1969; "Instruction on the Pastoral Care of People on the Move,"1969; "The Church and Human Mobility," 1978; "Refugees: A Challenge to Solidarity," 1992; "*Erga Migrantes Caritas Christi,*" 2004; "Guidelines for the Pastoral Care of Gypsies," 2005.

[156] He emphasized the inherent dignity of migrants and advocated for their integration into new societies while preserving their cultural identities. He is called "father of Migrants."

Pope John Paul II also addresses the more controversial topic of **undocumented migration** and the undocumented migrant. In his 1995 message for World Migration Day, he notes that such migrants are used by developed nations as a source of labour. Ultimately, the pope says, elimination of global underdevelopment is the antidote to illegal immigration. *Ecclesia in America*, which focuses on the Church in North and South America, reiterates the rights of migrants and their families and the respect for human dignity "even in cases of non-legal immigration."

Caritas in Veritate (2009)[157] addresses the complex issue of migration with a perspective rooted in social justice and solidarity. The encyclical highlights the importance of recognizing the dignity of every human person, regardless of their nationality or immigration status. "Every migrant is a human person who, as such, possesses fundamental, inalienable rights that must be respected by everyone and in every circumstance" (#62). In the face of a multifaceted issue that involves economic, social, and political factors, *Caritas in Veritate* urges us **to view migrants not as mere statistics or burdens, but as individuals with inherent rights and aspirations** (#26 & 35). Pope Benedict XVI pinpoints the need for a coordinated response that addresses the root causes of migration while also ensuring the rights and well-being of migrants themselves (#67). This requires not only policy changes but also a shift in attitudes and perceptions towards migrants. It offers a profound reflection on the migration issue, emphasizing the importance of empathy, cooperation, and respect for human rights (#25, 32, &45). By embracing these principles, we can work towards a more equitable and compassionate world where all people, regardless of their background, can thrive and contribute to the common good.

Evangelii Gaudium,[158] issued by Pope Francis in 2013, touches on many issues concerning the Church and society, including the plight of migrants (#210). In this apostolic exhortation, the Pope underlines the importance of welcoming migrants and their families

---

[157] *Caritas in Veritate*, is the third and final social encyclical by Pope Benedict XVI. It focuses on the relationship between human and environmental ecologies, linking charity and truth. Refer to https://www.vatican.va/content/benedict-xvi/en/encyclicals/documents/hf_ben-xvi_enc_20090629_caritas-in-veritate.html (accessed on 11.03.2025).

[158] https://www.vatican.va/content/francesco/en/apost_exhortations/documents/papa-francesco_esortazione-ap_20131124_evangelii-gaudium.html (accessed on 11.03.2025).

with compassion and solidarity. Pope Francis points out that all human beings are entitled to dignity and rights, regardless of their immigration status (#192). He maintains that migrants should not be seen merely as problems to be solved, but rather as individuals with dreams, aspirations, and the right to seek a better life. This perspective encourages communities to recognize the humanity of migrants and to support their integration rather than enforcing exclusion (#210). The surge in migration has often faced negative reactions at local and national levels, where there are fears about job competition, cultural integration, and social services. The Pope encourages societies to provide aid and support to these individuals and to recognize the contributions they can make through a lens of empathy.

Furthermore, Pope Francis underscores the need for policies that protect the rights of migrants (#190). He argues that nations should commit to ensuring safety and dignity for all individuals, creating a more inclusive society (#239). Initiatives aimed at providing education, healthcare, and employment opportunities for migrants can lead to richer communities for everyone. The encyclical presents a compelling message about the importance of supporting migrants. Pope Francis calls on individuals and governments alike to demonstrate compassion and solidarity with those who are vulnerable. By recognizing the inherent dignity of every person, regardless of their background, societies have the opportunity to enrich their cultural fabric and contribute to a more just and equitable world.

Fratelli Tutti[159] **(2020)** In his encyclical "Fratelli Tutti" released in 2020, Pope Francis discusses the importance of valuing and caring for migrants and refugees. The Pope highlights the global crisis of displacement and calls for a more compassionate and welcoming approach towards those who are forced to leave their homes in search of safety and better opportunities (# 37). He underlines the humanity and dignity of every individual, regardless of their nationality or immigration status, and urges the international community to come together in solidarity to address the root causes of migration and provide support and protection for those in need.

---

159 https://www.vatican.va/content/francesco/en/encyclicals/documents/papa-francesco_20201003_enciclica-fratelli-tutti.html (accessed on 11.03.2025).

Pope's Messages for the World Migration Day

The Church has celebrated the World Day of Migrants and Refugees each year since 1914.[160] Such World Day affords the opportunity to reflect on the conditions of migrants and refugees and gives an incentive to identify their priority needs. It is also essential to combat vigorously the criminal activities which exploit illegal immigrants. In his message, Pope John Paul II, in 1993-94 highlighted the complex realities of migration, addressing the causes and consequences.[161] The message centred on the need for increased awareness and compassionate responses towards migrants. In 1995, 1997, 2009, and 2024 importance was on the status of family unity in migration. The message called on nations to respect and uphold family ties amidst migration processes, and to provide support for families separated by migration. In 1996, 2006 and 2014 the attention was on the dignity of each migrant as a person and the need to protect their rights.

Pope Francis condemns the widespread fear and prejudice towards migrants, which often leads to discrimination, exclusion, and violence against these vulnerable populations. He challenges societies to overcome the mentality of "us vs. them" and instead embrace a culture of encounter, dialogue, and respect for diversity (# 41). The Pope calls on political leaders, policy-makers, and individuals alike to prioritize the common good and work towards building a more inclusive and just society that ensures the rights and dignity of all people, including migrants and refugees (# 141).

Fratelli Tutti serves as a powerful reminder of our shared responsibility to welcome and assist migrants and refugees, recognizing their inherent dignity and worth as fellow human beings (#127). The encyclical calls on individuals and communities to cultivate attitudes of compassion, solidarity, and hospitality towards

---

160 For each year's papal message please refer to, https://www.cliniclegal.org/sites/default/files/2023-04/Papal%20Messages%20for%20the%20World%20Day%20of%20Migrants%20and%20Refugees.pdf (accessed on 26.03.2025). Here one can find the messages from the year 1996 to 2022.

161 https://www.vatican.va/content/john-paul-ii/it/messages/migration/documents/hf_jp-ii_mes_19930806_world-migration-day-93-94.html (accessed on 26.03.2025). Only from 1996 original English version of the message is available in the Vatican site. However, in the following cite messages from 1978 on available. Refer to https://www.vatican.va/content/john-paul-ii/en/messages/migration.index.html (accessed on 26.03.2025).

those who are marginalized and in need of support (# 62, 67, 115-16, 90).

In 1998 to 2000 the messages called for global awareness and responsibility towards migrants and refugees, emphasizing solidarity and humanitarian action (1998), discussing the opportunities and challenges of migration (1999), highlighting the fundamental human rights of migrants, encouraging advocacy against exploitation and discrimination (2000). In the following year 2001 and 2007 the messages linked migration with peace, stressing that migratory movements can promote understanding among peoples if guided by justice and compassion. Promoted peace among diverse cultures and the need for tolerance and respect in host communities. In 2002 urged the Church to play an active role in welcoming, protecting, and advocating for migrants and their rights. In 2003, 2004 and 2013 the messages called on the world to view migrants as contributors to society, advocating for their inclusion and respect in communities, which will foster dialogue, understanding, and harmonious coexistence between cultures.[162] The messages in 2008, 2010-12 called for an inclusive society to visualize a new world, considering the migrants as resource for development and giving them a better future through policies that support fair migration process.

From 2015 to 2020, Pope Francis spoke of migrants who sojourned like the holy family, in hope seeking a better world to be welcomed, protected, promoted and integrated. In 2021-23, he focused on the importance of solidarity and inclusivity calling for a broader sense of community that embraces diversity and works towards the common good. The Pope highlighted the intrinsic connection among all human beings and the importance of compassionate outreach to migrants. Pope Francis has chosen "Migrants, missionaries of hope" as the theme for the 2025 World Day of Migrants and Refugees. Reflecting on "the courage and tenacity of migrants and refugees, who bear daily witness to hope in the future... contributing to revitalising their faith and promoting interreligious dialogue based on common values. They remind the Church of the ultimate goal of this earthly

---

[162] If the "dream" of a peaceful world is shared by all, if the refugees' and migrants' contribution is properly evaluated, then humanity can become more and more of a universal family and our earth a true "common home." Message of the Holy Father John Paul II for the 90th World Day of Migrants and Refugees, 2004, #6.

pilgrimage—the attainment of our future homeland."[163] Overall, the papal messages across these years consistently illuminate human dignity, rights, solidarity, peace, and the importance of welcoming migrants. They call the Church and society to action, encouraging advocacy, understanding, and the recognition of the contributions migrants make to communities.

Catholic teaching has a long and rich tradition in defending the right to migrate. Based on the life and teachings of Jesus, the Church's teaching has provided the basis for the development of basic principles regarding the right to migrate for those attempting to exercise their God-given human rights. Catholic teaching also states that the root causes of migration–poverty, injustice, religious intolerance, armed conflicts–must be addressed so that migrants can remain in their homeland and support their families.

In modern times, this teaching has developed extensively in response to the worldwide phenomenon of migration. Pope Pius XII reaffirms the Church's commitment to caring for pilgrims, aliens, exiles, and migrants of every kind in his apostolic constitution *Exsul Familia*, affirming that all peoples have the right to conditions worthy of human life and, if these conditions are not present, the right to migrate. "Then–according to the teachings of [the encyclical] *Rerum Novarum*–the right of the family to a life worthy of human dignity is recognized. When this happens, migration attains its natural scope as experience often shows.

While recognizing the right of the sovereign state to control its borders, *Exsul Familia* also establishes that this right is not absolute, stating that the needs of immigrants must be measured against the needs of the receiving countries: Since land everywhere offers the possibility of supporting a large number of people, the sovereignty of the State, although it must be respected, cannot be exaggerated to the point that access to this land is, for inadequate or unjustified reasons, denied to needy and decent people from other nations, provided of course, that the public wealth, considered very carefully, does not forbid this.

---

163 https://www.vaticannews.va/en/pope/news/2025-03/missionaries-of-hope-theme-world-refugee-day-2025-pope.html#:~:text=The%20Dicastery%20for%20Promoting%20Integral,attainment%20of%20our%20future%20homeland.%E2%80%9D (accessed on 11.03.2025).

Thus, migration presents complex challenges to the international community and individual states, leading to stricter migration laws and reinforced border controls. This shift focuses more on the problems immigrants create in host countries rather than the situation of emigrants in their home countries. Migration is increasingly seen as a social emergency, which persists despite current restrictions. Prudence in handling this issue should not lead to exclusion, as many migrants suffer and their dignity must be respected. International cooperation is needed to foster political stability and eliminate underdevelopment, addressing the economic and social imbalance driving migration. The Church views migrants through Christ's perspective, aiming to integrate them into a community based on justice and acceptance of God's word, without ethnic or social distinctions.

The host society's attitude is crucial, and public opinion should be informed about the migrants' true situation and the risks they face. It is important to combat racism and xenophobia and ensure legislation across countries is harmonized for a balanced solution. Administrative regulations should not unjustly force people into illegal situations, and adequate protection should be provided to those at risk if they return to their homeland. Thus, the Catholic Church's social teaching on migrants, as articulated in papal documents and writings over the last century, highlights the dignity of migrants, the need for solidarity, and the moral responsibility of nations to welcome and protect those in need.

Migration in the Light of the Word of God: The word of God and the Catholic social teaching it inspires illuminate an understanding–one that is ultimately full of hope–that recognizes the lights and shadows that are a part of the ethical, social, political, economic, and cultural dimensions of migrations between our two countries. The word of God and Catholic social teaching also bring to light the causes that give rise to migrations, as well as the consequences that they have on the communities of origin and destination. As Christians and believers, we are invited to put the social teachings of the Church into practice and accompany and assist the migrants and refugees.

7

Responses of National and International Agencies

Some of the major stakeholders who are supposed to attend to the issues of the migrants are the national governments. They are duty bound to gather information, collect necessary data, examine the state of affairs of the migrants and plan their response. In addition to the governments and their departments, there are national and international agencies who are trying to comprehend the reality of the migrants and respond to them. This section focuses on these aspects.

At the outset it needs to be stated that the Indian government does not have a policy on migration. Similarly, it does not have a policy on refugees. Due to this, its response has been ad hoc to say the least. Over the last 40 years, the civil society of India has been demanding for a policy on migrants. But the government has not come out with a policy on migrants. Here too, there are discriminations by the government of India. Yes, there are policies and programs for international migrants. There is a separate ministry for international migration but there is nothing for internal migrants. The issues of the internal migrants subsumed under the labour departments of state and central governments. Diagram 1 highlights some of the complaints of the migrants. There is no one area where they are subjected to ill-treatment. Here let us see what the government of India should do to protect them.

Diagram 1: Complaints of Labour Migrants[164]

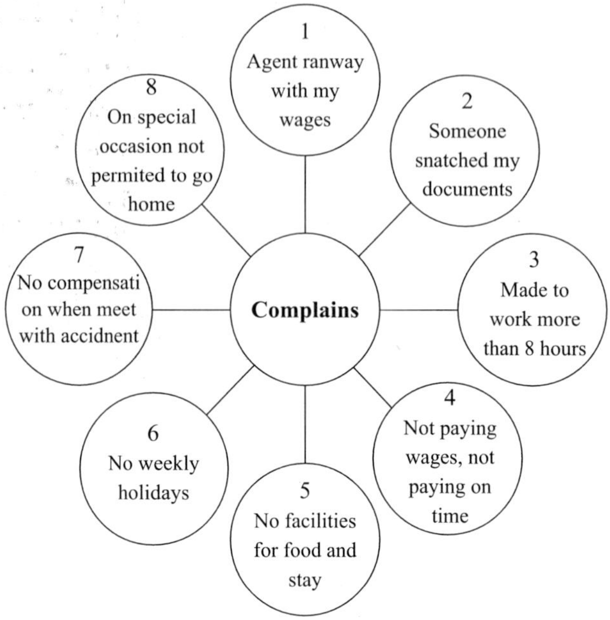

Response of Indian Government

In the 5th Section of this book, we elaborately examined the socio-economic and political implications of distressed migrants in India. We also presented the some of the efforts by the government to address the issues of the migrants. Here we will further elaborate upon these efforts and related them with the international responses.

Committees and Commissions

In India, several commissions and committees focus on labor welfare, including the National Commission on Labour (NCL), the Standing Committee on Labour, and various committees within the Ministry of Labour & Employment. The NCL was established twice, in 1966 and 1999, to review labor laws and suggest improvements. The Standing Committee on Labour, part of the Indian Parliament, also oversees labor-related matters. The table below highlights the commissions that were set up to look into the rights of the labourers and migrants.

---

[164] XISR. Migrant Labour Pre-Departure Training Module. Xavier Institute of Social Research: Patna. 2023.

S. No.	Commission/Committee	Objectives
1	Royal Commission on Labour, 1931[165]	To point out the need for systematic collection of labour statistics and collect data on labourers in India.
2	Labour Investigation Committee, 1946	To provide information about various social security schemes for labourers
3	National Commission on Labour, 1969	To proife detailed examination of all aspects of labour problems, both in the organised and unorganised sectors.
4	National Commission on Rural Labour, 1991	To gather information on the implementation of social legislation for rural labourers protection.
5	National Commission on Labour, 2002	General objectives: to bring labour reforms Specific objectives: (i) to suggest rationalization of existing laws relating to labour in the organized sector; and (ii) to suggest 'umbrella' legislation for ensuring a minimum level of protection to the workers in the unorganized sector. (iii) Also take into account rapid technological changes, globalization of economy, liberalization of trade and industry and emphasis on international competitiveness and the need for bringing the existing laws in tune with the future labour market needs and demands.
6	Working Group on Migration, 2017	To provide recommendations to try and build on the existing frameworks, to urge the implementation, to the maximum possible extent, of many relatively progressive statutory provisions and government schemes.

International Migrants and the Government of India

The Government has taken several initiatives like the *Pravasi Bhartiya Bima Yojana* (PBBY) and Pre-departure Orientation Training (P-DOT) in ensuring that Indian migrant workers undertake safe migration,

[165] As early as 1931, that is, much before independence the Royal Commission on Labour was constituted to address the issues of the labourers, who are also often migrants.

have decent working and living conditions in destination countries, are aware of their rights and have access to social security, reintegration of returnee migrants. various welfare schemes of the Government. To emphasise, Ministry also launched the '*Surakshit Jaayen, Prashikshit Jaayen*' – Go Safe, Go Trained' campaign in 2018 to raise awareness and facilitate safe and legal migration.

The *Pravasi Bhartiya Bima Yojana* (PBBY) is a mandatory insurance scheme aimed at safeguarding the interests of ECR category Indian migrant, that is, Emigration Check Required workers going for employment to 18 ECR countries. The scheme provides an insurance cover of INR. 10 lakh and other benefits in case of accidental death or permanent disability leading to job loss, at a nominal insurance premium of INR 275/- for two years or INR 375/- for three years validity. PDOT, that is, Pre-Departure Orientation and Training is a one-day training programme on soft skills imparted by Ministry of External Affairs (MEA) in collaboration with National Skill Development Corporation (NSDC), State Governments and other stake holders.

India Missions/Posts abroad also utilize the Indian Community Welfare Fund (ICWF) to provide the following services/assistance to the Indian diaspora in distress on a means tested basis:

(i) Transportation of mortal remains to India or cremation with the consent of the family;
(ii) Emergency medical care;
(iii) Legal assistance;
(iv) Boarding and lodging; and
(v) Air passage for stranded Indians.

The Government has established various mechanisms to enable Indian workers abroad to reach out in case they need any assistance. The workers can contact the Missions/Posts through various channels like walk-in, email, multilingual 24x7 emergency numbers, grievance redressal portals like MADAD, that is, MEA in Aid of Diaspora in Distress, CPGRAMS, that is, Centralized Public Grievance Redress and Monitoring System, eMigrate, that is, *An app by Ministry of External affairs* to ensure your safe employment abroad. and social media etc.

Pravasi Bhartiya Sahayata Kendras (PBSK) have been set up in New Delhi and at Dubai (UAE), Riyadh & Jeddah (Kingdom of

Saudi Arabia) and Kuala Lumpur (Malaysia) to provide assistance, guidance and counselling to Indian workers in distress.

Protection of vulnerable category migrants: The protection and welfare of Indian Emigration Check Required (ECR) category female migrant workers [including Domestic Sector Workers (DSWs)] is a foremost priority for MEA. In this direction, as additional safeguard measures, only the State-run recruitment agents are authorized to undertake the recruitment of ECR category female workers (including DSWs) for overseas employment. Further, a minimum age criteria of 30 years was put in place of ECR category female workers and DSWs for overseas employment to protect them from exploitation.

Indian Missions/Posts abroad have also established 24X7 Helplines including Toll Free Helplines, WhatsApp numbers and have launched mobile Apps to enable Indian nationals contact respective Indian Missions/Posts when in distress or in emergency situation.

The Government has also taken extra-ordinary measures for evacuating Indians from conflict zones. The Government evacuated 28594 Indian nationals from conflict-affected nations since 2021. However, the Ministry does not have data regarding the number of Indians who might have returned on their own, from conflict-affected nations.

Steps Taken by the Government with Regard to Migrant Labour during the Lockdown

During the lockdown, several inter-state migrant workers tried to return to their home state. Due to the suspension public transport facilities, migrants started walking towards their home state on foot. Subsequently, buses and Shramik special trains were permitted by the central government subject to coordination between states.[166] Between May 1 and June 3, more than 58 lakh migrants were transported through specially operated trains and 41 lakh were transported by road. Measures taken by the government to aid migrants include:

Transport: On March 28, the central government authorised states to use the State Disaster Response Fund to provide accommodation to traveling migrants. States were advised to set up

[166] [3] Order No. 40-3/2020 DM I (A), Ministry of Home Affairs, April 29, 2020, https://prsindia.org/files/covid19/notifications/4233.IND_Movement_of_Persons_April_29.pdf.

relief camps along highways with medical facilities to ensure people stay in these camps while the lockdown is in place.

In an order issued on April 29, the Ministry of Home Affairs allowed states to co-ordinate individually to transport migrants using buses. On May 1, the Indian Railways resumed passenger movement (for the first time since March 22) with *Shramik Special trains* to facilitate movement of migrants stranded outside their home state. Between May 1 and June 3, Indian Railways operated 4,197 Shramik trains transporting more than 58 lakh migrants. Top states from where Shramik trains originated are Gujarat and Maharashtra and states where the trains terminated are Uttar Pradesh and Bihar.[167] Note that these trends largely correspond to the migration patterns seen in the 2011 census data.

Food Distribution: On April 1, the Ministry of Health and Family Affairs directed state governments to operate relief camps for migrant workers with arrangements for food, sanitation and medical services. On May 14, under the *second tranche of the Aatma Nirbhar Bharat Abhiyaan*, the Finance Minister announced that free food grains would be provided to migrant workers who do not have a ration card for two months. The measure is expected to benefit eight crore migrant workers and their families. The Finance Minister also announced that One Nation One Ration card will be implemented by March 2021, to provide portable benefits under the PDS. This will allow access to ration from any Fair Price Shop in India.

Housing: The *Aatma Nirbhar Bharat Abhiyaan* also launched a scheme for Affordable Rental Housing Complexes for Migrant Workers and Urban Poor to provide affordable rental housing units under PMAY. The scheme proposes to use existing housing stock under the Jawaharlal Nehru National Urban Housing Mission (JnNURM) as well as incentivise public and private agencies to construct new affordable units for rent. Further, additional funds have been allocated for the credit linked subsidy scheme under PMAY for middle income group.

---

[167] "Indian Railways operationalizes 4197 "Shramik Special" trains till 3rd June, 2020 (0900hrs) across the country and transports more than 58 lacs passengers to their home states through "Shramik Special" trains since May 1", Press Information Bureau, Ministry of Railways, June 3, 2020, https://pib.gov.in/PressReleseDetail.aspx?PRID=1629043.

Financial Aid: Some state governments (like Bihar, Rajasthan and Madhya Pradesh) announced one-time cash transfers for returning migrant workers. UP government announced the provision of maintenance allowance of Rs 1,000.00 for returning migrants who are required to quarantine.

Directions by the Supreme Court

The Supreme Court reviewed the situation of migrant labourers stranded in different parts of the country, noting inadequacies and lapses in government response to the situation.

- On May 26, the Court issued an order to the central and state governments to submit a response detailing all measures taken by the respective governments for migrant labourers.
- On May 28, the Court provided interim directions to the central and state/UT governments for ensuring relief to the migrant workers: i) no train or bus fare should be charged to migrant workers, ii) free food should be provided to stranded migrants by the concerned State/UT government and this information should be publicised, iii) States should simplify and speed-up the process of registration of migrants for transport and those registered should be provided transportation at the earliest and iv) the state receiving migrants should provide last-mile transport, health screening and other facilities free of cost.
- Reiterating their earlier directions, on June 5 (full order issued on June 9), the Supreme Court further directed the Central and state/UT governments to ensure: i) transportation of all stranded workers wanting to return to their native place is completed within 15 days, ii) identification of migrant workers is immediately completed and the process of migrant registration be decentralised to police stations and local authorities, iii) records of returning migrant labourers are kept including details about place of earlier employment and nature of their skills, and iv) counselling centres are set-up at the block level to provide information about central and state government schemes and other avenues of employment. The Court also directed the state/UT governments to consider withdrawal of prosecution/complaints under Section 51 of

Disaster Management Act filed against migrant labourers who allegedly violated lockdown orders.

Migration as Reflected in Indian Policy before COVID-19[168]

Policy responses to internal migration have emerged in the context of India's federal governance system, where the duties of the union and the states are specified in the Constitution. The union government is responsible for matters related to interstate migration and is thus empowered to coordinate between the states. However, labour welfare, trade and social security fall in the concurrent list, which the union and the states must jointly address. Other policy areas such as education and health, which Indian citizens are universally entitled to, are usually addressed through centralised schemes designed and (at least partially) funded by the union government, with the states acting as implementers. States can also have their own schemes, but usually within a centralised statutory framework.[169]

In Indian policy, migration is strongly linked to work and is therefore governed by the Ministry of Labour and Employment through national legislation, of which the most crucial is the Interstate Migrant Workmen (Regulation of Employment and Conditions of Service) Act, 1979 (ISMWA). Labour-centric governance regards migrants as a subset of informal employment but has not yet resolved the challenges of delivering social protection to unorganised workers. For this purpose, the National Commission for Enterprises in the Unorganised Sector (NCEUS) has, over time, recommended the registration of migrant workers by local governments (Kannan, 2020). Additionally, the MGNREGS, introduced by the Ministry of Rural Development, seeks to reduce rural–urban migration by improving livelihood opportunities in source areas.

Other policy areas have also addressed migration. Areas related to human development like education, health and nutrition are designed for universal access. Under the Right to Education Act, 2009, the *Samagra Shiksha Abhiyan* (SSA), India's overarching public education scheme, accords priority to migrant children and

---

168 Mukta Naik. Tracing Internal Migration Governance in India Through a 'Mainstreaming' Lens. Sage Journal. Vol. 9, Issue 1. 2024.

169 Mukta Naik. Tracing Internal Migration Governance in India Through a 'Mainstreaming' Lens. Sage Journal. Vol. 9, Issue 1. 2024.

provides for seasonal hostels and residential schools at source of migration, worksite schools at destination of migration, peripatetic education volunteers and tracking of children through migration cards to improve continuity in education. The National Education Policy 2020 also explicitly recognised migrants among the disadvantaged groups that require attention and concurred with the SSA's emphasis on alternative and innovative education facilities for the children of migrants. Similarly, the Integrated Child Development Services (ICDS) scheme, which is inclusive of all children up to the age of six, specifically provides for migration certificates so that children can avail continued services at destination locations (CPR & UNICEF, 2021).

However, migrants' access to social welfare is uncertain because the logic of universalisation and eligibility contradict each other in practice. Localised political considerations introduce eligibility requirements like documentation to prove domicile (i.e., local residence status) for many government schemes. These too vary in design and implementation across levels of government, and rural and urban jurisdictions. Welfare schemes formulated and funded by the Government of India tend to be more universal, while state schemes tend to include domicile as eligibility criteria (CPR & UNICEF, 2021). For example, even though created under the centrally legislated Building and Other Construction Workers (Regulation of Employment and Conditions of Service) Act, 1996, state government-run boards for such workers prefer to register only their own residents for social welfare benefits and often render interstate migrants ineligible (Roy et.al., 2017).

Until very recently, access to the Public Distribution System (PDS) was also dependent on location, and beneficiaries could take rations only from specific fair price shops (Government of India, 2017a). At the same time, policy has been focused on preventing migration by strengthening rural development (Deshingkar et.al., 2008). Questions around how cities can be more inclusive towards migrants remain inadequately addressed (Kundu & Saraswati, 2012).

In 2016–17, soon after UN Habitat put out the New Urban Agenda, and in response to the growing momentum on implementation of the Sustainable Development Goals (SDGs), the Ministry of Housing and Urban Poverty Alleviation (now merged with the Ministry of Housing and Urban Affairs) constituted an inter-ministerial Working Group on Migration to 'address the impact of migration on housing, infrastructure and livelihoods.'[170] Affirming the right to free movement within India, the Working Group Report, submitted in 2017, emphasised the need for an overarching legislative framework that would include migrants as regular and contractual workers rather than distinguishing them as a specific category. The report proposed a comprehensive law for unorganised workers along the lines of NCEUS recommendations. Additionally, the report made a number of specific suggestions to extend social protection to migrants and facilitate access to services, especially food security, healthcare, education, skilling and employment, and financial inclusion. It suggested augmenting rental housing and hostels to address housing issues, and strengthening of data systems to measure internal migration (Government of India, 2017a).

The Economic Survey of 2016–17 also included a chapter on internal migration and labour mobility, which it considered central to the policy objective of leveraging India's demographic dividend (Government of India, 2017b). However, these recommendations and publications did not translate into substantive policy shifts.

Policy and Governance Responses to the COVID-19 Migrant Crisis

The COVID-19 migrant crisis did not spur a cohesive policy response to internal migration. The NITI Aayog convened a subgroup on the issue of migrant labour and drafted a policy document, which was not finalised. The union government's efforts to condense a large number of labour legislations into four comprehensive labour codes on occupation safety, health and working conditions, wages, and industrial relations, were also completed during the pandemic. These codes are intended to simplify access to justice. While they do expand social security to all organised and unorganised workers, including interstate migrant workers, they have been criticised for reducing protections for migrants by excluding intrastate migrant workers and raising threshold limits to

[170] It is rightly pointed out "The housing of migrant workers is a critical issue. While migrants are often held responsible for the growth of slums in cities, there is limited evidence to support that contention. Nevertheless it is also true that there are also limited options for migrant housing at destination."

exempt smaller units.[171] However, though they have been notified, the new labour codes are yet to come into effect. Besides these, numerous other policy reactions emerged as a result of the crisis. These built on existing schemes and frameworks and were located at multiple levels of government and across various sectors.

Registration and Tracking

Benefits under the ISMWA, the main legislation for interstate migrants, are dependent on a system of registration for migrants. Even though is it now subsumed under the Code on Social Security, 2020, the necessity for systems to register and enumerate migrants is well understood in the policy imagination. This notion was strengthened when stakeholders were unable to enumerate, locate and deliver relief to vulnerable migrants during the COVID-19 crisis. Several state governments relaxed criteria for registration under the Building and Other Construction Workers Act, which was a key conduit for direct cash transfers during the pandemic. At the central level, the Ministry of Labour and Employment's e-Shram digital portal for self-registration of unorganised workers became operational in August 2021, with the capacity to link individual beneficiaries.

At present, the website shows that nearly 293 million workers have registered on the portal (Government of India, 2024). While the portal is expected to ease the process of welfare delivery, it is not yet clear how interstate migrants will be specifically identified and serviced. Detailed migration tables from the 2011 Census are not available, the 2021 Census is delayed, and the National Sample Survey Organisation does not collect regular data on migration. Without a reliable statistical database, registration information cannot be triangulated. At the state level, several source states have intensified efforts to register migrants at source through panchayat-level registers.

For example, Jharkhand has institutionalised this in its Safe and Responsible Migration Initiative (SRMI) that uses registries to connect migrant households to social schemes. States like Jharkhand,

---

[171] D. Varma, K. Bharadkar & R. Mehrotr. India's new labour codes fail migrant workers whose vulnerability was highlighted by lockdown crisis. September 27, 2020. Scroll.in https://scroll.in/article/974137/indias-newlabour-codes-fail-migrant-workers-whose-vulnerability-was-highlighted-by-lockdown-crisis.

Chhattisgarh, Uttar Pradesh (UP), Bihar and Odisha also captured skills data about return migrants during the pandemic in order to design responses for livelihood support and skilling. Though it is not yet clear how this data is being specifically utilised, capturing the magnitude of return migration has helped craft politically astute policies for source states to reduce interstate migration.

A notable example here is UP's emphasis on local employment generation through industrial revival policies like the UP Industrial Investment and Employment Promotion Policy 2017, the UP Micro, Small and Medium Enterprises Promotion Policy 2017, and the One District One Product Policy, which extends the national Make in India policy. Beyond the purview of work and employment, in Maharashtra, the Women and Child Development Department (WCD) has developed a Migration Tracking System (MTS) that tracks seasonal women and child migrants from vulnerable source areas to their work destinations to provide continued service delivery for schemes related to maternal and child health and nutrition. This system was piloted in six districts and is now being scaled up across the state. Distinctively, it reverses the state's response from a demand-driven system to an accountable supply-driven system.

Portability

Labour migration experts have long recommended that all rights-based benefits and entitlements to Indian citizens must be portable, that is, access to welfare must be ensured regardless of location. The COVID-19 pandemic increased public awareness about the benefits of universally accessible health and nutrition services. This became particularly evident when government officials and civil society personnel engaged in relief operations realised that a large proportion of return migrants were women and children, shifting their perceptions away from the image of the single male migrant that had hitherto dominated the internal migration discourse. In response, tracking systems evolved to provide a practical mechanism to ensure portability in delivering universal public services. Similar mechanisms for portability are needed to ensure that children migrating with parents can access education.

While Sarva Shiksha provisions have been used by states like Odisha to run seasonal hostels for left-behind children of migrants to continue education, past efforts by states like Maharashtra and Gujarat to issue education cards to enable continuity in education across source and destination locations require revival and streamlining.[172]

Since 2021, the WCD in Maharashtra has been exploring how the Multi-Tasking Staff (MTS) can help improve schemes run by other state government departments and has shared learnings with the Ministry of WCD at the central level to improve the Poshan Tracker, an app that helps monitor anganwadis under the ICDS scheme. Such efforts demonstrate how the pandemic provided an impetus for experiences from new initiatives to travel across horizontal and vertical governance layers. During the pandemic, food security for unorganised workers who had faced livelihood losses was an urgent concern, and within this group, migrants were particularly affected. Previously, PDS rations, which a large number of poor Indians depend on for nutritional sustenance, could only be accessed at the specific fair price shop to which a household's ration card was linked. Seasonal and circular migrants suffered from food shortages during the pandemic because of this lack of portability; moreover, the scheme did not account for households being split across locations.

Initially notified in 2019, the implementation of the One Nation One Ration Card (ONORC) scheme was accelerated during COVID-19 as an important initiative to improve PDS access to seasonal migrants by addressing portability as well as enabling individual household members to access rations separately from households. The central government directed the states to distribute free food grains as part of its pandemic relief package. By using Aadhaar, a biometric-enabled unique identification system, as the backbone, state governments were directed to seed ration card databases with Aadhaar information. This was a precursor to implementing the One Nation One Ration Card (ONORC) scheme, whereby ration card holders could access supplies at any fair price shop in the country.

At present, the scheme has been adopted by all 36 states and union territories in India, and as of March 2023, over a billion transactions have taken place under it. Evaluations show that these numbers are still minuscule and the scheme faces logistical challenges, though Delhi has emerged as a state where a large number of interstate migrants have been able to access rations (Dalberg, 2022). Despite its

[172] CPR & UNICEF. Assessing Portability of Social Protection & Services among Child Migrants in India. Centre for Policy Research and UNICEF. 2021.

teething troubles, ONORC is a big step towards removing mobility-based exclusion.

Facilitation

Before the pandemic, many civil society organisations had been running migrant resource centres (MRCs), where reliable information and networks were provided to migrant workers. The Odisha government ran MRCs in destination locations. In Tirupur, Tamil Nadu, civil society organisations partnered with employers and local governments to do the same. The pandemic has revealed that the MRC model can address problems like information asymmetry and facilitate delivery of services to migrants. Additionally, common service centres (CSCs) were set up to connect citizens to government services through agents.

A different model for facilitation is being piloted in Ranga Reddy district of Telangana, where 9,000 migrants from Odisha working in brick kilns are being delivered a coordinated package of services through collaboration among the departments of education, health and family welfare, women and child welfare, labour, civil supplies, and law and order at the district level, with the support of corporate social responsibility (CSR) funding and civil society organisations. Another robust example of facilitation is the Government of Odisha's provision of a cadre of Odia teachers to accompany seasonal migrant households to destination states like Telangana and Tamil Nadu. These teachers ensure that children can continue education in their mother tongue. Such facilitation, in which non-governmental organisations (NGOs) play a significant role, goes a long way in ensuring uninterrupted education.

Housing

Recognising the need for cities to cater to seasonal migrants, the Ministry of Housing and Urban Affairs announced the Affordable Rental Housing Complexes (ARHC) scheme in 2020. The scheme invited private concessionaires to retrofit unoccupied public housing for rental purposes and build new affordable housing stock. Nearly 30 retrofitting projects and one greenfield project are in the pipeline, according to the scheme's official website.

India has developed several welfare policies to support migrants, targeting housing, healthcare, and skill development:

- **Pradhan Mantri Awas Yojana (PMAY):** Launched in 2015, this initiative aims to provide affordable housing to both urban and rural poor, including migrants, with a target of ensuring adequate housing by 2022 (Ministry of Housing and Urban Affairs, 2021).
- **One Nation One Ration Card (ONORC):** This scheme allows migrants to access food grains from any Public Distribution System (PDS) shop across India, helping ensure food security for those who frequently relocate for work (Department of Food & Public Distribution, 2020).
- **Affordable Rental Housing Complexes (ARHC):** A recent initiative designed to provide affordable rental housing for migrants and the urban poor, addressing their accommodation needs (Ministry of Housing and Urban Affairs, 2023).

Evaluation of the Effectiveness of These Policies: The effectiveness of these policies has been mixed:

- **Access to Benefits:** Migrants often struggle with bureaucratic hurdles and documentation requirements. For example, the ONORC scheme has faced challenges in implementation, with many unable to access rations due to the lack of a permanent address (P. Reddy, 2021).
- **Skill Development:** The PMKVY has had varied success. Despite offering training, job placement remains a challenge due to low demand in certain sectors. Many trained migrants have struggled to find employment (R. Patel, 2022).
- **Healthcare Access:** PMJAY provides substantial coverage, but many migrants are unaware of their eligibility or face difficulties accessing services due to the informal nature of their work and lack of a stable address (A. Sinha, 2021).
- **Housing:** The ARHC scheme holds promise but requires effective implementation and transparency in the allotment process to ensure migrants can access affordable housing (S. Sharma, 2023).

Over the years, many studies have revealed the hard fact that the migrant labourers find it extremely difficult to access the government schemes. This is due to a combination of factors, including a lack of awareness, bureaucratic hurdles, and the non-portability of entitlements. Many schemes are designed for specific locations, making it challenging for migrants to access them when they move. State specific schemes are focused on specific social groups. But even in accessing central government schemes, the migrants find it very difficult to access them.

Diagram 2: Poor Access to Central Schemes for Interstate Migrant Workers

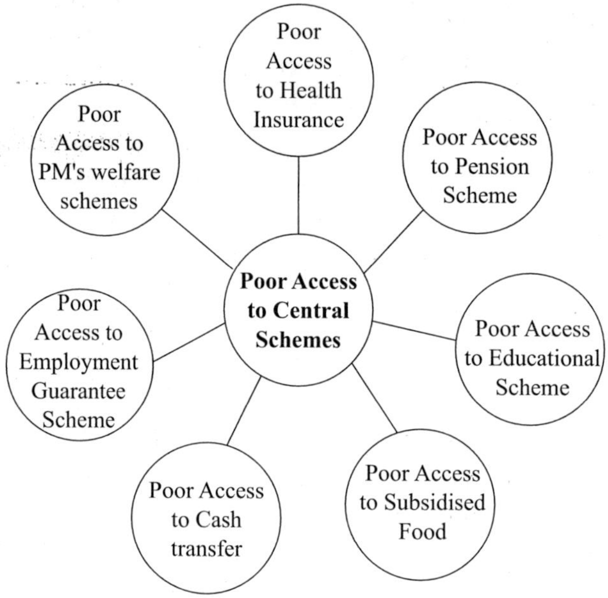

Call to Action for Policymakers to Enhance Support Systems for Migrants in India[173]

1. **Improve Access to Welfare Benefits:** Policymakers should streamline the implementation of welfare schemes like the One Nation One Ration Card (ONORC) to ensure that all migrants, regardless of their residential status, can access essential services. This involves reducing bureaucratic hurdles, improving documentation processes, and enhancing awareness among migrants about available benefits (P. Reddy, 2021).
2. **Address Housing Needs:** The Affordable Rental Housing Complexes (ARHC) scheme must be implemented with greater transparency and efficiency. Policymakers should

[173] Addressing Migration Challenges in India: A Call for Enhanced Policy Support. Centre for Development Policy and Practice. 27-09-2024.

ensure that rental housing is not only affordable but also meets the needs of migrants by being located near employment hubs and providing basic amenities (S. Sharma, 2023).

3. **Support Migrants in Legal and Social Integration:** Providing legal aid and facilitation centers, similar to those in Kerala, can help migrants navigate administrative challenges and understand their rights. Such centers should be expanded to cover more regions and offer comprehensive support, including legal assistance, job placement services, and access to social welfare schemes (J. Thomas, 2021).
4. **Mitigate Economic Vulnerabilities:** Migrants working in low-paying or informal sectors are particularly vulnerable to economic shocks. Policymakers should develop safety nets, such as emergency financial support or unemployment benefits, to protect these workers during economic downturns, such as those experienced during the COVID-19 pandemic (ILO, 2021).

Double Standard by the Government: There is clear indication of double standard in the response to the internal and external migrants. The Ministry of External Affairs (MEA) set up the India Centre for Migration (ICM) formerly known as Indian Council for Overseas Employment, as a 'not for profit' society under the Societies Registration Act 1860, in July 2008. The India Centre of Migration (ICM) serves as a research think-tank to Ministry of External Affairs (MEA) on all matters relating to international migration and mobility. But there is nothing like this for internal migrants.

With a staggering 450 million internal migrants (as of the 2011 census), migration has become integral to the political economy of India. India also has the largest diaspora in the world, numbering 18 million people. The modes, institutions, and ideological underpinnings of migration governance vis-à-vis both internal and international migration have witnessed substantial shifts and continuities ever since the ascendance of the NDA (National Democratic Alliance) led Modi government in 2014.[174]

---

[174] Irudaya Rajan and Anand Sreekumar. *Selective, Reactive and Liminal: An Overview of India's Migration Governance Over the Past Decade.* On Matters of Constitution. 21 April 2024.

Despite these gains, the internal migration governance has been hindered by a culture of ad-hocness, unsatisfactory policies and implementation as well as the invisibilization of dependents. Consider the legislative landscape in the first instance. The Interstate Migrant Workmen's Act of 1979 is the sole legislation which explicitly tackles the question of internal migration in India. However, this legislation is confined to contractor-driven migration. Informal migrant workers' rights are subsumed under varying labour laws which suffer from weak implementation. These weaknesses continue to persist. Rarely one hears about the issues of the migrants.

International Agencies and Policies

The International Labour Organization (ILO) Policies: The International Labour Organization (ILO) is devoted to promoting social justice and internationally recognized human and labour rights, pursuing its founding mission that social justice is essential to universal and lasting peace. Since 1919 the ILO brings together governments, employers and workers of 187 Member States, to set labour standards, develop policies and devise programmes promoting decent work for all women and men.

Several key policies have been established to ensure fair and equitable treatment for migrant workers.

1. **ILO Convention No. 97 (1949):** Article 1: Requires that migrant workers and their families be given employment terms no less favourable than those of nationals. Article 6: Mandates measures to prevent discrimination against migrant workers in employment and working conditions.
2. **ILO Convention No. 143 (1975):** Article 1: Ensures protection for migrant workers from discrimination, with equal rights and opportunities. Article 8: Guarantees that migrants receive the same work conditions and benefits as nationals.
3. **ILO Recommendation No. 151 (1975):** Paragraph 3: Advocates for the protection of migrant workers from discrimination and access to social services. Paragraph 12: Stipulates that migrant workers should have equal rights regarding working conditions and health and safety protections.

4. **ILO Global Compact for Migration:** Objective 6: Aims to facilitate fair recruitment and decent work conditions for migrant workers. Policy 6.2: Emphasizes transparency and respect for migrant workers' rights in recruitment and employment practices.
5. **ILO General Principles and Operational Guidelines:** General Principle 1: States that all migrant workers should have access to decent work, fair wages, safe conditions, and social protection. Operational Guideline 1.2: Calls for laws and regulations to protect migrant workers from exploitation and abuse.
6. **ILO's Fair Migration Agenda:** Principle 2: Ensures fair recruitment practices, protection against abuse, and equal workplace treatment. Principle 5: Promotes social protection and labour rights for all migrant workers, regardless of their migration status.

These policies aim to safeguard the rights of migrant workers, prevent discrimination, and ensure that they receive fair treatment and adequate protections in their host countries. Thus, from 1919 till date the ILO has been advancing social justice and decent work.

United Nations (UN) Policies and Frameworks

A. Global Compact for Safe, Orderly, and Regular Migration (GCM): Objective 7: Protect migrants from exploitation, ensure access to basic services, and promote safe working conditions. 2. Objective 8: Encourage the positive economic and social contributions of migrants and Diasporas. 3. Objective 15: Ensure migrants access essential services like education, healthcare, and social protection.

B. Global Compact on Refugees (GCR): 1. Solidarity and Responsibility Sharing: Framework for fair responsibility sharing among countries, addressing the needs of refugees and host communities. 2. Comprehensive Responses: Emphasizes holistic support for refugees, host communities, and tackling displacement causes.

C. UNHCR Mandate: 1. Protection: Ensure refugees' rights are upheld and they receive necessary assistance. 2. Durable

Solutions: Facilitate voluntary repatriation, local integration, and third country resettlement for refugees.

D. International Organization for Migration (IOM) Policies: 1. Migration Governance Framework (MGF): Guidance on effective migration management, policy coherence, and international cooperation. 2. Migration and Health Framework: Addresses migrant health needs and promotes inclusive healthcare policies.

E. UN Sustainable Development Goals (SDGs): 1. Goal 10: Reduce inequality and promote inclusive growth and decent work for all, including migrants. 2. Goal 16: Foster peaceful and inclusive societies, justice for all, and effective institutions in migration contexts.

F. UN Treaty Bodies and Special Procedures: 1. ICESCR: Guarantees just and favourable working conditions, including non-discrimination for all workers. 2. CERD: Obliges elimination of racial discrimination and guarantees equality before the law, including for migrants.

United Nations Development Programme (UNDP)

Migration and displacement crises often arise due to inadequate national and local government capacities, fragmented responses, and insufficient resources and coordination. In 2016, the UN General Assembly adopted the New York Declaration for Refugees and Migrants, committing to safe, orderly migration and addressing refugee needs, including easing host country pressures and expanding third country solutions.

UNDP committed to tackling the root causes of displacement, integrating migration into development policies, and supporting affected communities. At the 2016 World Humanitarian Summit, commitments were made to improve displacement responses, support durable solutions, and enhance financial and political backing for host countries. The 2018 adoption of the Global Compact for Migration, the Global Compact on Refugees, and the GP20 Plan of Action offers UNDP a chance to enhance its development focused approaches to migration and displacement.

UNDP's migration and displacement approach rests on the following three focus areas of the Strategic Plan:

a) Eradicating poverty in all its forms and dimensions, and keeping people out of poverty;

b) Accelerating structural transformations for sustainable development, especially through innovative solutions that have multiplier effects across the Sustainable Development Goals;
c) Building resilience to crises and shocks, in order to safeguard development gains.

The 2030 Agenda and the Sustainable Development Goals form the overall framework for implementation of the migration and displacement agenda. In line with this, UNDP's development approach to migration and displacement focuses on **Four Specific Areas as follows**:

1. Addressing Root Causes
2. Integration into Plans
3. Resilience Based Development
4. Community Based Re/integration

UNDP also strengthens policies through data and analysis, ensuring all displaced and migrant groups receive their rights and protections.

International Organization for Migration (IOM)

Adopted the Global Compact for Migration in December 2018, which is a nonbinding agreement, aims to improve migration governance, address challenges, and strengthen migration's role in sustainable development. It supports international cooperation, offers policy options for states, and allows flexible implementation based on national contexts. IOM works to ensure the dignity, safety and protection of people in the most challenging crisis response contexts in the world.

Established in 1951, IOM is part of the United Nations System and stands as the leading intergovernmental organization in the field of migration. With 175 member states, a further 8 states holding observer status and offices in 172 countries, IOM is dedicated to promoting humane and orderly migration for the benefit of all. It does so by providing support to migrants across the world, developing effective responses to the shifting dynamics of migration and providing advice on migration policy and practice.

The organization collaborates with governmental, intergovernmental and non-governmental partners to improve the resilience of people on the move, particularly those in situations of vulnerability. It also works closely with governments to manage all forms of mobility, and their impacts. This work includes operations in some of the most complex emergency settings in the world.

The IOM Constitution recognizes the link between migration and economic, social and cultural development, as well as to the right of freedom of movement.

UNICEF works around the world to help protect the rights of migrant and displaced children. "We provide life-saving humanitarian supplies in refugee camps. We run child-friendly spaces – safe places where children on the move can play, where mothers can rest and feed their babies in private, where separated families can reunite. We support national and local governments to put in place laws, policies, systems and services that are inclusive of all children and address the specific needs of migrant and displaced children, helping them thrive." The commitment of UNICEF towards migrant children are laudable. "A child is a child, no matter why she leaves home, where she comes from, where she is, or how she got there."

UNICEF believes, "Children should be safe from violence and be able to grow up with their families. They shouldn't have to miss school or be scared to visit the doctor. They shouldn't be discriminated against because of where they come from. They should be able to feel at home – wherever they find themselves and wherever home is. It also believes and works, "Children around the world, regardless of where they are from and why they have left their homes, should be treated the same."

UNICEF also collects, analyses and disseminates data and gathers evidence about the situation and individual experiences of children and young people on the move. It helps to keep families together. It works to end child immigration detention by helping governments put in place alternative community - and family-based solutions. It works with governments, the private sector and civil society. It empowers children and youth on the move with cutting-edge solutions, partnering with them and making their voices heard. It strongly believes and works, "The solutions exist, and they're attainable."

UNESCO is a specialized agency of the United Nations, working for world peace through global cooperation in education, science, culture, and communication. Its functions include promoting access to quality education, fostering scientific collaboration, safeguarding cultural heritage, and advocating for freedom of expression and information.

In addition to its regular work, UNESCO contributes to the well-being of migrants by promoting their cultural rights, ensuring access to education, and facilitating social integration. Though UNESCO does not have the mandate to work directly among the migrants it works to create a policy environment that supports migrants and recognize their qualifications. UNESCO places emphasis on the human face of migration. It addresses the implications of the movement of people within its fields of competence, firmly embedding its interventions in a human rights framework.

UNESCO's contribution emanates from its mission to promote the building of peace, eradication of poverty, sustainable development and intercultural dialogue through education, the sciences, culture, communication and information. The Organization places emphasis on the human face of migration and addresses the implications of the movement of people within its fields of competence, drawing on relevant human rights principles and standards. Its activities and programmes, carried out in collaboration with a large range of partners, including intergovernmental organizations, civil society groups and universities.

Global Migration Data Analysis Centre (GMDAC): Established in Berlin in September 2015 at the invitation of the Government of Germany, the International Organization for Migration's Global Migration Data Analysis Centre (GMDAC) responds to the call for better international migration data and analysis.

Timely data on migration are often scarce, making it difficult for decision-makers to develop effective migration policies. Even when migration statistics do exist, policymakers may not make full use of them, because data are often scattered between different stakeholders and between different countries. Sharing data effectively is often just as important as collecting data. Poor presentation of migration data can contribute to misperceptions about migration, and can distort public opinion. Better analysis and communication of the data are needed to promote a balanced debate on migration issues.

Objectives

1. Strengthen the role of data in global migration governance (e.g. Global Compact for Migration, Sustainable Development Goals).
2. Support IOM Member States' capacities to collect, analyse and use migration data.
3. Promote evidence-based policies by compiling, sharing and analysing IOM and other sources of data.

Office of the United Nations High Commissioner for Human Rights (OHCHR)

OHCHR works to promote, protect and fulfil the human rights of all migrants, regardless of their status, with a particular focus on migrants in vulnerable situations and at most risk of human rights violations. OHCHR promotes a human rights-based approach to migration, which places the migrant at the center of migration policies and governance, and seeks to ensure that migrants are included in all relevant national action plans and strategies, such as plans on the provision of public housing or national strategies to combat racism and xenophobia.

The Global Compact for Safe, Orderly and Regular Migration (A/RES/73/195), is the first intergovernmental agreement, prepared under the auspices of the United Nations, to cover all dimensions of international migration in a holistic and comprehensive manner. It was adopted at an intergovernmental conference on migration in Marrakesh, Morocco on 10 December 2018. Member States agreed to review the progress made at the local, national, regional and global levels in implementing the Global Compact at an International Migration Review Forum (IMRF) through a State-led approach and with the participation of all relevant stakeholders at the UN General Assembly. OHCHR has welcomed the Global Compact as an important framework for improved migration governance that puts migrants and their human rights at the centre and that provides a significant opportunity to strengthen human rights protection for all migrants, regardless of status.

OECD for Migration: The Organisation for Economic Co-operation and Development is an international organisation that works to build better policies for better lives. We draw on more than 60 years of experience and insights to shape policies that foster prosperity and opportunity, underpinned by equality and well-being. OECD works closely with policy makers, stakeholders and citizens to establish evidence-based international standards and to find solutions to social, economic and environmental challenges. From improving economic performance and strengthening policies to fight climate change to bolstering education and fighting international tax evasion, the OECD is a unique forum and knowledge hub for data, analysis and best practices in public policy. Its core aim is to set international standards and support their implementation – and help countries forge a path towards stronger, fairer and cleaner societies. It provides data and policy matters to OECD countries on migration.

Thus, it is a fact that both national and international governments and agencies have been trying to respond to the issues of the migrants. But their efforts do not seem to lead to the expected result. Interestingly, the Ministry of External Affairs in India has established the India Centre for Migration (ICM)[175] to conduct research and policy analysis on migration. This is also a fact while some of them work for and with them, some of them work only for them which does not allow them to be committed fully.

[175] It has been observed that many of these institutions are started in India with big fanfare and lofty ideas. But they do not serve the purpose of those population for whom these were set up. Often time, these institutions become employment centres for the upper caste and upper class children who have the opportunity for better English language learning and computer skills. They usually have technical skills but not social skills. These institutions are shown as centres that are created for the betterment of the migrants. But they achieve mighty little.

8

Christian Responses to Distressed Migration

Migration has been and is a historical and contemporary phenomenon. Migration has been and is an economic and social reality. Migration takes place in a political and cultural context. Migration and especially that of the distressed labour migration is a religious and spiritual fact. It also raises, ecclesiological and missiological questions, inviting all, especially those who believe in Jesus Christ to ponder over this dark reality and find measures to respond to the migrants in distress. Since, Jesus himself was a migrant,[176] he reflected in his life and mission, the distress and hope the labour migrants are subjected to in the present context. From this background, this sections tries to examine the Christian responses to distressed labour migrants.

Questions Christians should raise: In a grim situation such as that of the distressed labour migrants, these are the questions one raises which are more important than the answer one gets. Raising right question will lead to search for answer. Hence, as Christians these are the questions we need to raise.

- Who are the migrants?
- Why are they migrating?
- Why does God care so much about migrants?

[176] This book as stated in the preface and introduction, focuses squarely on the distressed labour migrants of India and the world. While doing so, it also relates the discourse with Jesus being a migrant in his birth, life and death. It is this parallel which this book tries to foreground for discourse and course of action.

- What does justice look like for these "strangers" among us?
- What do migrants have to do with me/us, and what difference could I/we possibly make in the lives of migrants?
- Why is migration such a conflictual issue for Christians, with some Christians and churches offering them sanctuary and others not in favour of the migrants?
- Is there a 'biblical' way to view migrants?
- Is there a 'religious' way to view migrants?
- Is there a 'spiritual' way to view migrants?
- How do we as Christians respond to the issues of the migrants?

Church's Response to Migrants[177]

As we have seen in the foregoing discussion, the issues of migration and refugees are currently major global challenges. They are also important aspects of the teachings of the Catholic Church, as evidenced by the many recent Church documents. These issues also came up in discussions at the Synod on Synodality convened by Pope Francis. In this section, we attempt to analyse the contemporary migration phenomena and its consequences leading to pathways for accompanying and assisting them. A common theme of various efforts to understand and respond to the issues of the migrants is the need to sensitize societies to the specific plight of migrants, threatening to marginalize them. Accompanying the migrants and caring for their integration has been a running theme of the Church's response to the migrants. For the Church this is both as a task and also as opportunities for host communities to actualize solidarity, fraternity, and cultural exchange.[178]

It will not be out of place to state that "All the world seems to be on the move." This was something that Pope Francis had in mind, when he claimed that "**perhaps one can speak of a third war, one fought piecemeal, with crimes, massacres, destruction.**" Thus, this was not a rhetorical ploy but an attempt to draw attention to these phenomena. These circumstances, combined with devastating poverty

[177] Though we have titled this section as Christian Response to Migrants, we due to our ignorance are concentrating only on the responses of the Catholic Church. We apologise to all the other churches.

[178] Rafal Cekiera and Mateusz. The Catholic Church and Its Approach towards Refugees and Migrants: An Analysis of the Presence of Migration Issues in the Synod's Syntheses on Synodality. Religions 2024, 15 (10).

and a lack of life prospects, provoke many to make risky attempts to find better places to live.[179]

The Synod on Synodality convened by Pope Francis provided an excellent opportunity to reflect on the perceptions of refugee phenomena, migration, and relations with newcomers among local churches. This topic was not addressed incidentally; it was frequently mentioned in synodal syntheses prepared by individual episcopates. A clear confirmation of the importance of this issue was the prayer vigil on October 19, 2023, which concluded the 13th plenary session of the Assembly of the Synod of Bishops led by Pope Francis. Francis encouraged them to pray that God would make Christians Good Samaritans towards all migrants and refugees.

The Church has been invited to '**Offer Hospitality without Grumbling**', taking clue from the Old Testament, e.g., "**Love the stranger then, for you were strangers in the land of Egypt**"—(Dt 10:19). Christian teaching on migrants and refugees does not leave aside the concrete social reality experienced at any given historical moment. While upholding the fundamental principle of protecting the life and dignity of every person without exception, regardless of origin, religion, or other peculiarities, the Catholic Church, in its official documents, repeatedly acknowledges that it is not always easy to "see Christ in the newcomer."

However, this does not in any way change the obligation to adopt open-minded attitudes and co-create a human brotherhood that transcends all boundaries. This requires courage—but it also requires concrete action based on an unprejudiced interest in the fate of another ("Accepting Christ..." pt. 120). Based on the challenges of a particular time, the Catholic Church's annual messages for World Migrant and Refugee Day are also updated with migration teaching.

In the report of the Assembly of the Synod of Bishops one of the suggestions emphasized the importance of the Catholic Church in the process of integrating migrants in societies affected by xenophobia and the distrust of migrants. This recommendation came about due to the heterogeneous experiences of individual countries in dealing with modern international mobility and its consequences. In analysing the synodal syntheses, five main themes were identified within which migration and refugee issues were addressed:

[179] Pope Francis warns on 'piecemeal World War III'. BBC. 13 September, 2014.

1. The awareness of the importance of the problem among the faithful;
2. The marginalization of refugees and migrants;
3. Meeting "face to face" with migrants and refugees;
4. Refugees and migrants as an opportunity for the Catholic Church;
5. Intra-church problems related to migration.

The synodal efforts led to the following understanding and call for action: The contemporary migration phenomena are seen by the Holy See as a *kairos,* a specific "sign of the times." Hence it is crucial that individual local churches skilfully recognize this challenge. It was recognised that there is the weakness of ties with such people within religious communities and calls for the creation of pastoral care with a stronger emphasis on integration issues.

Caring for those on the margins of society is at the very core of the Church's ministry. The synod documents devote considerable space to people who may feel excluded from society. Some churches recognised the need to reach out to those particularly vulnerable to social exclusion, such as the following: "women, members of the LGBTQIA+ community, Travellers/Mincéirs, migrants and refugees."[180] If this has to take place, there has to be pastoral reforms. It also demanded the Catholics to establish contacts and ties with specific refugee and migrant groups. Further, there was also the felt need to create open spaces for encounters with people who do not feel a connection with the Church. Church also feels the need to create 'neutral ground', places designed to allow dialogue with people of all faith and no-faith.

The Christian community over the years recognised this fact that refugees and migrants often experience social exclusion. The first fundamental task is to recognize their situation, that is, to recognize the plight of the migrants and their vulnerability to marginalization. This sensitization is meant to lead not just to some form of charitable involvement in aid but to authentic encounters with them. It should lead to integration—a complex, multidimensional process. It is relevant not only in the situation of an inter-religious encounter but also among coreligionists with different cultural

[180] LGBTQI Refugees. Women's Refugee Commission.

backgrounds, coming from different countries. If this is lacking, the result can be various tensions or even ghettoization. On the other hand, integration practices are self-generating and also bring much satisfaction and concrete fruits to the host community.

Taking this conversation further, John Paul II wrote in his Message for the 88th World Day of Migration in 2002, "The parish represents the space in which a true pedagogy of meeting with people of various religious convictions and cultures can be realized. In its various expressions, the parish community can become a training ground of hospitality, a place where an exchange of experiences and gifts takes place. This cannot but foster a tranquil life together, preventing the risk of tension with immigrants who bring other religious beliefs with themselves."[181]

Catholic Ministries Serving Migrants and Refugees

Some Christians even after all these teachings and practices raise questions about the mission to the migrants. It is important to clear this doubt. Catholics serve migrants and other newcomers in accordance with our sincerely held religious beliefs, abiding by the teachings of Jesus Christ, affirming the inalienable rights and dignity of every person, and providing Christian charity as a visible sign of God's love and mercy to those in need.

In the wake of World War II, Pope Pius XII boldly recognized that the "émigré Holy Family of Nazareth, fleeing into Egypt, is the archetype of every refugee family.[182] Pope Francis has said that chapter 25 of Matthew's Gospel, which calls us to **"welcome the stranger," is "a constant admonition to see in the migrant not simply a brother or sister in difficulty, but Christ himself, who knocks at our door.** Consequently, even as we work to ensure that in every case migration is the fruit of a free decision, we are called to show maximum respect for the dignity of each migrant; this entails accompanying and managing waves of migration as best we can,

[181] John, Paul, II. 2002. Message of the Holy Father John Paul II for the World Day of Migrants and Refugees 2002.

[182] *Exsul Familia Nazarethana*. Apostolic Constitution. Pope Pius XII – 1952.

constructing bridges and not walls, expanding channels for a safe and regular migration."[183]

In *Strangers No Longer*, the U.S. and Mexican bishops also aligned themselves with the "religious and social service providers who, without violating civil law, attempt to respond to the migrant knocking at the door" (no. 4). They explicitly encouraged these "signs of hope" by calling on pastors and lay leaders to ensure support for immigrant families, urging communities to offer migrant families "hospitality, not hostility," along their journey, commending Church communities that establish migrant shelters that provide appropriate pastoral and social services to migrants, and urging local dioceses to sponsor pertinent social services for newcomers, particularly affordable legal services (no. 42).[184]

The Services Catholic Organizations Provide to Migrants

The types of services offered by the Catholic and Christian organisations to the migrants vary. But the Church regularly and consistently cooperates in the administration of humanitarian aid with local, state, and federal governments. Church agencies work along with the community based organisations, civil society organisations, non-governmental organisations, etc. They also join the UN and international agencies to respond to the issues of the migrants. At the national, diocesan and parish level, many efforts are made to work for the migrants.

Catholic organizations along the U.S.-Mexico border, for example, may provide a meal, clean clothes, a shower, medical attention, and temporary shelter for newly arrived migrants. Some Catholic organizations also advise recently arrived migrants on the individual steps they can take to reunite with family or reach the location of their immigration proceedings. Catholic organizations provide resettlement and integration services to newly arrived refugees, helping them to find lawful employment, enroll children in school, learn English, and navigate life in their new communities.

Clergy administer the Sacraments to those in immigration detention. Many Catholic organizations across the country provide

---

[183] 'Free to choose whether to migrate or stay'. Pope Francis. World Day of Migrants and Refugees Message 2023.

[184] USCCB. Strangers No Longer: Together on the Journey of Hope. January 22, 2003.

services to noncitizens who have suffered human trafficking. Catholic organizations also provide affordable immigration legal services, helping qualified individuals to naturalize as U.S. citizens, prepare their cases for immigration court, and more. These programs are designed to assist noncitizens with navigating legal obligations placed upon them by the U.S. immigration system and to promote compliance with applicable laws.

Church also is involved in legal assistance to the migrants and making all stake holders aware of various legal restrictions and provisions. For example, Pope Francis stated, "As the Church accompanies migrants and refugees on their journey, she seeks to understand the causes of migration, but she also works to overcome its negative effects, and **to maximize its positive influence on the communities of origin, transit and destination."**[185] This also highlights the need to work in source, transit and destinations.

This needs to be reiterated that the Church does not encourage unnecessary or irregular migration. Church is clear of the fact that its duty is not to encourage or discourage migration. "Ideally, unnecessary migration ought to be avoided; this entails creating in countries of origin the conditions needed for a dignified life and integral development."[186] It is ultimately the individuals, families and communities who want to migrate, need to migrate and forced to migrate. But it is committed to accompany them.[187] Moreover, the Church regularly uplifts the need to address the root causes of migration and provides recommendations in this regard, in addition to the efforts of Caritas International, Catholic Relief Services, and other organisations.

---

[185] Message of His Holiness Pope Francis for the 104th World Day of Migrants and Refugees. 15th August 2017.

[186] Encyclical Letter, 'Fratelli Tutti – On Fraternity and Social Friendship' of the Holy Father Francis. October, 2020.

[187] In the year 2002, when some of us began to work among the migrant domestic workers in New Delhi, we were also caught up in similar situation. Some of the church leaders got irritated and kept on telling the migrant domestic workers mostly from central India not to migrate. But young women migrated in thousands. After understanding their state of affairs in source and destination, we were strongly convinced not to tell them to migrate or not to migrate. But we began to accompany and assist them.

Concrete Commitment to the Marginalised and Migrants

The Church made efforts to convert its social teachings into action in the following manner: During his leadership, Paul VI expected and urged the universal church and its Episcopal 'Conferences' to become a loving and serving church. The following 3 initiatives highlight this fact: 1) Three synods held: in 1969 - Cooperation between the Holy See and the Episcopal Conferences - 1971 – Justice in the World - and 1974 - Evangelization in the Modern World - deal with issues that are related to human development, wellbeing dignity. 2) His address to the national and regional conferences of bishops encouraged and directed them to give the poor and the oppressed central place in their pastoral concerns. 3) Following from these, he established the Pontifical Commission for Justice and Peace in 1967. This commission became the agent through which the church intervenes in justice and peace issues both within the church and in the world. He wrote "to awaken in the people of God full awareness of their mission today. In this way they can further the progress of poorer nations and international social justice, as well as help less-developed nations to contribute to their own development."[188]

International Catholic Migrant Commission: The International Catholic Migration Commission (ICMC) is an international non-governmental organization working in the areas of migration and refugee assistance and advocacy. ICMC was founded in 1951, in the wake of the massive human displacement caused by the Second World War. For nearly 75 years, the International Catholic Migration Commission (ICMC) has operated in many countries to protect and serve, in the name of the Church, uprooted people, including refugees, asylum seekers, internally displaced people, victims of human trafficking and migrants — regardless of faith, race, ethnicity or nationality.

ICMC has a long history of well-established partnerships with the U.S. and other governments, civil society, and other Catholic-inspired groups to serve through advocacy and direct support. In this framework – and since our founding – ICMC has played a key role in international refugee resettlement. With the unprecedented general suspension of funding for the U.S. Refugee Admissions Program and foreign assistance, like many other humanitarian organizations,

[188] Pope Paul VI. *Populorum Progressio*. March 26th, 1967.

ICMC must make the difficult decision to downsize by cutting critical services to refugees and people displaced by war and persecution in several countries in the world. ICMC is complying with the U.S. stop-work orders while looking for ways to overcome these huge challenges.

Even when the funding its work was stopped, ICMC continued to work. The inspiration came from Pope Francis. 'I exhort all the faithful of the Catholic Church, and all men and women of good will, not to give in to narratives that discriminate against and cause unnecessary suffering to our migrant and refugee brothers and sisters. **With charity and clarity, we are all called to live in solidarity and fraternity.'**[189]

Efforts by the Mexican and US Churches to Stand by the Migrants: The Episcopal conferences of Mexico and the US jointly issued the followed document, "Strangers No Longer: Together on the Journey of Hope: A Pastoral Letter Concerning Migration from the Catholic Bishops of Mexico and the United States."[190]

The bishops acknowledge that while "globalization" has led to greater and freer flows of goods, technology, capital, and information, the migration of people has become more restrictive, even as the new world economy requires a more mobile labor pool. The proposed five principles which will guide the Church's view on migration issues.

1. ***Persons have the right to find opportunities in their homeland*:** All persons have the right to find in their own countries the economic, political, and social opportunities to live in dignity and achieve a full life through the use of their God-given gifts. In this context, work that provides a just, living wage is a basic human need.
2. ***Persons have the right to migrate to support themselves and their families*:** The Church recognizes that all the goods of the earth belong to all people. When persons cannot find employment in their country of origin to support themselves and their families, they have a right to find work elsewhere

[189] Letter of The Holy Father Francis to the Bishops of the United States of America. 10 February 2025.

[190] Delivered on the fourth anniversary of Ecclesia in America, January 22, 2003, Washington, D.C., U.S.A., and Mexico City, Mexico.

in order to survive. Sovereign nations should provide ways to accommodate this right.

3. ***Sovereign nations have the right to control their borders*:** The Church recognizes the right of sovereign nations to control their territories but rejects such control when it is exerted merely for the purpose of acquiring additional wealth. More powerful economic nations, which have the ability to protect and feed their residents, have a stronger obligation to accommodate migration flows.
4. ***Refugees and asylum seekers should be afforded protection*:** Those who flee wars and persecution should be protected by the global community. This requires, at a minimum, that migrants have a right to claim refugee status without incarceration and to have their claims fully considered by a competent authority.
5. ***The human dignity and human rights of undocumented migrants should be respected*:** Regardless of their legal status, migrants, like all persons, possess inherent human dignity that should be respected. Often they are subject to punitive laws and harsh treatment from enforcement officers from both receiving and transit countries. Government policies that respect the basic human rights of the undocumented are necessary.

The Pontifical Council for the Pastoral Care of Migrants and Itinerant was a pontifical council of the Roman Curia. It was established by Pope John Paul II on 28 June 1988, and was dedicated to the spiritual welfare of migrants and itinerant people (people travelling from place to place). This council was to bring the pastoral concern of the Church to bear on the special needs of those who have been forced to leave their native land or who do not have one. It also sees to it that these matters are considered with the attention they deserve."

The aim of the council was: Determine and provide, by common agreement and united effort, suitable means and directives to cater to the *spiritual* needs of those members of the faithful who, because of their way of life, are not adequately catered to by the ordinary pastoral ministry of parochial *clergy* or are entirely deprived of it, including migrants, exiles and refugees, foreign students, seafarers and fisherman, air travelers and crews, airport staff and related workers, nomads, circus and travelling show people; develop suitable pastoral programmes to provide for the spiritual life of people in the world of tourism and pilgrimages and all the people using roads and railways or living on the streets.

Documents of Holy Fathers on Migration[191]

Message of His Holiness Pope Francis for the World Day of Migrants and Refugees 2022

Message of His Holiness Pope Francis for the World Day of Migrants and Refugees 2021

Message of His Holiness Pope Francis for the World Day of Migrants and Refugees 2020

Message of His Holiness Pope Francis for the World Day of Migrants and Refugees 2019

Message of His Holiness Pope Francis for the World Day of Migrants and Refugees 2018

Message of His Holiness Pope Francis for the World Day of Migrants and Refugees 2017

Message of the Holy Father Pope Francis (2016) "Migrants and Refugees Challenge Us. The Response of the Gospel of Mercy"

Message of the Holy Father Pope Francis (2015) 'Church without Frontiers, Mother to All'

Message of the Holy Father Pope Francis (2014) 'Migrants and Refugees: Towards a Better World'

Message of the Holy Father Pope Benedict XVI (2013) 'Migrations: Pilgrimage of Faith and Hope'

Message of the Holy Father Pope Benedict XVI (2012) 'Migration and the New Evangelization'

Message of the Holy Father Pope Benedict XVI (2011) 'One Human Family'

Message of the Holy Father Pope Benedict XVI (2010) 'Minor Migrants and Refugees'

---

[191] https://www.cliniclegal.org/sites/default/files/2023-04/Papal%20Messages%20for%20the%20World%20Day%20of%20Migrants%20and%20Refugees.pdf.

Message of the Holy Father Pope Benedict XVI (2009) 'St. Paul, Migrant, Apostle of the Peoples' Message of the Holy Father Pope Benedict XVI (2008) 'Young Migrants'

Message of the Holy Father Pope Benedict XVI (2007) 'The Migrant Family'

Message of the Holy Father Pope Benedict XVI (2006) 'Migrations: A Sign of the Times'

Message of Saint Pope John Paul II (2005) 'Intercultural Integration'

Message of Saint Pope John Paul II (2004) 'Migration with a View to Peace'

Message of Saint Pope John Paul II (2003) 'For a Commitment to Overcome All Racism, Xenophobia and Exaggerated Nationalism'

Message of Saint Pope John Paul II (2002) 'Migration and Inter-Religious Dialogue'

Message of Saint Pope John Paul II (2001) 'The Pastoral Care of Migrants, A Way of Accomplishing the Mission of the Church Today'

Message of Saint Pope John Paul II (2000)

Message of Saint Pope John Paul II (1999)

Message of Saint Pope John Paul II (1998)

Message of Saint Pope John Paul II (1997)

Message of Saint Pope John Paul II (1996) 'Undocumented Migrants'

Effective from 1st January 2017, the work of the council was assumed by the Dicastery for Promoting Integral Human Development.

Caritas Program for Migrants: For 70 years, Caritas has accompanied migrants, refugees, asylum seekers, and internally displaced along their journey. Operating in 200 countries and territories, Caritas confederation is active in the countries of origin of people on the move, promoting programmes aimed at eradicating the causes of migration; it accompanies migrants in the countries they pass through on their journey, offering them food and water, shelter, psychological support and also information about their rights and the dangers they will face along the way; and it welcomes migrants in the countries of arrival, helping them to integrate.

Caritas will also continue advocating with and for them for regular and safe pathways of migration and for enhanced protection, urging governments to recognise their right to citizenship in the host communities and, finally, assisting them in case of voluntary return. And during this COVID-19 pandemic, "Caritas organisations intensified their efforts to ensure that all people on the move were assured of their right to access to care and basic necessities. Caritas also advocates on issues affecting refugees and migrants. We work to build awareness on refugee issues through building local relationships with refugee and migrant groups and through our international partnerships responding to the needs of displaced people."[192] Corresponding to Caritas International located in Rome, there are also national Caritases who carry out similar responses.[193]

International Organisation for Migrants (IOM): The Holy See is the universal government of the Catholic Church and operates from Vatican City State, a sovereign city-state founded following the signing of the Lateran Pacts between the Holy See and Italy on February 11th 1929, whose territory consists of a walled enclave within the city of Rome, Italy. It became an IOM Member State in December 2011. As stated in January 2012 by Pope Benedict XVI in his address to the members of the diplomatic corps last December the Holy See strengthened its longstanding cooperation with the International Organization for Migration by becoming a full member.

This is a sign of the commitment of the Holy See and the Catholic Church, alongside the international community, in the search for suitable solutions to this phenomenon which presents a number of aspects ranging from the safeguarding of the dignity of persons to concern for the common good of both the communities which receive them and those from which they come."

The Director of the IOM Coordinating Office for the Mediterranean and Chief of Mission in Italy is also the Representative

---

192 https://www.caritas.org/caritas-programmes-for-migrants/.

193 It is regrettable to state that the Indian Caritas due to internal and external challenges is not able to do what it was supposed to do or what it was doing. With the imposition of doing away with Foreign Contributions Regulations Act (FCRA) by the present government of India, it has lost the opportunity of drawing support from other Caritases to carry out its works. Due to internal scams and scandals, this organisation is in shambles and not able to fulfil its objectives.

to the Holy See. IOM's main counterpart at the Holy See was the Pontifical Council on Migrants and Itinerant People.

Throughout the years, IOM has worked in close cooperation with the Catholic organizations: in particular with organizations such as the International Catholic Migration Commission (ICMC), Caritas, the Scalabrinians Missionaries, the Capuchin Missionaries, the International Union of Superiors General, Jesuit Migrant Service, and others.[194] These partnerships are focused both on sensitization and information events – such as conferences, meetings with diasporas, etc. – and on on-the-field activities – such as missions in post-conflict countries or the participation in Refugee Resettlement Programmes.

IOM Rome had a long cooperation with the International Union of Superiors General (UISG) in the implementation of the project "Counter-Trafficking Training Programme for Religious Personnel", a six-year project funded by the US State Department's Bureau for Population, Refugees and Migration (PRM) – that allowed more than 500 Catholic women religious in 31 countries in Europe, Africa, South and Central America and Asia to be trained in the prevention and assistance of trafficked victims. The religious trained under this project have established the first inter-congregational worldwide network of Catholic women religious, called "Talitha Kum", meaning in Amharic "Stand up, woman."

In addition to these global forums, organisations, etc., there are also country specific organisations. One such is the 'Goda Grannar', that is, Good Neighbours project in Sweden, which was established in the Autumn of 2015 following the arrival of a large number of migrants in Stockholm. When a local mosque began helping the migrants by providing food and shelter, they were contacted by volunteers from a local church who wished to support them in their work. The collaboration between the groups soon showed that additional forms of help could be provided, such as language classes and a support service offering both legal advice and community information.

---

[194] There are many other organisations and agencies who are working among the migrants. Due to lack of space and lack of knowledge about them, we are not able to profile them here.

Council of Catholic Bishops of India (CCBI) Commission for Migrants

The Catholic Church of India is administered through two organizational structures called the Catholic Bishops Council of India (CBCI) and the CCBI. While the CBCI takes care of the labour issues, the CCBI takes care of the migrant issues. Pastoral care of migrant families was one of the major concerns of the CCBI after the implementation of the Pastoral Plan in 2013. The 74th Executive Committee meeting of the CCBI held at Delhi and the 75th Executive Committee meeting held at Bangalore decided to have Migrant Commission for the CCBI. The members of the 29th Plenary Assembly held from 31st January to 8th February 2017, Bhopal voted for the Migrant Commission. The Migrant Commission of the CCBI was established on 2nd May, 2017. This Commission closely works with the International Catholic Migration Commission, Rome.

Some of the objectives are: a) To provide pastoral care, support, help, guidance, counselling and assistance for all categories of refugees and migrants in India, like interstate and cross boarder migrants; b) To form animators, formators and trainers for the pastoral care of the migrants and refugees; c) To network with various types of government and non-governmental agencies for the betterment of the migrants and refugees in our country; d) To facilitate and promote job opportunities for migrants and monitor the minimum and just wages are implemented to all migrant workers; e) To organise awareness programmes about forced labour and human trafficking and to give assistance to the migrants who are the victims of forced labour and human trafficking, etc.

Global Catholic Sisters are actively involved in assisting migrants, offering support and advocacy on issues like family separation and anti-immigrant sentiment. They provide direct services, such as shelter, food, and legal assistance, and advocate for policies that protect migrants' rights. Additionally, they engage in public education and outreach to counter fear and promote empathy towards migrants.

Many women religious either as individuals or as members of their congregations work among the migrants in various parts of India. They also join the diocesan and regional forums of the Catholic

Church to respond to the issues of the migrants. Some of them also align with other religious organisations at the local, parish, diocese and national levels.

VIVAT International: 25 Years of Faith in Action. In 2025, VIVAT International, an organization of the Divine Word Society (SVD) marks 25 years of transformative advocacy for justice, peace, and sustainable development. As a faith-based network rooted in local communities and active on the global stage, it is celebrating a legacy of courage, compassion, and commitment and renewing its mission for the years ahead. VIVAT International was a creation of the Divine Word Missionaries and the Missionary Sisters Servants of the Holy Spirit along with 12 religious congregations in the year 2000. This is a non-governmental organisation that advocates the cause of the migrants and the marginalized at the United Nations.[195]

Don Bosco for Migrants (DB4M)[196] is an initiative of the Salesian Provincial Conference of South Asia for collaboration and networking of the efforts of the Salesian Family in India to reach out to migrant workers. Most of the provinces have setup "Migrants Desks" and launched various initiatives to address the plight of migrant workers.

Following their charism, the Salesians began reaching out to children living on the streets, creating shelters near railway and bus stations. Children from various states across India were found in major cities such as Delhi, Kolkata, Mumbai, Chennai, and Bangalore. Currently, they are supporting over one lakh children through Child Care Institutions (CCIs) across India. From this foundation sprang the migration ministry which was the outcome of the National YaR Seminar on the theme "Migrant Youth/Children in the Unorganized Sector," which was held in Guwahati in March 2012. This theme was revisited in February 2015 as part of the broader theme "Reaching the Unreached - the 18+ Young at Risk" for the YaR National Seminar of 2016.

At the Don Bosco Bicentennial Salesian Family Congress in September 2015, a call was made for the entire Salesian Family to

---

[195] In the year 2010, Prakash Louis was instrumental in organising a three day consultation in the Indian Social Institute, Bengaluru on the theme of migration based on which concrete action plans were worked out and followed up.

[196] DB4M Ministry with Migrants in India A Framework for Action. dbyarforum.org.

unite in addressing the concerns of migrants in India. This call was promptly taken up by the Salesian Provincial Conference of South Asia (SPCSA) for follow-up action. They also have a national helpline for the migrants.

DB4M focuses on the safety, well-being, and dignity of migrant workers in India. DB4M reaches out to vulnerable internal migrants across various sectors, including construction, brick kilns, loaders and unloaders, housekeeping, domestic work, garment manufacturing, sanitation, massage parlours, spas, malls, salons, and the hotel industry. Currently, it operates 43 migrant help desks across India, with 33 managed by the Don Bosco Fathers and the remaining desks run by other religious organizations and NGOs.

Migrant Assistance and Information Network (MAIN)[197] is the outcome of the felt-need for a concerted, collective and innovative response to reach out to the distress migrant workers; inter-state and intra-state. Being essentially a partnership model, MAIN would work in collaboration with individuals, NGOs / CSOs / CBOs, institutions, religious congregations, dioceses, networks, etc. at various levels. This was an initiative taken by the Jesuits of South Asia.

It works closely with state governments by developing a replicable and sustainable model of Accompanying, Serving and Advocating for the cause of distressed migrants. MAIN visualizes itself becoming a state-run programme eventually to address the issues of distress migrants in the long run across India. The objectives of MAIN are: a) To accompany the distress migrants by setting up a helpline system, which will be a credible rallying first point of contact for distress migrants; b) To serve the distress migrants by responding to their distress calls and assisting them with various services, primarily through partners; c) To advocate for the causes of distress migrants with all relevant stakeholders, including government, by analysing the distress calls and report generated, gaps in services/ entitlements, and also critical challenges being faced by them.

Its structure is as follows: 1) Central Hub – based in New Delhi; 2) Zonal Hubs – one based in Bagaicha, Ranchi and the other in ISI, Bengaluru to coordinate the various efforts; 3) State Hubs – there are

---

[197] www.mainindia.org.

at present 22 state hubs[198] located in various states of India. Each of the Hub would be the pivot around which the action takes place at the ground level, reaching out to the distress migrants through link person/s from among migrant workers and to assist them with various services to the level possible.

Like the Global Sisters – India, VIVAT International, DB4M and MAIN, there are other church agencies and organisations who collaborate and network with church, religious, ngos, movement and trade unions, etc. Organisations, institutions and agencies who form a broader network are: CBCI, CCBI, Diocesan migrant commissions, OMIs, SAJ, SDBs, Jesuits, Sacred Heart Brothers, OFM, SVD, FMA, MSMHC, UFC, SCN,[199] from the faith based organisations. Along with these, there are also coalition with secular organizations like Save Tirupur, Ajeevika Bureau, Apna schools, Pratham, Nirman Mazdoor Panchayat Sangh, Delhi, Uorgnaised Workers Federation - TN, National Federation Unorganised and Migrant Workers - Delhi, Bandkam Shramik Sankalan Samiti -Vipulji,[200] Gujarat. Thus, on a conservative note, there are over 300 organizations part of the local, district, state and national level migrant protection forums.

The World Council of Churches

The World Council of Churches is a fellowship of churches which confess the Lord Jesus Christ as God and Saviour according to the scriptures, and therefore seek to fulfil together their common calling to the glory of the one God, Father, Son and Holy Spirit. It is a community of churches on the way to visible unity in one faith and one eucharistic fellowship, expressed in worship and in common life in Christ. It seeks to advance towards this unity, as Jesus prayed for his followers, "so that the world may believe." (John 17:21). The World Council of Churches (WCC) is the broadest and most inclusive among the many organized

---

[198] There is the Bihar Migrant Hub where Prakash Louis works as state coordinator along with other staff. Though Bihar Migrant Hub is supposed to work among and for migrants moving out of Bihar, due to its contacts, it is able to assist migrants from all over India.

[199] These are some about whom, we have some information from the Catholic Church of India. There are many others, who work among the migrants whose responses are acknowledged here with gratitude.

[200] There are also many individuals, institutions, agencies who work among the migrants from various faith based, social concern based organisations. Their contributions are also recognised.

expressions of the modern ecumenical movement, a movement whose goal is Christian unity. One of the areas of interventions by the WCC is the issue of migrants through its affiliate churches.

The Mission from the Margins solidarity programme facilitates and encourages theological reflection and action on issues brought about by the increasing migration and movements of people. While migration has always been a fact of life, it raises new economic, political, cultural and ecclesial concerns in today's globalized world. New forms of migration, including trafficking, development-induced displacement, and climate-induced displacement threaten the human dignity of millions of people.

Migration in a globalized world raises questions about interfaith relations, identity, justice, racism, advocacy and *diakonia*. The World Council of Churches seeks to engage and challenge the churches in their work with migrants, including refugees, internally displaced people and victims of trafficking. As the connections between xenophobia and racism are particularly strong, it emphasizes understanding new migration phenomena in a framework of transformative justice, which grew out of the WCCs work on overcoming racism..

Africa-Europe Forum Calls on Churches to Enhance Protection of Migrants

The Second Africa-Europe Ecumenical Forum on Migration was held 17-21 March in Addis Ababa, Ethiopia, organized by the All Africa Conference of Churches and the Churches' Commission for Migrants in Europe (CCME). The forum built on the outcomes of the first forum held in Hamburg, Germany, in March 2023. "We affirm that migration is an integral part of humanity, yet it remains an area fraught with injustices," reads a communique released by the forum. "We remain steadfast in opposing the criminalization and weaponization of migration and resisting migration management policies that disregard human dignity and safety."

The forum discouraged exploitative migration practices that hinder many from experiencing the love and goodness of God. "We noted the growing frustration among a significant proportion of young Africans who are seeking every possible avenue to migrate in pursuit of employment and better living conditions," reads the communique.

Muslim Organisations Working among the Migrants

Interfaith efforts between Chilkur Balaji Temple in Hyderabad and the Helping Hand Foundation help achieve shared community health goals. (WNV/Helping Hand Foundation)

One voluntary organization in Hyderabad, the Helping Hand Foundation (HHF), has had a significant impact in the city, especially among minorities.

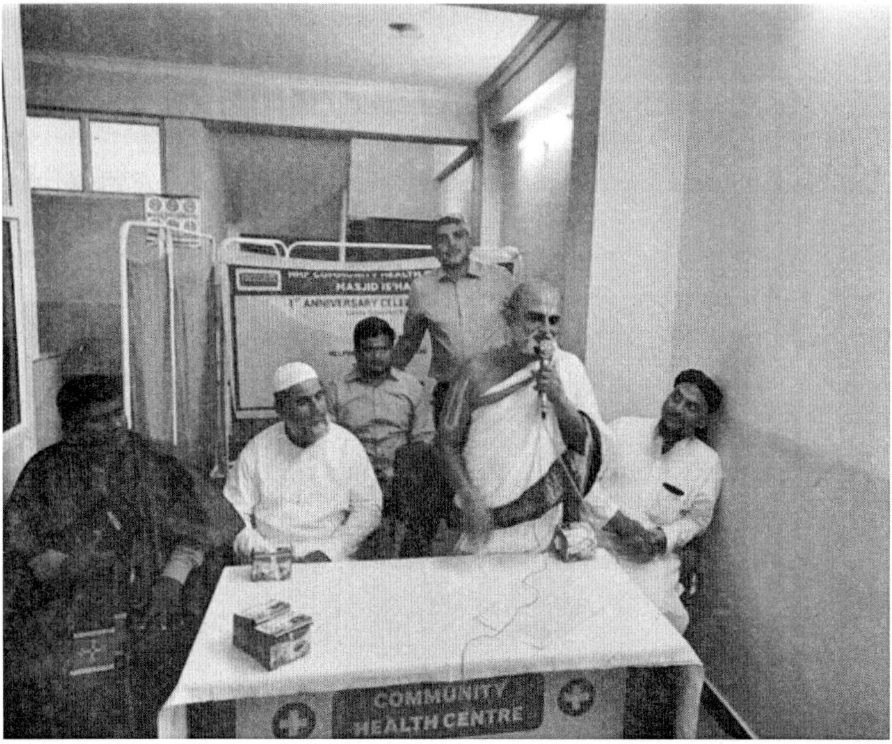

Islamic Relief is a faith-based relief and development agency working to save and transform the lives of some of the world's most vulnerable people. Established in 1984, we now work in over 45 countries assisting individuals, families and communities through emergency response and development projects that typically help over 10 million people each year.

Hindu Organisations Working among the Migrants

Hindrise Social Welfare Foundation is working on providing healthcare, education, basic amenities, and legal assistance to Pakistani Hindu refugee families in India. We are performing our operations in the Majnu ka Tila camp.

Aajeevika Bureau is a public service organisation committed to protecting the rights and well-being of migrant workers in India's vast informal workforce. Aajeevika was conceived in response to the growing, all-pervasive reality of migration becoming central to the survival of rural poor. Despite their enormous contributions to India's economic prosperity, migrant workers remain on the margins – they earn meagre wages, work and live in precarious conditions, lack legal rights and do not avail of basic social security or services. Aajeevika Bureau seeks to bring lasting change in these conditions confronting migrant workers and their communities – both in their rural homes and in their urban destinations. Aajeevika Bureau though is not a typical Hindu organisation, its main team members are Hindus but move beyond religion to work for the migrants.

Khalsa Aid is a non-profit Sikh humanitarian organization that provides disaster relief, keenly supports refugees, and tirelessly works to aid communities globally. Founded in 1999, it operates under the principle of selfless service, no matter who one is.

Mobile Creches: Set up in 1969, Mobile Creches' runs day-care programs for children of migrants working in construction sites across Delhi NCR (Gurgaon, Ghaziabad, Noida). The centres focus on health, nutrition and education of these children.

Jan Sahas: In the last 15 years, Jan Sahas has worked with 1 million+ migrant communities to ensure their social protection and safe migration. Their efforts are towards reducing forced labour conditions by raising awareness within the communities, helping them access social schemes, rehabilitation and bring system reforms. Jan Sahas currently works in 48 districts across India.

9

Recommendations and Conclusions

In the foregoing pages, we tried to see, observe, understand and articulate the issue of migration and the lives and the struggles of the migrants of the world in general and that of India in particular. As a case study, we examined the state of affairs of the distressed labour migrants of Bihar. We tried to profile the issues of the migrants from a social, economic, political, educational, cultural, spiritual, biblical, theological, ecclesiological, missiological point of view so that we get a fair picture of the lives and struggles of distressed migrant labourers. We do not claim to have a comprehensive understanding of this hard reality. But it is an attempt to spell out these so that our individual and collective efforts to accompany and assist them is on sound ground, based on facts and figures, motivated by a positive sense of their liberation and emancipation.

In this final section of this book, we will reiterate some of the observations and recommendations and make some concluding remarks. These recommendations are not new. Many individuals and institutions have been making recommendations based on their experience and studies carried out on migrants. Moreover, these recommendations are made not from the point of view of seeing women as objects but as subjects whose rights and dignify need to be the point of debate and program of action. Here these recommendations are made to retell those recommendations so that actions follow.

Build Synergy Between Migration and Development Policies and Programs[201]

- labour legislation should be enforced more strictly, with necessary simplification and modification of laws where necessary.
- panchayats could act as a resource pool for migrants residing in their area, maintaining a register of migrant workers and working with NGOs to cut transaction costs and upgrade the workers' skills.
- a labour market authority should be set up to monitor the labour markets of the major labour-importing countries, carry out negotiations on labour contracts, and study the nature of emerging skill requirements.
- the 1983 Emigration Act should be liberalised to bring it into line with current market conditions, and to remove the motive for recruitment agents to operate outside of the law
- advocacy campaigns should aim to address stereotypes and misapprehensions about migrants and to raise their political voice.

Promoting Human Security to Prevent Exploitative Migration. The Following Approaches are Needed

- to approach the dynamic processes of exploitative migration;
- to develop inter-regional and inter-state[202] networks for information sharing and coordinated actions;
- to develop a good data base so that policies and programs could be based on hard facts;
- to combine with internet networks, personal contacts permitting the sharing of human experiences, and;
- to identify target groups in developing common strategies to address the issues of distressed migrants anywhere.

---

[201] Ravi Srivastav, et.al. Internal Migration in India and the Impact of Uneven Regional Development and Demographic Transition across States: A Study for Evidence-based Policy Recommendations. Institute for Human Development: New Delhi. 2020.

[202] For instance, there are over 4,000 labour migrants from Bhagalpur district of Bihar alone in Goa. They are paid better than Bihar but their safety and security, dignity and rights are not upheld. If the Government of Bihar and the Government of Goa or their labour departments make an Memorandum of Agreement (MoA), then this can be brought under safe and regulated migration.

Women, Gender and Migration

Poverty and attendant issues of powerlessness mediate women's migration. While gender provides the conceptual tool for mapping differential experiences of social reality, by identifying poverty and migration as significant axes around which social relations and process unfold. There is a complex layers of needs, networks and choices that come into play in poverty-driven migration.

In the given patriarchal social milieu of Bihar, India and the world, it is imperative that one understands the vulnerability of women and girl children and put social, economic and legal measures to protect their rights and dignity. Women are vulnerable in their original location, transit and destination. Distressed migrants are also subjected to this. But women are doubly vulnerable. Hence, a comprehensive understanding and measures need to be put in place.

- There is the need to interrogate perspectives that focus on the issue of voluntariness, as well as those that give a determining role to economic structures, thereby reducing migration to a passive response.
- Need to focus on structural and ideological factors, especially state policies, forming the contexts of migration.
- Conceptualise women's migration not merely in terms of degradation or improvement in women's social marginality, but as a process of restructuring of gender relations.
- Since many women migrate to work as domestic workers outside their countries, some nations like Sri Lanka, Indonesia and Philippines may get branded as 'nations of servants.' Similarly, some states like Jharkhand, Chhattisgarh and Odisha may get branded as 'women domestic workers' state.'
- For the international women migrants, the India Centre for Migration organises pre-departure training and awareness programs, workshops, etc. But this is absent for the internal migrants. It is recommended that both the central and state governments mandate this to the labour department and include the civil society organisations to engage in this preparation.

Employment-Based Migration: A system that is transparent and that protects the rights of workers should be formulated specifically for distressed migrants. Within this, these are recommended:

- Five kilograms of grains per person and one kilogram of chana per family per month for two months for migrants who are not state card beneficiaries nor covered by the National Food Security Act. Or at least, the labourer and or his family finds work.
- Mahatma Gandhi National Rural Employment Guarantee Scheme (MGNREGS) opportunities for those who return to their native place. If not for ever but at least as long as they are in their homes and not migrate.
- Nation-wide implementation of the One Nation One Ration Card scheme at the earliest, thus, enabling national portability of the ration card.
- Affordable Rental Housing Scheme for migrant workers under the Pradhan Mantri Awas Yojana (PMAY). The ILO in its study in 2020, unearthed the fact that migrant workers were themselves marginal owners with slim profit margins, and were not in a position to fully compensate for the loss of wages or waive rent payments.
- Skill enhancement for migrants according to their ability and experience so that they are able to find better paid work to save themselves and their families.[203] This will not be successful as long as there is no delivery by the stakeholders and access by the migrants. The Niti Ayog or the erstwhile Planning Commission of India itself has come out with an elaborate document on "Empowering Migrant Workers through Skill Development and Livelihood Generation: Best Practices from States and Districts."[204] Niti Ayog highlights one initiative in Katihar district titled, *Jeevika Yuva Paramarsh Sah Sansaadhan Kendra* Initiative. If this is true and successful, similar ones can be replicated.
- Often time it has been observed that skill development is mostly oriented towards international migration. For

[203] For more on this, refer to ILO. Skills for migrant workers. 22 April 2024.

[204] Niti Ayog. 2020.

instance, Skill Development Initiative for Potential Migrants from the North-Eastern States of India was a pilot project in eight North-Eastern states in partnership with International Organization for Migration (IOM). The project has designed seven International Vocational Qualifications (IVQs) in hospitality sector for use in India and established a Skills Training Certification Resource Centre in Guwahati (Assam) in 2012. But there is nothing like this for internal migrants. Youth both boys and girls work in hospitality sector in a big way from the northeast. But they have to enroll themselves in a highly expensive private institutions or learn the job while working. This places restrictions on their opportunity to get the job and earn a living for themselves and their families.

Family-Based Migration: More and more families are migrating from distressed conditions to further distressed conditions in an unknown land. There are some families, who migrate for better economic, educational, health care, employment opportunities. But that number is less and even if they migrate with families, they have support system. The families of distressed labour migrants need special assistance to ensure safety and security, education and employment, food and health care if they decide to remain or to move out as a family. Family unity also is weakened when the children and the women of migrants are left unprotected both in their own place or where they migrate to.

Ensure the flow of remittances from the migrants to the families. It is a hard reality that the formal financial institutions like the banks are not friendly to the migrants in their financial dealings. Due to this, the migrants are forced to opt for informal financial institutions who fleece them. Sometimes acquaintances or villagers or relatives, do not submit the money, the migrant earns with lots of hardship. This leads to fight among the migrants and their families. They try to settle the matter through the police and court who see this as an opportunity to cheat them and even take exceptional fees or bribe.

Public Policy Challenge and Responses

The realities of migration stare before India and the world. Within India, internal migration is on the increase and the distress of the migrants too. Hence, Indian government need to come out with a comprehensive policy responses implemented in unison between the state and central governments. Due to electoral politics, relationship between these two is weakened.

At times, it appears that we are only addressing the symptoms and leaving out the root causes. With this method, we will not reach anywhere. Hence, it is important to arrive at consistent and comprehensive policy frameworks to address the root causes and look for permanent solutions.

As we have stated in the foregoing pages, persons should have the opportunity to remain in their homeland to support and to find full lives for themselves and their families. This is the ideal situation for which the country must strive: one in which migration flows are driven by choice, not necessity. Paramount to achieving this goal is the need to develop the economies of source states, especially those that are economically and socially backward. If this is put in place, the country would see marked reduction in distressed migrants.

Integral development in the source states within the country should be a major goal of the governments so that labour migrants with employment opportunities that will allow them to remain at home and to support themselves and their families is a reality. Faith based and secular organisations have consistently singled out economic inequality between nations as a global disorder that must be addressed. This is also the case within a country where regional disparities exist which forces the labourers to migrate. Policies and programs which create living-wage jobs is vital in migrant producing states. Targeted development projects in backward districts and regions of India should form a priority of the government so as to reduce the risk of migration. Projects and resources particularly should be targeted to the agricultural sector, small businesses and self-employment in backward regions so as to bring in everyone within the ambit of integral development.

Often time, interstate border regions are the focal point of migration. Starting from housing, health care, employment, education of children, etc., do not catch the attention of many. Hence, consciously additional resources also should be directed toward communities on the borders. For children from these border regions, the Mother Tongue Based Multi Lingual Education (MTBMLE) is an option for education.

Creating Legal Avenues for Migration

- Labour legislation should be enforced more strictly, with necessary simplification and modification of laws where necessary.[205]
- A labour market authority should be set up to monitor the labour markets of the major labour-importing countries, carry out negotiations on labour contracts, and study the nature of emerging skill requirements.
- Advocacy campaigns should aim to address stereotypes and misapprehensions about migrants and to raise their political voice.
- Establishing institutional mechanisms for inter-state coordination. This is not just for recruitment for employment but to ensure that the rights of the migrants are respected and enforced.
- Improving enforcement of labour laws. Instead of doing away with the existing labour laws and introducing codes which ultimately appear to do away with the labour laws, the government should set up reimagined labour enforcement agencies and impose punitive measures if these laws are not put into practice or violated.
- Adopting a four-pronged approach for better protection of rights of workers that defines the roles and responsibilities of the state, employers, workers cum trade unions and civil society organizations and emphasizes the use of social dialogue and collective bargaining for promoting the rights of migrant workers.
- Ensuring access and portability of social security schemes, for example, access to public distribution networks, subsidized ration in destination areas, accessing housing, water and sanitation, etc.

Lessons Learnt from COVID-19

A careful reader of the risk faced by the migrants and returnee migrants realises the many vulnerabilities they were subjected to and also some of the best practices. The COVID-19 pandemic highlighted

---

[205] Abhishek Pandey. Legal Rights of Migrant People in India. Social Science Research Network. April 10, 2020.

significant disparities in the health and economic well-being of poor migrant communities, emphasizing the need for targeted interventions and inclusive policies. Migrants, particularly low-skilled labourers and those in precarious situations, faced disproportionate risks of infection and adverse outcomes due to factors like overcrowded living conditions, limited access to healthcare, and employment in essential but hazardous roles.

Since, the governments and the officials do not bother about internal migration, they do not bother about regulating it in anyway. In the light of these circumstances, it is imperative to reconsider the tagline of "safe, orderly, regular migration," which was initially promoted by the International Organization for Migration (IOM), used in discourses on the Sustainable Development Goals (SDGs), and more recently adopted by the World Health Organization (WHO) as a comprehensive and inclusive response to COVID-19.[206] Instead, the appropriate policy approach should be 'safe, just, and regular migration,' as the absence of justice and respect for human rights jeopardizes human security and health everywhere.

It is also a fact that building migrant-inclusive health is politically challenging. However, without an inclusive approach, our ability to respond adequately and equitably to any future emergencies will be severely hampered. This has to be done not only by those involved in health care sector but by all the stakeholders so that if something like COVID-19 outbreak happens, we are prepared and migrants and returnee migrants are not subject to unbearable hardships.

There is an urgent need to improve migrant-disaggregated data base pertaining to health and vaccination. If this is available a priori, in emergency situations, one can concentrate on response than looking for data. For instance, the present government of India which claims to '*Vishwaguru*', that is, the one who can teach the world, admitted shamefully that the government does not have data on the migrant labourers.[207] While this was a fact, this statement also helped the government to escape from its obligations.

---

[206] WHO . Refugees and migrants in times of COVID-19: mapping trends of public health and migration policies and practices. Geneva: World Health Organization; 2021.

[207] Govt. has no data of migrant workers' death, loss of job: 1.04 crore migrant workers returned to home States during lockdown, Minister tells LS. The Hindu. 14/09/2020.

Any healthcare organisations and or governments managing future health emergency responses should ensure any interventions and messaging are co-designed with local migrant communities to ensure maximum uptake and access. Unless delivery and access of factual informations are sent out the migrants would further be subjected to misinformation. This also applies for all other sectors like employment, return home, employment at home, precautions to be maintained in crisis situations, etc.

Years of experience in researching and working among the migrants opens up this focal point that action by governments to address the structural barriers that lead to the marginalisation of distressed individual and group of migrants, including action on the intersection of caste, class, ethnicity, gender, disability, sexuality, education, language, region and age. For this to happen, action by local and national media, advocacy, and governmental organisations to reframe the negative narrative on migration and positively view the contribution of the migrants who build homes, roads, hospitals, factories, schools and above all the nation.

Much before COVID-19, UNESCO came out with a document titled, 'Social Inclusion of Internal Migrants in India' and demanded for distribution of identity cards; affordable housing; informal credit systems and institutions; social inclusion of migrants, their families and children; address political apathy towards them and do away with uncontrolled exploitation.[208] But the government of India only talks about these in seminars, conferences but does not address them. The adamant manner in which the government of India is not formulating a National Migrant Policy is a proof of the fact that the migrants do not matter to these leaders but want their labour.

The government of India should have the humility to learn from many countries and NGOs within India who came out with some of the best practices to respond to the migrants during and after COVID-19. For example, The Migrant Support Program of the Gramin Vikas Trust in collaboration with the Department for International Development (DFID)[209] came out with innovative responses. Some of them are:

---

[208] UNECSO. Social Inclusion of Internal Migrants in India. 2013.

[209] Migrant Support Program. Gramin Vikas Trust and DFID. 2022. DFID is a British organisation which is concerned about the citizens of India, while India's politicians do not bother about them.

protection by providing ID cards; communication facilities through mobile phones; factual information to migrants; information to contractors on the availability of labour; facilitating remittances; skill upgradation; awareness creation, etc.

Human Dignity and Human Security Based Migration

Four areas which should receive a priority attention in ensuring human security should be an overarching recommendations when it comes to distressed migrants. They are:

1) **human security** threatened by **poverty** and **lack of development;**
2) **human security** threatened by **lack of employment, proper and appropriate wages, housing and health care facilities**;
3) **human security** undermined by **drug trafficking** and **trafficking of women and children**; and
4) **human security** seriously jeopardized through **human rights violation.**

Four areas which should receive a priority attention in ensuring human dignity should be an overarching recommendations when it comes to distressed migrants. They are:

1) **human dignity** threatened by **poverty** and **lack of development;**
2) **human dignity** threatened by **lack of employment, proper and appropriate wages, housing and health care facilities**;
3) **human dignity** undermined by **drug trafficking** and **trafficking of women and children**; and
4) **human dignity** seriously jeopardized through **human rights violation.**

Migrants Issues are Human Rights Issues

Under this perspective, enlarge the scope of migrants' issues as human rights issues. The human rights of migrant workers and their families include the following universal, indivisible, interconnected and interdependent human rights:

- The human right to work and receive wages that contribute to an adequate standard of Living.

- The human right to freedom from discrimination based on race, national or ethnic origin, sex, religion or any other status, in all aspects of work, including in hiring, conditions of work, and promotion, and in access to housing, health care and basic services.
- The human right to equality before the law and equal protection of the law, particularly in regard to human rights and labor legislation, regardless of a migrant's legal status.
- The human right to equal pay for equal work.
- The human right to freedom for sufficient food so as to have the necessary physical and mental power to work.
- The human right to freedom from forced labor.
- The human right to protection against arbitrary expulsion from the place of employment.
- The human right to return home if the migrant wishes.
- The human right to a standard of living adequate for the health and well-being of the migrant worker and his or her family.
- The human right to safe working conditions and a clean and safe working environment.
- The human right to reasonable limitation of working hours, rest and leisure.
- The human right to freedom of association and to join a trade union.
- The human right to freedom from sexual harassment in the workplace.
- The human right to protection during pregnancy from work proven to be harmful.
- The human right to protection for the child from economic exploitation and from any work that may be hazardous to his or her well-being and development.
- The human right of children of migrant workers to education.[210]
- The human right of children not to be employed in hazardous work.

[210] This is only possible when the officials and governments of place of origin and destination join together, agree upon this and make necessary arrangements for classes.

- The human right of migrants and their families to reunification.
- The human right of migrants and their families for a family wage.
- The fundamental human right of the migrants for safety, security and dignity.[211]

Conclusions

Sheer number of distressed labour migrants have grown over the years. While on the one hand their contribution to the economy has multiplied, but their vulnerability and exploitation has increased many fold. There may be a meagre improvement in their material conditions. Low and erratically earned wages, informal and casual work engagements, hazardous work leading to poor health conditions, and an all-pervasive presence of labour intermediaries creating debt bondage among migrant workers continue to characterize the experience of seasonal migrants.[212]

The absence of essential services and provisioning for migrants – housing, nutrition, sanitation, healthcare and legal aid – have created a paradigm of extraction rather than investment in workers' potential, productivity and agency. It has been a major coping, accumulation as well as adaptive strategy for the poor and marginalized migrants of India.

All the facts and figures, data and discussions, point to the central thesis of this book that the distressed migrant labourers are subjected to innumerable oppression and exploitation. Their rights are there to be violated. While, lip service is done for their contribution to nation building, their lives and struggles are not point of deliberations and much less action. All these point to this biblical and theological truth that the distressed labour migrants are the Jesus the Migrant Today. It is they who are crucified at every day, every level and every way.

This questions, what we can do is something that haunts us as Christians and human beings. Let us conclude this book with some possible answers.

---

[211] Taken and enlarged from the article of Abhishek Pandey. Legal Rights of Migrant People in India. Social Science Research Network. April 10, 2020.

[212] ILO. Road map for developing a policy framework for the inclusion of internal migrant workers in India. International Labour Organisation. 2020.

1. Personal

- Let us get beneath the political narratives and public proclamations. Lean into the hard stories of migrants who are human beings like us.
  - Migrant labourers who used to travel on the top of the trains since the unreserved compartments are full and overcrowded.
  - To understand the risks people undertake to move from their origin to destination often time to an unknown place, unwelcoming neighbours, exploiting agents, taskforce managers, cheating owners, etc.
  - For a glimpse into the challenges that the distressed migrants face in an unknown place without local identity card due to which they can neither get an accommodation, open bank account or access social securities.
  - The various ways and means they are cheated by everyone which leaves them totally depressed and exhausted.
  - The unhealthy conversation by the locals, labourers and trade unions who conceive migrant labourers as competitors.
  - The way the local police suspect them, arrest them without warrant and ill-treat them and even torture them.

2. Societal

- Demand from state and central governments to formulate a comprehensive 'National Migrant Policy.'
- Set up Migrant Resource Centres wherever sizeable number of migrants are located, jointly done by the origin and destination states.
- Demand that the governments of source and destination states will prioritise their responses to the migrants in terms of employment, wages, affordable housing, public distribution systems, health care, education of children, etc.
- Organise study groups that examines the state of the distressed migrants in their location so that they plan for their accompaniment and assistance.
- Once we have sufficient understanding, we need to plunge into our responses to the distressed migrants.

In all these, keep in focus the invitation of Pope Francis, "Welcome, Promote, Accompany and Integrate the migrants and refugees." This book, "Jesus the Distressed Migrant Today" invites us all to be open to welcome, protect and promote their rights and dignity. It invites us to accompany and assist them. Further, it gives an open invitation to be integrated with the migrants whoever they are, wherever they are from and whatever they do.

References

Aajevika Bureau. (2014). *Their Own Country: A Profile of Labour Migration from Rajasthan.* https://aajeevika.org/wp-content/uploads/2023/10/Their-Own-Country.pdf.

Adogame, Afe. (et.al, edited). (2019). *Migration and Public Discourse in World Christianity*. Minneapolis: Fortress Press.

Ahn, Ilsup. (2019). *Theology and Migration*. Leiden: Brill.

______ (2024). 'Migration and Christian Theology', *St Andrews Encyclopaedia of Theology*. Edited by Brendan N. Wolfe et.al.

Alfaro, Sammy. (2022). 'Incarnation and Redemption: Jesus the Migrant', in *The Church and Migration: A Theological Vision for the People of God.* Edited by Daniel Montañez and Wilmer Estrada Carrasquillo. Cleveland, TN: Centro para Estudios Latinos Press, 63–73.

Allard, Silas W., Kristin E. Heyer, and Raj Nadella (eds). (2022). *Christianity and the Law of Migration*. New York: Routledge.

Appiah, Bernard Otopah (2019). *A Socio-Theological Approach to Migration and Integration: Perspectives of African Church Communities in Britain*. Bernard Appiah:

Arya, Sadhna and Roy, Anupama. (2006). *Poverty, Gender and Migration*. New Delhi: Sage Publications.

Azam, Saleem. (2021). *Forced Migration on the Basis of Extremism: Forced Migration and Extremism*.

Baggio, Fabbio, and Agnes M. Brazal. (2009). *Faith on the Move: Toward a Theology of Migration in Asia*. Quezon City: Ateneo de Manila University Press.

Bala, A. (2017). "Migration in India: Causes and Consequences". *International Journal of Advanced Educational Research*, 54-56.

Barber, William J., II. (2016). *The Third Reconstruction: How a Moral Movement Is Overcoming the Politics of Division*. Boston: Beacon Press.

Basumatary, Songram (2018). *Migration in Perspectives: Towards Theology of Migration from the Margins*. Christian World Imprints: New Delhi.

Bhabha, Jacqueline. (2014). *Child Migration and Human Rights in a Global Age. Human Rights and Crimes against Humanity.* New Jersey: Princeton University Press.

Bharadwaj, R., Somnath Hazra, Mohan Reddy, Shouvik Das and Daljeet Kaur. (2021). Connecting Dots: Climate change, migration and social protection. IIED.

Boda, Mark J. and Ames, Frank Ritchel. (2015). *The Prophets Speak on Forced Migration: Ancient Israel and its Literature.* Atlanta: SBL Press.

Bora, R. S. (2014). "Migrant Informal Workers: A Study of Delhi and Satellite Towns." *Modern Economy*, 5(05), 562.

Breman, J. (1996), *Footloose Labour: Working in India's Informal Economy*, Cambridge: Cambridge University Press.

Bretherton, Luke. (2006). 'The Duty of Care to Refugees, Christian Cosmopolitanism, and the Hallowing of Bare Life', *Studies in Christian Ethics* 19, no. 1: 39–61.

C. Das, K., & Saha, S. (2012), *Inter-state Migration and Regional Disparities in India.*

Cahill, Lisa Sowie. (1980). 'Toward a Christian Theory of Human Rights', *Journal of Religious Ethics* 8: 277–301.

Campese, Gioacchino. (2008). '¿Cuantos Más?: The Crucified Peoples at the U.S.-Mexico Border', in *A Promised Land, A Perilous Journey: Theological Perspectives on Migration*. Edited by Daniel G. Groody and Gioacchino Campese. Notre Dame, IN: University of Notre Dame Press, 271–298.

Carmona, Victor, and Rober W. Heimburger. (2022). 'The Border, Brexit, and the Church: US Roman Catholic and Church of England Bishops' Teaching on Migration, 2015–2019', *Journal of Moral Theology* 11, no. 2: 15–44.

Carroll R., M. Daniel. (2008). *Christians at the Border: Immigration, the Church, and the Bible*. Grand Rapids: Baker Academic.

Carroll, M Daniel. (2020). *The Bible and Borders: Hearing God's Word on Immigration*. US: Blackstone Publication.

Carroll, M Daniel and Bacote Vincent E (edited). (2021). *Global Migration and Christian Faith: Implications for Identity and Mission. Eugene:* Wipf & Stock Publishers.

Castles, Stephen., Hein de Hass, and Mark J. Miller. (2014). *The Age of Migration: International Population Movements in the Modern World*. New York: The Guilford Press. 5th edition.

Chandrasekhar, S., & Sharma, A. (2014). "Urbanization and Spatial Patterns of Internal Migration in India." *Indira Gandhi Institute of Development Research*, 1-39.

Chinchilla, Norma Stoltz, Nora Hamilton, and James Loucky. (2009). 'The Sanctuary Movement and Central American Activism in Los Angeles', *Latin American Perspectives* 169, no. 36: 101–126.

Collier, Elizabeth W., Strain, Charles R. and CRS. (2017). *Global Migration: What's Happening, Why, and a Just Response*. Anselm Academic: Wionna.

Cosan Eke, Denzil and Eric Mr. Trinka. (2023). *Religion, Religious Groups and Migration*. London: Transnational Press.

Cragg, HyerRan Kim and Choi, EunYoung. (2014), *The Encounters: Retelling the Bible from Migration and Intercultural Perspectives*. Daejanggan Publisher: Yangchon-ri.

Cruz, Gemma Tulud. (2010). *An Intercultural Theology of Migration: Pilgrims in the Wilderness*. Boston: Brill.

Cruz, Gemma Tulud. (2013). 'A New Way of Being Christian: The Contribution of Migrants to the Church', in *Contemporary Issues of Migration and Theology*. Edited by Elaine Padilla and Peter C. Phan. New York: Palgrave-Macmillan, 95–120.

Cruz, Gemma Tulud (2014). *Towards a Theology of Migration: Social Justice and Religious Experience*. London: Palgrave Macmillan.

Cruz, Gemma Tulud. (2021). *Christianity Across Borders: Theology and Contemporary Issues in Global Migration*. New York: Routledge.

Dutta, Amrita. *Continuity and Change: Migration and Development in India.* The Case of Bihar. Ph D. Thesis. 2019.

De La Torre, Miguel A. (2009). *Trails of Hope and Terror: Testimonies on Immigration*. Maryknoll, NY: Orbis.

De La Torre, Miguel A. (2016). *The U.S. Immigration Crisis: Toward an Ethics of Place*. Eugene, OR: Cascade Books.

Deshingkar, Priya. et.al. *Circular Migration in Madhya Pradesh: Changing Patterns and Social Protection Needs*. European Journal of Development Research. February 2008.

______ and Akter, S. (2009), Migration and Human Development in India, Human Development Research Paper 2009/13, *New York: United Nations Development Programme*.

______ (2010). "Migration, remote Rural Areas and Chronic Poverty in India". *Overseas Development Institute*, Working Paper 323. Accessed on 10 August, 2017, from http://www.chronicpoverty.org/uploads/publication_files/WP163%20Deshingkar.pdf.

Dias, Darren J. and Mannion, Gerard, et.al. (2021). *The Church, Migration and Global (in) Difference: Pathways for Ecumenical and Interreligious Dialogue*. Switzerland AG: Springer Nature.

Ellacuría, Ignacio. (1993). 'The Crucified People', in *Mysterium Liberationis: Fundamental Concepts of Liberation Theology*. Edited by Ignacio Ellacuría and Jon Sobrino. Maryknoll, NY: Orbis, 580–604.

Faetanini, M., & Tankha, R. (2013). *Social Inclusion of Internal Migrants in India*. Delhi: UNESCO.

Frederiks, Martha and Nagy, Dorothy. (2016). *Religion, Migration and Identity: Methodological and Theological Explorations: 2 (Theology and Mission in World Christianity, 2)*. Netherlands: Brill Academic Publications.

Firth, David G. (2019). *Including the Stranger: Foreigners in the Former Prophets*. Downers Grove: InterVarsity Press.

Gaikward, Nikhar and Gareth Nellis. The Majority-Minority Divide in Attitudes toward Internal Migration: Evidence from Mumbai. American Journal of Political Science. Volume 61, Issue 2, April 2017.

Gangadhar, Nikhil. (10 July 2015). "City Becoming Death Trap for Migrant Labourers." Accessed on 10 March, 2017, from http://m/deccanherald.com/articles.php?name=http%2F%www.

deccanherald.com%2Fcontent%2F488631%2Fcity-becoming-death-trap-migrant.html.

Gopalakrishnan, Shankar and Sreenivasa, Priya. (2009). *The Political Economy of Migrant Labour*. New Delhi: Sruti.

GoI (2017). Report of the Working Group on Migration in India. Government of India: Ministry of Housing and Urban Poverty Alleviation.

Gonzallez, Karen, et.al. (2019). *The God Who Sees: Immigrants, the Bible, and the Journey to Belong*. Harvey: Herald Press.

Grigsby, Nadine, et.al. (2024). *Survival: Inspirational Immigrant Stories*. Georgia: Thanx A. Mills, LLC.

George, Sam, and Godfrey Harold. (2021). 'Motus Dei (The Move of God): A Theology and Missiology for a Moving World', *Pharos Journal of Theology* 102: 1–12.

Gledhill, Ruth. (2010). 'Archbishop Asks Christians to View Migrants as a Gift', *The Times*. 24. 14 May.

Groody, Daniel G and Campese, Gioacchino. (2008). A *Promised Land, A Perilous Journey: Theological Perspectives on Migration.* Notre Dame: University of Notre Dame Press.

______ (2009). 'Crossing the Divide: Foundations of a Theology of Migration and Refugees', *Theological Studies* 70, no. 3: 638–667.

______ (2022). *A Theology of Migration: The Bodies of Refugees and the Body of Christ*. Maryknoll, NY: Orbis Books.

______ (2002). *Border of Death, Valley of Life: An Immigrant Journey of Heart and Spirit*. New York: Rowman & Littlefield Publishers.

Gregory of Nyssa. (1978). *The Life of Moses*. Translated by Abraham J. Malherbe and Everett Ferguson. New York: Paulist Press.

Guajardo-Hodge, Alejandra. (2022). 'An Ethic of Embrace: Welcoming the Stranger,' in *The Church and Migration: A Theological Vision for the People of God*. Edited by Daniel Montañez and Wilmer Estrada Carrasquillo. Cleveland, TN: Centro para Estudios Latinos, 89–101.

Haan, Arjan de. (January 2011). "Inclusive Growth? Labour Migration and Poverty in India." *International Institute of Social Studies*, Working Paper 513.

______ Arjan de. (1999), "Livelihoods and Poverty: the Role of Migration, A Critical Review of the Migration Literature", *Journal of Development Studies* 36(2), 1-47.

Haberfeld, Y., Menaria, R. K., Sahoo, B. B., & Vyas, R. N. (1999). "Seasonal Migration of Rural Labour in India." Population Research and Policy Review, 18(5), 471-487.

Hagan, Jacqueline Maria. (2012). *Migration Miracle: Faith, Hope, and Meaning on the Undocumented Journey.* London: Harvard University Press.

Haker, Hille and Greening, Molly, et.al. (2018). *Unaccompanied Migrant Children: Social, Legal, and Ethical Perspectives.* Maryland: Lexington Books.

Hamilton, Mark W. (2019). *Jesus, King of Strangers: What the Bible Really Says About Immigration.* Grand Rapids: William B. Eerdmans Publishing Company.

Hanciles, Jehu J. (2016). 'Singing the Song of the Lord on Foreign Soil: What the Early Centuries Tell Us about the Migrant Factor in the Making of Global Christianity', in *Christianities in Migration: The Global Perspective.* Edited by Elaine Padilla and Peter C. Phan. New York: Palgrave Macmillan, 37–53.

______ (2021). *Migration and the Making of Global Christianity.* Grand Rapids: William B. Eerdmans Publishing Company.

Heimburger, Robert W. (2018). *God and the Illegal Alien: United States Immigration Law and a Theology of Politics.* New York: Cambridge University Press.

Hein, Aimee Allision (2024). *Theology in Motion: Migration, History and Responsibility.* Minneapolis: Fortress Press.

Heyer, Kristin E. (2010). 'Social Sin and Immigration: Good Fences Make Bad Neighbours', *Theological Studies* 71: 410–436.

______ (2012). *Kinship Across Borders: A Christian Ethics of Immigration.* Washington D.C.: Georgetown University Press.

______ (2016). 'The Promise of a Pilgrim Church: Ecclesiological Reflections on the Ethical Praxis of Kinship with Migrants', in *Church in an Age of Global Migration: A Moving Body.* Edited by Susanna Snyder, Joshua Ralston, and Agnes M. Brazal. New York: Palgrave Macmillan, 83–98.

Hiebert, Theodore. (2023). 'The First Immigrants: The Migratory Roots of Biblical Identity', *Interpretation: A Journal of Bible and Theology* 77, no. 1: 61–73.

Hilkert, Mary Catherine. (1995). 'Cry Beloved Image: Rethinking the Image of God', in *In the Embrace of God: Feminist Approaches to Theological Anthropology*. Edited by Ann O'Hara Graff. Maryknoll, NY: Orbis, 190–204.

Hirway, I., Singh, U.B., & Sharma, R. (2014). *Migration and Development Study of Rural to Urban Temporary Migration to Gujarat.* Ahmedabad: Centre for Development Alternatives.

Hudwai, Shafeeq. (14 May 2016). "With no One to Address their Concerns, Migrant Labourers in Kerala Face Tough Odds to Earn a Livelihood." Accessed on 10 March, 2017, fromhttp://twocircles.ner/2016may14/1463219290.html.

ILO. (2007). *International Labour Standards on Migrant Workers' Rights*. Bangkok: International Labour office. Accessed on 10 August, 2017, from http://www.ilo.org/wcmsp5/groups/public/---asia/---robangkok/documents/publication/wcms_146244.pdf

ILO. (2010). International Labour Migration: A Rights-based Approach. Geneva: International Labour Office. Accessed on 10 August, 2017, from http://digitalcommons.ilr.cornell.edu/cgi/viewcontent.content.cgi?article=1086&context=intl.

ILO. (2020). Road Map for Developing a Policy Framework for the Inclusion of Internal Migrant Workers in India. Geneva: International Labour Organisation.

ILO. (2024). Gendering Internal Labour Migration Corridors Migrant Women Workers in Southern India's Garment Industry.

International Migration Report. (2015). Accessed on 10 March, 2017, from http://www.un.org/en/development/desa/population/migration/publications/migrationreport/docs/MigrationReport2015.pdf.

International Organisation for Migration. (2011). *Key Migration Terms*. Accessed on 10 March, 2017, from http://www.iom.int/key-migration-terms.

International Organization for Migration. (2022). 'The World Migration Report of 2022', https://worldmigrationreport.iom.int/wmr-2022-interactive/.

Johnstone, Patrick, et.al. (2018). *Serving God in a Migrant Crisis: Ministry to People on the Move. Madison:* InterVarsity Press.

K. Vinayakam, & Sekar, S. P. (2013). "Rural To Urban Migration in an Indian Metropolis: Case Study Chennai City." *Journal of Humanities and Social Science*, 32-35.

Kaalund, Jennifer. (2020). Reading Hebrews and 1 Peter with the African American Great Migration: Diaspora, Place and Identity. Scotland: T&T Clark Ltd.

Kahl, Werner. (2022). 'Migration Experiences, Gospel Interpretation, and the Emergence of Multiethnic Faith Communities in Early Christianity: Acts and Paul', in *Migration and Diaspora Formation: New Perspectives on a Global History of Christianity*. Edited by Ciprian Burlăcioiu. Berlin: De Gruyter, 17–36.

Keller, Catherine. (2015). *Cloud of the Impossible: Negative Theology and Planetary Entanglement*. New York: Columbia University Press.

Kerwin, Donald and Berschutz, Jill Marie (2009). *And You Welcomed Me: Migration and Catholic Social Teaching*. Maryland: Lexington Books.

Kinukawa, Hisako. (2014). *Migration and Diaspora: Exegetical Voices of Women in Northeast Asian Countries.* Atalanta: Society of Biblical Literature.

Kitani, Kanan. (2020). 'Jesus the Paradigmatic Migrant', in *Christian Theology in the Age of Migration: Implications for World Christianity*. Edited by Peter C. Phan. New York: Lexington Books, 129–150.

Krehbiel, Susan. (2017). 'Sanctuary as Resistance and Solidarity', *Network News*. 20–21. August edition.

Kundu, A. (2007). "Migration and Urbanisation in India in the Context of Poverty Alleviation." *International Conference and Workshop on Policy Perspectives on Growth, Economic Structures and Poverty Reduction.* Beijing.

Lee, J. Fitzgerald. (2013). *The Great Migration: The Origin of the Jewish People and Materials Towards the Solution of a World Problem.* Whitefish: Literary Licensing, LLC.

Louis, Prakash. (2019). *Catholic Social Teachings: Towards a Catholic Faith in Action.* New Delhi: Indian Social Institute.

______ (2022). *Distress Migrants of Bihar: Factors, Causes and Responses*. XISR: Patna.

______ (2025). *Pope Francis: A Pastor, Prophet and Shepherd. A Global Champion of Dignity, Right, Peace, Fraternity, Openness, Inclusion & Common Home.* Varanasi: Marina Publications.

Maity, Kingsuk. et.al. (2018) *Male Out-Migration and its Impact on Women Empowerment in West Bengal*. Economic Affairs, Vol. 63, No. 2, pp. 459-467.

Marion, Jean-Luc. (1995). *God Without Being*. Translated by Thomas A. Carlson. Chicago: University of Chicago.

Mazumdar, I. Neetha, N. Agnihotri, I. (2013), Gender and Migration in India, *Economic and Political Weekly,* XLVIII (10), March 9, 2013.

Mishra, Deepak Kumar (Ed). (2016). *Internal Migration in Contemporary India*. New Delhi: Sage.

Montanez, Daniel (Author) and Estrada-Carrasquillo, Wilmer (Editor). (2022). *The Church and Migration: A Theological Vision for the People of God*. Centro para Estudios Latinos Press: Cleveland.

Moses, W. Jonathan and Rajan, S. Irudaya. (2012). "Labour Migration and Integration in Kerala." *Labours Development*, 19(1), 1-18.

Mukherji, Shekhar (Ed.). (2013). *Migration in India: Links to Urbanisation, Regional Disparities and Development Policies*. Jaipur: Rawat Publications.

Nanko-Fernández, Carmen. (2015). 'Roman Catholic: A "Documented" Response: Papal Teaching and People on the Move', in *Immigrant Neighbours Among Us: Immigration Across Theological Traditions*. Edited by M. Daniel Carroll R. and Leopoldo A. Sanchez M. Eugene, OR: Pickwick, 1–21.

Nguyễn, VănThanh, and John M. Prior. (2014). *God's People on the Move: Biblical and Global Perspectives on Migration and Mission.* Eugene, OR: Pickwick Publications.

______ (2020). 'Migration in the New Testament: The Quest for Home', in *Christian Theology in the Age of Migration*. Edited by Peter Phan. New York: Lexington Press, 69–86.

______ (2021). *What Does the Bible Say about Strangers, Migrants and Refugees*. New York: New City Press.

NSSO. (2013). Migration in India July 2007-June 2008. Report No. 533. Ranchi Master Plan 2037.

Oden, Amy G. (2001). 'And You Welcomed Me: A Source Book on Hospitality in Early Christianity', Nashville, T. N.: Abingdon Press.

Palma, Paul J. (2023). *Grassroots Pentecostalism in Brazil and the United States: Migrations, Missions and Mobility – Christianity and Renewal.* Gurgaon: Palgrave Macmillan.

Pandey, Abhishek. (2020). Legal Rights of Migrant People in India. Social Science Research Network. April 10, 2020.

Phan, Peter C. (2013). 'The Experience of Migration as Source of Intercultural Theology', in *Contemporary Issues of Migration and Theology*. Edited by Elaine Padilla and Peter C. Phan. New York: Palgrave Macmillan, 179–209.

______ (2016). 'Deus Migrator—God the Migrant: Migration of Theology and Theology of Migration', *Theological Studies* 77, no. 4: 845–868.

______ (2022). *Christian Theology in the Age of Migration: Implications for World Christianity.* Maryland: Lexington Books.

Platt, David, et.al. (2016). *Counter Culture: A Compassionate Call to Counter Culture in a World of Poverty, Same-Sex Marriage, Racism, Sex Slavery, Immigration, Abortion, Persecution, Orphans and Pornography.* Illinois: Tyndale House Publishers.

Pohl, Christine D. (1999). *Making Room: Recovering Hospitality as a Christian Tradition*. Grand Rapids: Eerdmans.

Prior, John and Nguyen, Vantthanh (2014). *God's People on the Move: Biblical and Global Perspectives on Migration and Mission.* Eugene: Pickwick Publications.

Rajan, S. Irudaya and P. Sivakumar. (2018). *Youth Migration in Emerging India.* Hyderabad: The Orient Blackswan.

Rajendra, Tisha M. (2017). *Migrants and Citizens: Justice and Responsibility in the Ethics of Immigration.* Grand Rapids: Eerdmans.

Reynolds, Thomas E. (2006). 'Welcoming Without Reserve? A Case in Christian Hospitality', *Theology Today* 63: 191–202.

Rieger, Joerg. (2020). *Theologies on the Move: Religion, Migration, and Pilgrimage in the World of Neoliberal Capital*. New York: Lexington Books.

Rivera-Pagán, Luis N. (2019). 'Xenophilia or Xenophobia: Toward a Theology of Migration', in *Migration and Public Discourse in World Christianity*. Edited by Afe Adogame, Raimundo C. Barreto, and Wanderley Pereira da Rosa. Minneapolis: Fortress Press, 191-214.

Romero, Robert Chao and Burris, Stephen. (2022). *Migration, Mission, and Ministry: An Introduction*.

Rowlands, Anna. (2012). 'The State Made Flesh: Catholic Social Teaching and the Challenge of UK Asylum Seeking', *New Blackfriars* 93: 175–192.

Roy, Sumita and Gopa Samanta. (2020). Informal Labours in Kolkata City: Migration from Undivided Bihar and Uttar Pradesh. Space and Culture: India.

Sainath P. (2009). More Migrations, New Destinations, The Hindu, July 11, 2009, URL: http://www.thehindu.com/todays-paper/tp-opinion/more/migrations-newdestinations/article226404.ece, Accessed on 25th July 2018.

Schmiedel, Ulrich. (2020). 'Coalitional Church: Ecclesiology in the Age of Migration', in *Christian Theology in the Age of Migration: Implications for World Christianity*. Edited by Peter C. Phan. New York: Lexington Books, 151–166.

Senior, Donald. (2008). '"Beloved Aliens and Exiles": New Testament Perspectives on Migration', in *A Promised Land, A Perilous Journey: Theological Perspectives on Migration*. Edited by Daniel Groody and Gioacchino Campese. Notre Dame, IN: Notre Dame University Press, 20–34.

Shaik, Zeeshan. (5 December 2016). "Every 3rd Indian Migrant, Most Headed South." Accessed on 10 March, 2017, from http://indianexpress.com/article/explained/tamil-nadu-kerala-daily-wages-migrant-population-4410694/.

Sherwood, Yvonne. (2018). 'Migration as Foundation: Hagar, the "Resident Alien", as Euro-America's Surrogate Self', *Biblical Interpretation* 26, no. 4–5: 439–468.

Singh, G. (2016), "Surging Internal Migration in Punjab: Emerging Policy Issues". *International Journal of Engineering Technology. Management and Applied Science.* 158-168.

Singh, Ruchi. (2021). *Exodus of Men from Rural Uttar Pradesh.* London: Transnational Press.

Slater, Gary. (2023). *Our Common, Bordered Home: Laudato Si' and the Promise of an Integrated Migration-ecological Ethics.* Ferdinand Schoningh Wilhelm Fink: Midwest.

Snyder, Susanna. (2012). *Asylum-Seeking, Migration and Church: Explorations in Practical, Pastoral and Empirical Theology.* United Kingdom: Routledge.

Snyder, Susanna, Agnes M. Brazal, and Joshua Ralston. (2016). *Church in an Age of Global Migration: A Moving Body*. New York: Palgrave Macmillan.

Sobrino, Jon. (1994). *The Principle Mercy: Taking the Crucified People from the Cross*. Maryknoll, NY: Orbis.

Soerens, Mathew and Yang, Jenny et.al (2018). *Welcoming the Stranger: Justice, Compassion and Truth in the Immigration Debate*. US: Inter-Varsity Press.

Southwood, Katherine. (2018). 'This Man Has Come into My House: Hospitality in Genesis 19; 34; and Judges 19', *Biblical Interpretation* 26: 469–484.

Stoeber, Michael. (2003). 'Transformative Suffering, Destructive Suffering and the Question of Abandoning Theodicy', *Studies in Religion* 32, no. 4: 429–447.

Strine, Casey A. (2018). 'The Study of Involuntary Migration as a Hermeneutical Guide for Reading the Jacob Narrative', *Biblical Interpretation* 26: 485–498.

Sutherland, Arthur. (2006). *I Was a Stranger: A Christian Theology of Hospitality*. Nashville, TN: Abingdon Press.

Sweeden, Nell Becker. (2015). *Church on the Way: Hospitality and Migration.* South Africa: Pickwick Publications.

Sunam, Ramesh. (2022). *Transnational Labour Migration, Livelihoods and Agrarian Change in Nepal*. London: Taylor & Francis.

Tassello, Giovanni Graziano. (2010). Church's Social Teaching on Migration: Issues and Challenges. Rev. Inter. Mob. Hum., BrasÌlia,

Ano XVIII, Nº 35, p. 229-246, jul./dez. 2010. https://www.redalyc.org/pdf/4070/407042012012.pdf.

Tan-Chow, May Ling. (2007). *Pentecostal Theology for the Twenty-First Century: Engaging with Multi-Faith Singapore.* Hampshire: Ashgate.

Tanner, Kathryn. (2010). 'Economy of Grace', *Word & World* 30, no. 2: 174–181.

The Economic Survey of India. (2016-17). Chapter 12, *India on the Move and Churning: New Evidence.* Govt. of India.

Truong, Thanh-Dam, Des Gasper. (2013). Migration, Gender and Social Justice: Perspectives on Human Insecurity. New Delhi: Springer.

UNESCO. (2013). *Social Inclusion of Internal Migrants in India.* Accessed on 10 August, 2017, from http://unesdoc.unesco.rog/images/0022/002237/223702e.pdf.

UNESCO. Social Inclusion of Internal Migrants in India at 4, UNESCO, New Delhi, June 2013.

______ Internal Migration in India Initiative, Policy Brief, UNESCO 2012, available at 2http://www.unesco.org/new/fileadmin/MULTIMEDIA/FIELD/New_Delhi/pdf/Policy_briefs_full_low_01.pdf.

USCCB. Migration & Catholic Social Teaching. United States Council of Catholic Bishops. https://www.usccb.org/resources/migrationandCST.

Uroko, Favour C., Mary J. Obiorah, and Success Nnadi. (2021). 'Migration Ethics in Genesis 47:1–12 as a Limelight for Nigerian Migrants', *Verbum Et Ecclesia* 42, no. 1: 1–8. https://doi.org/10.4102/ve.v42i1.2188.

______ Strangers No Longer: Together on the Journey of Hope. A Pastoral Letter Concerning Migration from the Catholic Bishops of Mexico and the United States. January, 2003.

Vasquez, Jorge. (2018). *Ruth The Immigrant: An Unconventional Interpretation of the Biblical Book of Ruth.* IFLE Instituto de Formación de Líderes Espirituales.

Wayl, Emmanuel. (2016). Migration in Christianity. Events of Migration in the New Testament. Karachi: Green Verlag.

WHO. Refugees and migrants in times of COVID-19: mapping trends of public health and migration policies and practices. Geneva: World Health Organization; 2021.

World Economic Forum. (2007). *Migration and Its Impact*. World Economic Forum.

Walczak, Jakub. (2021). 'The Conditions of Christian Hospitality', *The Way* 60, no. 3: 85–97.

Walls, Andrew F. (2002). 'Mission and Migration: The Diaspora Factor in Christian History', *Journal of African Christian Thought* 5, no. 2: 3–11.

Webb, Stephen H. (1996). *The Gifting God: A Trinitarian Ethics of Excess*. New York: Oxford University Press.

Yong, Amos. (2011). *Who Is the Holy Spirit? A Walk with the Apostles*. Brewster, MA: Paraclete Press.

Zehnder, Markus. (2021). *The Bible and Immigration: A Critical and Empirical Reassessment.* Eugene: Wipf and Stock Publishers.

Websites

http://www.forcedmigration.org/papers/

htpp://www.migrationindia.org

www.migrationpolicy.org

https://holyseemission.org/index.php

https://www.migrationdataportal.org/

https://www.un.org/en/global-issues/migration

https://worldmigrationreport.iom

https://migrationnetwork.un.org/

https://www.gfmd.org/